T0119190

HORNS
OF THUNDER

THE LIFE AND TIMES
OF JAMES M. GOODHUE
INCLUDING SELECTIONS
FROM HIS WRITINGS

BY MARY WHEELHOUSE BERTHEL

St. Paul   *1948*
MINNESOTA HISTORICAL SOCIETY

2004 reprint of 1948 edition by the Minnesota Historical Society.

www.mhspress.org

The Minnesota Historical Society Press is a member of the
Association of American University Presses.

♾ The paper used in this publication meets the
minimum requirements of the American National Standard
for Information Sciences—Permanence for
Printed Library Materials, ANSI Z39.48-1984.

International Standard Book Number 0-87351-518-8 (paper)

Library of Congress Control number: 48009671

Foreword

THE THUNDERINGS OF JAMES MADISON GOODHUE, JOURNALIST
and prophet, sound across a century in this recording of his
writings taken from his own trumpet, the *Minnesota Pioneer*.

In *Horns of Thunder* we of today can hear the sounds of
pioneering, of the rise of city and state and region, of the
fashioning of democratic government and institutions, and of
the play of diverse talents in the life of Minnesota a hundred
years ago.

To Goodhue, the primary purpose of the frontier press was
"to mirror back to the world, the events, the peculiarities and
the whole features of the new world by which it is surrounded."
In serving that purpose faithfully and vigorously, Goodhue
also mirrored the pioneer scene on to a far future. His future
is our present. Here, in this centennial book of Minnesota, are
reflected the hopes and dreams of the founders of a common-
wealth. Here, too, is a challenge to take stock of the progress
made in ten decades. Have the hopes and dreams come true?
What has Minnesota made of itself? What answer can we give
to Goodhue? What is the judgment of history? Such questions
echo from Goodhue's horns of thunder with an insistence that
recalls the angel trumpeting thunder in the vision of St. John.

Horns of Thunder is not only the voice of Minnesota's infant hopes; it is also the biography of a remarkable man. In its
pages Goodhue comes alive — provocative, courageous, exuberant in thought and phrase, intelligent in his reading of the
future. He comes alive as a man of "rowdy and irreverent"
humor; as a booster to whom "a month in Minnesota, in dog-
days" was "worth a whole year anywhere else"; and as a city
and state planner whose ideas rolled like thunder into the ears
of the Minnesota pioneers.

The flavor of Goodhue's piquant personality and the vivid-
ness of his writings are caught on every page of *Horns of
Thunder*. St. Paul, said Goodhue on one occasion, "is stretching like a young giant after a nap." Calling for a resurvey,
he deplored the town's "skewdangular" lots. Bad government
appointees were "infamy upon stilts." Boring speeches were
"as long as the ears of the human donkeys that get up and
bray them." An epigram sums up the Minnesota career of a
dishonest official: "He stole into the Territory, he stole in the
Territory, and he stole out of the Territory."

In this book are recorded the concrete ideas of a community
builder who never ceased to specify the reforms and improvements he wanted, such as a town clock, a jail, streets
a hundred feet wide, bridges, roads, telegraph lines, railroads,
a water system, a fire company, and schools much better than
the river wharf whose graduates, he said, received their diplo-
mas from the devil.

Minnesota and the West owe much to James Madison
Goodhue. Here, from the hand of Mrs. Berthel as author and
editor, is a tabulation of the debt in a centennial book that
is a delight to read — a probing study of Minnesota in its
colonial era, a judicious gleaning of the writings of one of the
giants in the Territorial earth.

THEODORE C. BLEGEN

Introduction

AS A PUBLICATION OF THE MINNESOTA HISTORICAL SOCIETY commemorating the Minnesota Territorial Centennial of 1949, this book has a three-fold purpose: to portray the personality and contributions of one of the territory's outstanding leaders; to mirror Minnesota Territory in its early years; and to show how one pioneer newspaper exemplified the personal journalism of a century ago.

The first six chapters of the book are biographical, and, because Goodhue was so deeply involved in Minnesota politics, which influenced his conduct of the *Minnesota Pioneer* in no small way, they tell something of the story of the bitter factional quarrels that were characteristic of the early years of the territory. The remaining chapters consist of selections from Goodhue's writings in the *Pioneer*, accompanied by background information necessary to make them understandable to the reader of today. In her selection of materials from the *Pioneer*, the present editor has needed to discipline herself to refrain from including only the more entertaining and spirited of Goodhue's editorials and excluding all others — a course which would fail to reveal the man, the newspaper, and the infant Minnesota in their broader and true lights. The capitalization, punctuation, and spelling of the quoted material have been reproduced as they appeared in the *Pioneer*, except that obvious typographical errors have been corrected. In some instances long paragraphs have been broken up in the interests of readability, and missing words and letters have been supplied in brackets.

The illustrations in the book need a word of explanation. Those in the text, unless otherwise indicated, are reproductions of pen-and-ink sketches made by Robert O. Sweeny in the spring of 1852, which give us an excellent visual record of early St. Paul. Sweeny was a St. Paul druggist, and more of an artist than some of these crude drawings, made on the backs of prescription blanks, reveal. The Minnesota Historical Society has, in addition to the originals of these drawings, a number of charming little water colors by Sweeny. Credit for the half-tone illustrations will be found under the pictures themselves, most of which are herewith reproduced for the first time. The printing press on the cover, the jacket, and the title-page is the work of Francis Lee Jaques, famous for his paintings and drawings of birds and other outdoor subjects. Through his generosity and interest, he has devoted his talented hand to a reproduction of the old hand press in the museum of the Minnesota Historical Society, which may or may not have been Goodhue's original press, but which was at least the same primitive type of press that was used to print the *Pioneer*.

MARY WHEELHOUSE BERTHEL

Minnesota Historical Society
St. Paul

Table of Contents

List of Illustrations

THE MAN

1. A New Englander Goes West

SOME THIRTY FRAME SHANTIES AND LOG CABINS, STRAGGLING along dirt trails atop a white bluff above the Mississippi River, constituted the little hamlet of St. Paul on March 3, 1849, when Minnesota Territory was born. But to the inhabitants of the place, March 3 was just another day, important only because it was one day nearer the end of their long winter's isolation, when the opening of the river would bring steamboats with supplies and news from the outside world.

It was not until April 9 that the first boat of the season steamed up to the St. Paul levee and brought to the expectant villagers gathered there the long-awaited news, already a month old to the outside world, that the bill for the establishment of Minnesota Territory had become a law.[1] And on the same boat came the vanguard of the immigrant hordes that were to swarm into Minnesota throughout that season and many seasons to come, hopeful men and women from "the states," intent on making their homes and fortunes in a land of new opportunity. They brought with them, gradually, to that frontier community in the wilderness, the adjuncts of civilization — living comforts and conveniences, industries, churches, schools, newspapers.

Among the early arrivals that spring was a man who was to take a leading part in the affairs of the young territory, guiding its people in laying their political and social foundations, influencing their opinions, showing them the beauties and potentialities of Minnesota, suggesting measures for developing their resources and industries; thundering at them,

[1] An excellent description of the reception of the news at St. Paul is given in an article in the *Minnesota Pioneer* of April 28, 1849, entitled "The Breaking up of a Hard Winter" and signed "D. L." (David Lambert). Files of the *Pioneer* and of the other Minnesota newspapers referred to on following pages are in the possession of the Minnesota Historical Society.

cajoling them, entertaining them; and, after three brief years, leaving on them the impress of a rare and robust personality. James Madison Goodhue, a "burly stout-jawed" man nearing forty, arrived in St. Paul on April 18 with a printing press, and ten days later he issued the first number of the first newspaper published in the territory, the *Minnesota Pioneer*.[2]

Goodhue was well fitted by background and training, as well as by temperament and native talent, for the editorship of a frontier newspaper. He was born in Hebron, New Hampshire, on March 31, 1810, a descendant of William Goodhue, who emigrated from England to Ipswich, Massachusetts, about 1635, and the sixth of nine children of Stephen and Betsey Page Goodhue. Piety, sturdiness of character, and deep respect for education characterized his forebears, most of whom were leaders in their communities. His father, a merchant in Hebron, "was a man of good education and gentlemanly bearing," who, before settling in Hebron, had taught school in Sanbornton, New Hampshire. Goodhue's mother, who was the daughter of the Reverend John Page, a Congregational minister in Hebron, died when the boy was nine years old, and his father remarried the next year.[3]

About Goodhue's boyhood existing records give meager information. His preparatory education is placed variously in schools at Amherst and Woburn, Massachusetts, and Hebron and Meridan, New Hampshire. In 1828 he entered Amherst College from Newton, Massachusetts, where his family was then living, and he was graduated in 1833, having remained out of school in 1830–31. At college he was distinguished

---

[2] *Pioneer and Democrat* (St. Paul), April 28, 1859. Thomas M. Newson, in his *Pen Pictures of St. Paul*, 101 (St. Paul, 1886), describes Goodhue as "a good-sized man, given a little to a rocking motion when he walked."

[3] Jonathan E. Goodhue, *History and Genealogy of the Goodhue Family*, 11, 62 (Rochester, New York, 1891); M. T. Runnels, *History of Sanbornton, New Hampshire*, 2:314 (Boston, 1881); *Vital Records of Newton, Massachusetts, to the Year 1850*, 452 (Boston, 1905); John H. Stevens, "Recollections of James M. Goodhue," in *Minnesota Historical Collections*, 6:493, 494.

more for his physical strength and histrionic ability than for his scholastic accomplishments. John H. Stevens, whose "Recollections" of Goodhue were published in 1894, wrote that "while at school no man could, from a dead stand, leap so high over a pole as he. He never was worsted in an encounter with fists." During his college days, according to Stevens, he gave evidence of possessing a remarkable "theatrical talent" and "noble imitative faculties." [4]

His course of study was primarily classical, with much emphasis on composition, declamation, and debate. Courses in French, mathematics, rhetoric, history, political economy, logic, philosophy, "the philosophy of natural history, with its application to natural theology," and the natural sciences were required of all students, in addition to the many courses in Greek and Latin. At the end of his freshman year he gave as a declamation in competition for a prize an "Extract from Randolph's Speech on Retrenchment"; but it is not recorded that he won the prize. He was a member of a student literary society, the Alexandrian, and a contributor to the *Sprite*, a periodical issued by a group of Amherst students. He did not belong to Chi Delta Theta, whose members were chosen from those who had earned the highest grades; nor was he one of the twenty-two members of his class of thirty-eight who received "appointments" for commencement, which were given in the order of rank of scholarship. [5]

For several years following Goodhue's graduation from Amherst information about his whereabouts and activities is indefinite and contradictory. Out of many conflicting statements there emerge a few facts, and some probabilities. Goodhue himself is authority for the information that he was in the

[4] *Minnesota Historical Collections,* 6:494–496.
[5] Stevens, in *Minnesota Historical Collections,* 6:495; W. L. Montague, ed., *Biographical Record of the Alumni of Amherst College,* 98 (Amherst, 1883); Amherst College, *Catalogues,* 1829, p. 9; 1831, p. 7; 1892–93, p. 111; George R. Cutting, *Student Life at Amherst College,* 66, 81, 135 (Amherst, 1871); Rena M. Durkan, secretary to the president of Amherst College, to the writer, May 19, 1937.

West as early as 1831; that he fought in the battle of Bad Axe in the Black Hawk War in August, 1832; and that he visited St. Louis in 1833. It may be that he spent in the West the year that he remained out of college, 1830–31, and summers thereafter until his graduation. During the winter following his graduation, according to Stevens, he read law and taught school in Elmira, New York, and, "after further study of the law in New York City, was admitted to the bar." According to Goodhue's own statement, in 1839 he was farming in Illinois; and Stevens wrote that "he passed some three years in Plainfield, near Joliet," where, "to supply his want of means, he cultivated the black soil." It may be surmised that during those years he worked on the farm of his uncle, Ezra Goodhue, who lived in Plainfield, Illinois, where he had settled in 1832.[6]

In the fall of 1841 Goodhue was practicing law in Platteville, Wisconsin, a little town in the lead region in the southwestern part of the territory. Stevens met him there in October of that year; and on November 27 his card appeared for the first time in the *Galena* (Illinois) *Advertiser:* "J. M.

[6] Stevens, in *Minnesota Historical Collections,* 6:496; Montague, ed., *Record of Amherst Alumni,* 98; *History of Will County, Illinois,* 237, 484 (Chicago, 1878); *Grant County Herald* (Lancaster, Wisconsin), March 23, 1844, July 31, 1847; *Pioneer,* July 19, August 30, 1849. The *Record of Amherst Alumni* states that Goodhue studied law in New York City "with Mr. Burr"; that he was admitted to the bar "about 1840"; that he first practiced law in Galesburg, Illinois; and that he was a colonel of a Wisconsin regiment. The writer has found no verification of these statements. It may be that the title of "colonel," usually associated with his name in newspapers and correspondence of the times, was a complimentary one bestowed upon him by his friends as a result of service in the Black Hawk War. The bar records of New York and Illinois fail to reveal Goodhue's name among persons admitted to the bar in those states. According to records of the clerk of the Minnesota Supreme Court, he was admitted to the Minnesota bar on January 15, 1850; but there is no evidence that he practiced his profession in the territory. He wrote to Henry H. Sibley on January 10, 1851: "I have myself been a member of the bar for more than a dozen years." The letter is in the Sibley Papers, in the possession of the Minnesota Historical Society. W. W. McMaster, in his *60 Years on the Upper Mississippi,* 156 (Rock Island, Illinois, 1893), states that Goodhue lived in Galena "for two or three years," but he does not indicate when he lived there.

Goodhue, Attorney and Counsellor at Law, Platteville, W. T." A card in the *Wisconsin Whig* (Platteville) announced that "James M. Goodhue, Attorney, at law," practiced his profession in Grant, Crawford, and Iowa counties, and would "attend the Supreme Court at Madison, and make application for persons claiming the benefit of the Bankrupt Law." [7]

Goodhue's law practice was not so heavy as to consume all his energy, for he found time for writing and lecturing. Communications on various subjects from his pen appeared in the *Galena Advertiser* and the *Grant County Herald*, published at Lancaster, Wisconsin; and the *Advertiser*, in the issues from November 14, 1843, to January 2, 1844, published serially "Struck a Lead. An Original Tale by James M. Goodhue." [8] The story is one of romance and adventure in the lead mining region in the early 1840's. Most of the characters are adventurers of various kinds and conditions drawn to the lead mines to make their fortunes by hook or crook. The hero, a young man of dubious principles, reforms, wins his fortune and the lovely lady of his affections, and becomes a pillar of the church, while the villains of the tale are buried alive in a mineral hole. As literature, the novel has little merit; but descriptions of a steamboat race on the Mississippi River, of Galena, life in the lead district, mining methods, and the workings of the law on the frontier give it some interest and historical value. With the publication of the last installment, the *Grant County Herald* of January 13, 1844, came to the defense of the mining region with the following comment:

"A mistake has gone abroad in regard to the distinctive character of the country comprising, and the people inhabiting, the Mining District, highly detrimental to both. . . .

[7] Stevens, in *Minnesota Historical Collections*, 6:492; *Wisconsin Whig*, April 27, 1842. The State Historical Society of Wisconsin has a file of the *Galena Advertiser* and two issues of the *Whig*, as well as files of the other Wisconsin newspapers referred to on following pages.

[8] Many years after Goodhue's death the novel was published in book form, under the title *Struck a Lead; An Historical Tale of the Upper Lead Region* (Chicago, 1883).

"Six years ago 'Struck a Lead' would have been as characteristic as it was eloquent: and it is perhaps to a few scenes rarely eclipsed in genuine recklessness and brutality that the Col. found material for the formation of his rare characters, and that has given to the present population of the Upper Mines a reputation in no way enviable, except by the veriest barbarians."

During the 1830's and 1840's interest in phrenology was widespread. Articles on the subject and advertisements of lectures on phrenology and "phrenomnemotechny" were frequent in the newspapers of the times. Phrenologists traveled about giving "examinations and oral descriptions" for fifty cents, and "the same with marked chart" for a dollar.[9] On February 19, 1842, Goodhue delivered a public lecture before the Young Men's Debating Club in Galena. From under his lecture desk he brought forth from time to time a dog's skull, on which he pointed out bumps and characteristics to illustrate his talk, under the pretense that each time he was exhibiting a different human skull. A few days later the *Galena Advertiser* observed that Goodhue had been lecturing on phrenology "before different societies here" and had "got the reputation of being a great wag," a remark that brought forth from the lecturer an indignant letter to the editor: [10]

". . . I have never, either in Galena or elsewhere, sought nor gained the reputation of 'a wag.' I have a character to sustain, both personal and professional, which I respect, and others shall respect. It is true, I have used ridicule in attacking the pretended science of Phrenology. I did consider and do *now* consider it the appropriate weapon to attack fools with. . . .

"If there be 'waggery' in exposing such ridiculous hum-

[9] See, for example, the *Galena Advertiser*, November 25, 1837, August 26, 1842, and September 27, 1844.

[10] McMaster, *60 Years on the Upper Mississippi*, 157; *Galena Advertiser*, February 19, 26, March 5, 1842. Goodhue delivered the same lecture in Platteville and Mineral Point, Wisconsin. *Mineral Point Free Press*, April 19, 1842.

buggery to public scorn; if it be waggish to show up the absurdity of believing, without proof, in the complex multi-plicity of the organs of thought; if it be *droll* to maintain that unity, individuality and identity of ourselves of which all are conscious; if it be *droll* and *funny* to defend well established principles of mental philosophy, against the crude specula-tions of travelling quacks, who are alike ignorant of mind or of anatomy, then charge the drollery where it belongs — to the subject, and not the lecturer."

In later years many a "travelling quack" was to squirm under Goodhue's gibes.

Platteville was visited by an epidemic of smallpox in the winter of 1843-44. Nearly half of the five hundred inhabitants of the town, Goodhue among them, contracted the disease, and many of the cases proved fatal. The citizens, thoroughly alarmed, held a meeting at which they took measures to elimi-nate the disease and appointed a committee to care for the sick and bury the dead. Whether or not Goodhue, before he was stricken or after his recovery, was a member of the com-mittee has not been recorded; but, according to Stevens, he gave assistance to one victim, at least, Henrietta Kneeland, a young woman who taught in the village school, and the result was their marriage on December 21, 1843. Goodhue was to find in his wife a courageous helpmate, who, in addi-tion to her household duties and the care of their three young children, could, when necessity demanded, "set type to avoid a delay in the issue of the Pioneer, and now and then with a baby on her left arm, sit at the editor's desk and write edito-rials" of "merit and ability." She has been described as "a queenly woman, a motherly woman, and an intelligent wo-man."[11]

[11] *History of Grant County, Wisconsin,* 691 (Chicago, 1881); *Galena Advertiser,* December 15, 29, 1843; *Grant County Herald,* December 30, 1843; William P. Murray, "Memories of Early St. Paul," in the *St. Paul Pioneer Press,* November 9, 1899; Stevens, in *Minnesota Historical Collections,* 6:497. Rebecca M. Cathcart, in "A Sheaf of Remembrances," in *Minnesota Historical*

Soon after his marriage Goodhue decided that Lancaster, the seat of Grant County, offered larger opportunities in his profession than did Platteville. On May 3, 1844, he wrote to Cyrus Woodman of Winslow, Illinois, that he would remove to Lancaster the following week, and he invited Woodman to form a partnership with him to practice law there. "The people of Lancaster," he wrote, "are quite anxious that I should reside there. . . . I am satisfied that we can do a good business there; — that we can if we desire, have one or two county offices." Woodman did not accept the invitation; but Goodhue carried out his intention and opened a law office in Lancaster later that month.[12]

Collections, 15:545, describes Mrs. Goodhue as "a woman of unusual intellectual ability and very great social qualities. She not only kept her household in order, but could edit her husband's newspaper in an emergency."

[12] The letter is in the Woodman Papers, in the possession of the State Historical Society of Wisconsin. Goodhue's professional card in the *Grant County Herald* was dated at Lancaster for the first time in the issue of May 18, 1844. Woodman the same year entered into partnership with Cadwallader C. Washburn in Mineral Point. Ellis B. Usher, "Cyrus Woodman: A Character Sketch," in *Wisconsin Magazine of History*, 2:393–412 (June, 1919).

2. Wisconsin Editor

LANCASTER WAS THE HOME OF THE GRANT COUNTY HERALD, A weekly newspaper that had been established in the spring of 1843. It was a four-page, five-column sheet made up for the most part of materials clipped from other newspapers and periodicals, typical of country papers of the time. Except for communications from readers, a few paragraphs on local matters, and now and then a brief and uninspired editorial on a topic of the day, the paper was innocent of original matter. At the time of Goodhue's arrival, the publisher, J. D. Spalding, was struggling, with indifferent success, to perform the editorial duties that had fallen upon him with the departure of the editor some weeks earlier.

With the issue of July 6, 1844, it must have been apparent to the most unobservant of the *Herald's* readers that something had happened to give the paper new life, a fact that became more obvious with each succeeding issue. The editorial page assumed a distinct individuality. Vitality and good-natured humor pervaded the page, and the writing was fluent and original. The tone of the paper became more local. Items describing the surrounding country and near-by communities, the crops raised in the vicinity, and the agricultural possibilities of the region were frequent; and vigorous editorials called upon the people to build and improve roads and bridges, to raise farm produce for the home market, to amend laws, and, above all, to establish a system of common schools. Most of the articles and paragraphs on the editorial page were signed "G." beginning with the issue of July 13; but "G.'s" identity was not disclosed until October 12, when the *Herald*, issued under the new name *Wisconsin Herald and Grant County Advertiser*, published a statement, signed by Goodhue, that his "editorial connection with this paper, terminated with the last number," and a comment by Spalding that Goodhue had given up his work on the *Herald* because his time was "necessarily taken up by business in his profession, the law."

Goodhue had made a spirited campaign for new subscribers for the *Herald*, which evidently met with great success. In the issue of August 31 he wrote that the paper had begun its career with a subscription list of 250 names, which had "remained about stationary — until within a few weeks. Of late the Herald has attracted some attention from *abroad*, and we have received flattering encouragement from several quarters." Now and then he printed evidences of such "flattering encouragement," among them a letter from a new subscriber who wrote of the *Herald* as "the best newspaper extant," and the following, quoted from the *Racine Advocate:* "There is a certain writer who has all the vivacity and eccentricity of Randolph, the sound common sense of *Madison*, the naturalness and simplicity of Irving, and, withal a continual and abundant flow of the choicest humor. Wherever he paints, you will observe the good hue." [1] When Lucien B. Leach, who had taken over Goodhue's editorial duties, left the paper the following spring he wrote:

"The paper will enter into the new year of its existence, in a healthy and improved condition, having, in the course of the last volume been much enlarged and its circulation greatly increased. At No. 16, Vol. 2, J. M. Goodhue, commenced writing for the *Herald*, under the operation of whose pen, the paper began to *look up*, and has continued to increase in patronage to the close of the volume. At No. 30, Mr. G. discontinued writing for the paper editorially, but not till after establishing for himself a brilliant reputation far and wide, as a clear, pleasing and able writer." [2]

The talent that this brief and happy experience in jour-

[1] *Herald,* September 7, 21, 1844.
[2] *Herald,* March 8, 1845. The paper had been enlarged to six columns.

nalism had brought to light was not allowed to remain long dormant. On August 2, 1845, the *Herald* appeared with Goodhue named as copublisher and editor; and a month later, in the issue of September 13, under the heading "Palinurus Overboard!" he published this announcement:

"When Æneas left the realms of queen Dido and his vessel was cleaving the blackened waves of the deep sea, the pilot, Palinurus, fell asleep and tumbled overboard; after which Æneas took upon himself the duty and business of pilot. In like manner Mr. Spalding, the pilot of the Herald, has fallen overboard — and the helm is in the hands of the Editor — now sole proprietor also of the little craft; — who will endeavor to steer her safely on her voyage between Scylla and Charybdis. No longer water-logged nor sailing in the calm of a dead sea, we have fitted up the Herald with a *propeller* — and now with a fair breeze of popular favor, we hope to see her ride the waves of the future 'like a thing of life.' "

Thenceforth the *Herald* was in truth "a thing of life," a sprightly and entertaining sheet, reflecting in its columns the lusty personality of its editor.[3]

Goodhue called upon his patrons to sustain him "in a full, fair, untrammeled expression of thoughts upon all subjects embraced in the range of newspaper discussion," and announced his intention of making the *Herald* "an exponent of the history, events, the progress and the business of the county of Grant." He lamented the lack of knowledge about Wisconsin in the country at large and blamed the press of the region for being "too feeble to throw its rays abroad." For this appalling situation there was but one remedy: "*to sustain the press of the North-west;* to give it dignity, talent, force, momentum, saleableness, that will drive back the tide of stupid periodical

[3] Goodhue continued to practice law for a time after he took over the editorship of the *Herald,* which printed his card up to and including the issue of September 25, 1847: "James M. Goodhue, Attorney and Counsellor at Law, and Notary Public." Beginning with the issue of October 9, 1847, his card read: "James M. Goodhue, Notary Public and Land Agent."

stuff that is flowing into the North-west and impeding the motions and activity of our *own* presses, with stagnant, stinking backwater."[4]

For the enlightenment of the outside world the *Herald* published descriptive articles about Wisconsin and editorials extolling the climate, resources, and prosperity of the Northwest and its superiority over California and Oregon, which were then drawing on the populations of the East. Editorials and paragraphs on agricultural conditions, schools, the mines, and local politics, events, and needs carried out the editor's determination to make the paper "an exponent" of the county. In spite of Goodhue's strictures on "stupid periodical stuff," exchange papers and periodicals continued to provide the *Herald* with articles on a wide variety of subjects, ranging from "The Progress of Steam" to "The Ladies of Lima." Especially numerous were articles on travel and description, which included much material on Mexico, California, and Oregon, and a series of lectures on China. While it was the editor's stated policy not to print "tales," now and then there appeared in the *Herald* stories under such titles as "Lillian More; or the Blighted Bud," by Fanny Forrester, and "The Broken Hearted, or a Night of Years; a Tale of Sad Reality," by Grace Greenwood. Most of the paper's fiction, however, consisted of humorous accounts and amusing nonsense.[5]

The *Herald* was dependent on exchange papers also for news of the outside world, much of which was delivered by the slow mails when it was no longer news. Foreign and domestic items from exchanges were either clipped in full on the front page, or abstracted in a series of short paragraphs on the editorial page. Domestic items consisted largely of curious and unusual occurrences and sensational catastrophes, the latter headed "Melancholy Accident," "Horrid Murder," or "Awful Catastrophe," according to the fashion of newspapers

[4] *Herald*, August 2, September 13, 1845, August 1, 1846.
[5] *Herald*, February 13, August 7, September 11, 1847, July 15, 1848.

of the day, and followed by an adequate number of exclamation points to indicate the degree of melancholy, horror, or awfulness of the incident. The president's messages were printed on the first page, as were the governor's messages and notable speeches made in Congress and in the Wisconsin legislature. Much space was devoted to news of the Mexican War during the years it was in progress.

Concerning the Mexican War, Goodhue in the summer of 1846 expressed the opinion that it was well for the United States to extend "its right arm into Mexico that our neighbors may gaze and tremble at the vastness of its muscles and the iron strength of its grip   . but if our government intends to extinguish Mexican nationality, it shall succeed — never!" A year later he was accusing the administration of "heedlessly, recklessly, blindly" plunging the country into "a war of conquest, such as our Constitution never contemplated," of conducting the war "in a spirit at once niggardly and cruel," and of protracting it "wantonly and unnecessarily." The main object of the war, he wrote, was "a conquest of a market for slaves. . . . In obedience to the laws . . . we will rally by and defend our flag . . . but before high Heaven, we protest against the mission on which it is sent." [6]

The first local matter of importance to engage Goodhue's attention was a movement launched in 1846 to divide Grant County, against which he waged vigorous war in the *Herald*. A meeting held at Beetown to discuss the subject was broken up by a noisy delegation from Lancaster, who feared for the prestige of their town as the county seat if Grant should be divided.[7] Goodhue's part in the affair is revealed in a communication printed in the Platteville *Independent American* of January 16, 1846:

"Mr. Goodhue detained the meeting [*until the arrival of the Lancaster delegation*] with a very lengthy speech, which

[6] *Herald*, August 22, 1846, September 11, October 23, November 6, 1847.
[7] *Herald*, January 10, 24, 1846.

was full of tautology — departing entirely from his usual course of short and pithy speeches, and methodical arguments. Hence, the opinion was imbibed, by many that the whole scheme for breaking up the meeting had been previously concocted. However, the Col. denies being privy to such an understanding. — As he is a gentleman and a man of veracity, his denial will remove suspicion."

For some time after Goodhue took over the paper there was no party organization in Grant County, and local affairs as reflected in the *Herald* remained uncolored by politics, although the editor was a delegate to the Wisconsin Whig territorial convention in 1845. Little editorial attention was given to national affairs, except for a comment now and then on the Mexican War. On July 19, 1847, the Whigs of Grant County met in convention and passed a resolution requesting Goodhue to publish a Whig paper; and in its next issue, that of July 24, the *Herald* printed the proceedings of the meeting, in which Goodhue had taken an active part, and announced that it would support the Whig party. Thenceforth the *Herald* took a lively interest in politics, lauding all Whig men and measures and hurling editorial missiles at all things Democratic, from the administration down to the least local office-seeker. A special object of Goodhue's denunciation was Moses M. Strong, who was an unsuccessful Democratic candidate for delegate in 1847. In 1848, when Strong was running for district judge, Goodhue wrote of him: "The electors all know him. He is as much distinguished for *integrity* as for *sobriety*. If this is not recommendation, it is his fault — not ours." [8]

Early in January, 1846, a bill for an enabling act for Wisconsin was introduced in Congress, and a few weeks later the territorial legislature passed an act for a statehood referendum in April. In anticipation of the formation and adoption of a state constitution, Goodhue in February and March published

[8] *Herald*, August 5, 1848.

a series of able editorials on state organization, in which he dealt with the legislative, executive, and judicial branches of state government. In general, he professed "little faith in innovations and experiments in government" and declared himself opposed "to altering existing and well known laws, unless such alteration be clearly beneficial." Among the provisions that he advocated was a small legislative body, "ample authority" and a term of four years for the governor; adherence to "the great frame work of law now existing in England and America"; the election of judges by the people and a fair remuneration for them; and a minimum number of courts to meet "the absolute necessities of justice." [9]

In the fall of 1846 a convention of delegates, a majority of whom were Democrats, prepared a constitution for the approval of the people. This constitution Goodhue denounced as "radical, wrong, with a tendency to break up the very foundations of social life" — "a monster" begotten at the expense of the people. The article prohibiting the incorporation of banks and the issuance of notes as money, he wrote, "alone ought to kill the Constitution." In an editorial headed "The Petticoat Constitution" he assailed the article giving married women the right to their separate property: if the convention had attempted "to Amazonize women and emasculate the lords of creation, they could not have done it more effectually." He was particularly incensed that "a fine strip of territory" had been "bartered away" by the convention when it advocated for the western boundary of the new state a line east of the present boundary, which would have excluded from Wisconsin "all the waters of the St. Croix, a river destined hereafter to connect an immense trade between lake Superior and the Mississippi." [10] On November 28 he wrote

[9] *Herald*, February 14, 21, 28, March 7, 14, 1846. These editorials are reprinted in Milo M. Quaife, ed., *The Movement for Statehood, 1845–1846*, 343–351 (*Wisconsin Historical Collections*, vol. 26 — Madison, 1918).

[10] Louise P. Kellogg, "The Admission of Wisconsin to Statehood," in Quaife, ed., *Movement for Statehood*, 26; Frederic L. Paxson, "Wisconsin — A

in the *Herald,* under the heading "The Constitution": "It is
expected shortly that a tape-worm will come away from the
Convention at Madison, in Committee of the Whole, which it
will take three hours to wind upon a clock-reel; after which
that august Body will rise." His opinion of the convention and
all its works was summed up in the latter part of his "New
Year's Address," in the *Herald* of December 31, 1846: [11]

> So failed our Great Convention, met at Madison,
> *Where Moses threw his cane at one McGone:* [12]
> Where Hunkers, Tadpoles, Crawfish, took their pay,
> *Then stooped to steal themselves four bits a day!*
> There rogues for bankrupts fixed a cunning plan
> To keep their gains and gain whate'er they can.
> To make the wife change places with her lord
> And consummate a general scheme of fraud.
> They knocked all paper currency "to fits,"
> *Then paid their board off, with certificates!*
> Refused to make our boundary the St. Croix,
> And *docked* the State, one member to annoy.
> This extra service of the State to pay
> They vote themselves an extra half per day,
> Place their abortive Constitution on a hearse
> Then like a school of cuttle fish, disperse.
> As at the rising of some radiant star
> Whose trembling rays, glad millions hail afar,
> Dense fogs from swamps and stagnant fens arise
> And hide its welcome radiance from their eyes;
> So has the host of vaporing demagogues,
> Obscured Wisconsin in its nauseous fogs.

Constitution of Democracy," in the same work, 37; *Herald,* December 5, 19,
1846, January 9, 20, 1847. The boundary advocated by the convention of
1846 was a line starting from the first rapids of the St. Louis River and
running southward to a point fifteen miles east of the most easterly point in
Lake St. Croix, thence south to Lake Pepin, and on down the main channel
of the Mississippi.
    [11] This has been reprinted also in Milo M. Quaife, ed., *The Struggle over
Ratification, 1846–1847,* 624 (*Wisconsin Historical Collections,* vol. 28 —
Madison, 1920).
    [12] On the altercation between Moses M. Strong and James Magone, see
Milo M. Quaife, ed., *The Convention of 1846,* 557 (*Wisconsin Historical
Collections,* vol. 27 — Madison, 1919).

"The world," cries one, "is too much governed, or has been;"
'Tis not as true as that the world *drinks too much gin!*
When shall we see triumphant virtue's cause?
An honest Constitution? vigorous laws?
When drunken black-legs, leave our public halls!
When the vile Dynasty of rowdies, falls!

The constitution of 1846, as Goodhue had predicted, was
rejected by the electorate, and a second convention met in
December, 1847. The *Herald* published its proceedings, but
devoted comparatively little editorial attention to them. Because many of his objections to the old constitution were met
in the new one, and perhaps because the Whig voice was
more influential in the convention of 1847–48, Goodhue made
only one criticism of the second constitution, but that criticism
was highly significant. The constitution of 1848 accepted the
boundary prescribed by the Wisconsin enabling act, which
was the present Wisconsin-Minnesota line, but included a
proviso expressing a preference for a line running from the
first rapids of the St. Louis River to the mouth of the Rum
River, and thence down the Mississippi, which would have
given the whole St. Croix Valley to Wisconsin. In January,
1848, the citizens of the St. Croix Valley, at a meeting held in
St. Paul, drew up a memorial to Congress protesting against
the Rum River line and proposing instead "A line drawn due
south from Shagwamigan [*Chequamegon*] bay, on Lake Superior, to the intersection of the main Chippewa river, and
from thence down the middle of said stream to its debouchure
into the Mississippi." Goodhue printed the proceedings of the
meeting in the *Herald* of February 26, and on March 25 he
published an editorial sympathetic with the "natural and right-
ful" wishes of the St. Croix people "to become a portion of
Minnestota [*sic*] territory instead of being embraced in the
State of Wisconsin," and expressing approval of the boundary
suggested by the St. Paul convention. The line that Goodhue

then favored was even farther to the east than was the one against which he had protested so vigorously two years earlier. By that time he had probably conceived the idea of removing to Minnesota, should the contemplated territory be established.[18]

Goodhue, in common with other newspaper publishers of his day, had difficulty in collecting payment for subscriptions to the *Herald*. He informed his readers that he would take "lumber, wood, or any kind of produce" at the market price in payment for subscriptions; and time and again he advertised his need for cash, cordwood, corn, or oak boards from subscribers. Now and then a reminder appeared in the midst of a paragraph on an alien subject, as, for instance, the following, headed "Sickness":

"Let medical books alone and attend daily to the dictates of your own experience, if you wish to keep well. Avoid all excesses — all exposures — eat and drink only what agrees with you . . . and pay what you are owing at the Herald office, if you would avoid sickness, doctors' bills and death."

Occasionally he published the name of a subscriber who left town without paying his subscription. When milder methods failed, he threatened to sue backward subscribers, or he gave notice that payment in advance would be required on all subscriptions, advertising, and job work. "As for credit," he announced on one occasion, "we will not trust our *grand-father*." But he evidently found the latter course impractical,

[18] Kellogg, in Quaife, ed., *Movement for Statehood*, 27–29. The manuscript proceedings of the St. Paul meeting are in the possession of the Minnesota Historical Society. The memorial may be found in 30 Congress, 1 session, *Senate Miscellaneous Documents*, no. 98 (serial 511). On April 28, 1848, Goodhue wrote to John H. Tweedy, delegate to Congress from Wisconsin, that the "general sentiment prevailing here, in regard to the northern [western] boundary of Wisconsin, is favorable to the line petitioned for by the people of St. Croix." The letter is in the Tweedy Papers, in the possession of the State Historical Society of Wisconsin. A history of the boundary between Wisconsin and Minnesota is given by William W. Folwell in his *History of Minnesota*, 1:489–495 (St. Paul, 1921).

JAMES MADISON GOODHUE
[From a photograph, presumably of a daguerreotype, in the museum of the
Minnesota Historical Society.]

THE FALLS OF ST. ANTHONY IN 1851

[From a photograph, owned by the State Historical Society of Wisconsin, of a water color by

for not long after each such announcement, appeals and threats to dilatory subscribers became as frequent as ever.[14]

Like other papers then and now, the *Herald* was probably supported chiefly by advertising, for nearly half of its space was devoted to advertisements. Another source of income was the job printing done at the *Herald* office; and in 1848 and 1849, at least, the paper, according to the fiscal report of Grant County, got the lion's share of the county printing. On one occasion Goodhue capitalized on a murder committed by Robert D. Brewer in Beetown by publishing in pamphlet form "a very complete report" of the murderer's trial, "illustrated by a diagram of Beetown — and also a sketch of Brewer's life, and his account of the killing . . . taken down in his own language. — Price 1 dime." [15]

Goodhue's hope of securing a county office, which he had expressed in his letter to Woodman, was realized almost at once, for in 1844 and 1845 he was district attorney of Grant County.[16] He held no other county office while he lived in Wisconsin, although twice later he was a candidate for office. On June 20, 1847, he published in the *Herald* the following announcement over his signature:

"The subscriber, believing that he can if elected, discharge properly the duties of the office of Collector of the county of Grant, and wishing, by visiting the various parts of the County, at the same time to prepare for publication in 'The Herald' a more full and minute description of all the different parts of the County and its earliest settlement so as to give additional interest and value to his journal, offers himself as a

[14] *Herald*, November 8, December 4, 27, 1845, September 26, October 10, November 7, December 12, 1846, April 17, June 5, 19, 1847, March 25, 1848, March 10, 1849.
[15] *Herald*, May 9, 1846, January 20, 1848, March 3, 1849. The following announcement appeared in the *Herald* for January 22, 1848: "An immense crowd of job work this week, must be our excuse for any lack of *news* in our columns."
[16] *Herald*, August 17, 1844, April 5, 1845; *History of Grant County*, 499.

candidate at the next election, for the office of Collector of the county of Grant."

The editor of the Platteville *Independent American*, J. L. Marsh, saw in this announcement an opportunity for revenge on one who had at various times belabored and ridiculed him. Among other matters that must have rankled in his breast was Goodhue's repeated reference to the *American* as "the Independent American and Jew David's Plaster," because of an editorial puff of the nostrum, "Jew David's or Hebrew Plaster," that Marsh had published. On June 26 Marsh announced his own candidacy for collector by reprinting Goodhue's announcement verbatim, except for the substitution of "The American" for "The Herald" and his own signature for Goodhue's. In his next issue Goodhue graciously placed Marsh's name above his own in the list of candidates, but remarked that "the few who had not seen the Herald supposed that the American printer had hired some one who *could* construct a paragraph, to write it for him; whereas it was merely an exhibition of mimicry." Marsh retorted that it was his intention to test "the comparative popularity of the *pettifogger* and the *mimic*."

Goodhue's campaign activities were cut short in August when the last illness of his father called him east. Meanwhile four more candidates for collector had entered the field. Both editors were defeated in the election, Marsh standing fourth and Goodhue fifth. Apparently the citizens of the county cared little about paying the traveling expenses of a newspaper editor for the enhancement of his journal, even though he should serve them as their collector at the same time. "We boast of running in a larger crowd of defeated candidates, than can be scared up in the wide world," wrote Goodhue. "If misery loves company, we ought to be in ecstacies." [17] In 1848 he was a candidate for probate judge, and again he was

[17] *Herald*, February 7, March 14, 28, May 30, June 27, August 15, October 3, 1846; *Independent American*, August 15, 1846.

defeated. In the *Herald* of November 25 he thanked the electors who had voted for him. "God forbid," he wrote, "that
any of them should die, especially in this county, or within
the next two years."

During the winter of 1848–49 Goodhue was doubtless following the debates in Congress on the Minnesota bill and laying plans for the removal of his press to St. Paul as soon as
the bill should become a law. While his conduct of the *Herald* had won for him a reputation throughout the Northwest
as a journalist of ability and had made his paper an influential
political factor in southwestern Wisconsin, the financial rewards were not large.[18] Moreover, the outlook for the future
development of the lead-mining region was unpromising in
the later 1840's. The reduction in 1848 in the tariff on lead,
which encouraged the competition of Spanish lead in the
American market, and the increasing cost of operating the
mines at the lower levels, resulted in a large emigration of lead
miners to California.[19] On the other hand, the new territory to
the northwest offered great promise for future development.
St. Paul, its designated capital, had an advantageous position at
the head of navigation on the Mississippi River, and it was the
common belief that, with the establishment of a territorial
government, immigrants would pour into the region in countless numbers; and an opportunity to obtain the public printing,
a financial boon to any newspaper, awaited its pioneer journalist.

No hint of Goodhue's intended removal from Lancaster appeared in the *Herald*, which suspended publication with the
issue of March 17, although in February the editor had issued
a prospectus for the paper to be published by him in St. Paul.

[18] In a letter written to Henry H. Sibley on May 6, 1849, Elihu B. Wash-
burne of Galena wrote of Goodhue: "He is one of the most entertaining
editors in the country and will make you a most interesting paper." The letter
is in the Sibley Papers.

[19] Joseph Schafer, *The Wisconsin Lead Region*, 107, 108, n. (*Wisconsin
Domesday Book, General Studies*, vol. 3 — Madison, 1932).

Unfortunately no copy of the prospectus has been found; but in the *Prairie du Chien Patriot* of April 4, 1849, appeared this announcement:

"Goodhue & Ditmars [20] have issued a prospectus for a whig paper at St. Paul, Minnesota, to be called the 'Epistle of St. Paul,' the first number to be issued in the month of April. Mr. Goodhue, for the last five or six years has published a paper at Lancaster, and is a ready and vigorous writer. The Herald has been discontinued and the materials of the office 'packed up' for St. Paul."

When the paper was issued it was not Whig, nor was its name "The Epistle of St. Paul." [21]

[20] In a few issues of the *Herald* beginning with that of November 11, 1848, "E. H. Ditmars, printer" followed Goodhue's name at the top of the page. His name disappeared from the paper in the spring of 1848, and no evidence has been found that he was with Goodhue after the establishment of the *Pioneer*.

[21] Goodhue's reason for discarding the title "The Epistle of St. Paul" is given below, on page 249. His son James made the following statement in the *St. Paul Pioneer* of January 28, 1868: "Mr. Goodhue printed in Lancaster a prospectus which was distributed in Minnesota, called the 'Epistle of St. Paul,' but . . . Stillwater and St. Anthony objected to this name for the paper, as being entirely local in its significance."

3. The Pioneer is Launched

ST. PAUL AS GOODHUE FOUND IT UPON HIS ARRIVAL IS BEST DE-scribed in his own words, reprinted elsewhere in this book.[1] Minute as it was, it was the capital of a vast territory extending westward to the Missouri and White Earth rivers, and embracing much of present-day North and South Dakota. But the only part of that broad area that was open to white settlement in 1849 was the triangle between the St. Croix and the Mississippi rivers as far north as the latitude of the mouth of the Crow Wing; the remainder was still Indian country. Besides St. Paul, the principal settlements were at Stillwater, Little Canada, and St. Anthony, which was later absorbed by Minneapolis. According to a census taken in June, 1849, when the population had been augmented by several boatlands of immigrants, the number of people in the whole territory was under five thousand, and St. Paul had fewer than a thousand. It was not until June 1 that the Whig governor, Alexander Ramsey, who had been appointed by the president, declared the territorial government established and announced the names of the other appointed officers.[2]

In a carpenter shop on the north side of Third Street, between Robert and Jackson streets, Goodhue set up his press and began the publication of Minnesota's first newspaper. "We print and issue this number of the Pioneer," he wrote, "in a building through which out-of-doors is visible by more than five hundred apertures; and as for our type, it is not safe from being pied on the galleys by the wind." A few weeks later a better location was found for the *Pioneer* office, in the second story of a frame building on the south side of Third Street, between Robert and Minnesota streets, where it re-

[1] See especially pages 135–137, 246–251, below.
[2] Folwell, *Minnesota*, 1:250, 351, 352.

mained for about a year. Soon after Goodhue's arrival in St. Paul he bought a lot extending from Bench (later Second) Street to Third, just below Wabasha Street, and built a small house, unlathed and unplastered. There he brought his family — his wife and three small children, the two-year-old twins,

GOODHUE'S SECOND HOUSE

James and Mary, and Edward, a year old. The house in 1850 became the middle section of the *Pioneer* office, the editorial office being at the end facing Bench Street at first, and later, in the fall of 1850, at the Third Street end. At that time the family removed to a better house on the northeast corner of Third and St. Peter streets.[3]

    [3] *Pioneer*, August 29, November 21, 1850, April 15, 1852; Murray, in the *St. Paul Pioneer Press*, November 9, 1899; Newson, *Pen Pictures*, 102; J. Fletcher Williams, "The Press in Minnesota," in Minnesota Editors and Publishers Association, *Proceedings*, 1870, p. 36; Goodhue to Sibley, July 30, September 14, 1850, Sibley Papers. Goodhue's youngest child, Edward, died in October, 1849. A daughter, Eve, was born in 1851. *Pioneer*, November 1, 1849.
    The fate of Goodhue's original printing press has long been the subject of controversy. One version has it that it was purchased in 1858 or 1859 and taken to Sioux Falls, South Dakota, to print the *Dakota Democrat*, and that its remains now rest in the Masonic Museum at Sioux Falls. According to another

William Pitt Murray, who arrived in St. Paul in December, 1849, found that "the working force of the Pioneer was James M. Goodhue, owner, editor, manager, town reporter, compositor, pressmen and distributor, [and] two journeymen and a printer's devil."[4] It was Goodhue's practice on the day the *Pioneer* was issued to take his papers over his arm and deliver them himself to his St. Paul subscribers, in the process gathering news for the next issue, observing changes in the rapidly growing community, noting its needs, and sounding the views of the townsmen on all matters pertaining to the territory.[5] The publication day of the *Pioneer* was doubtless eagerly awaited, for it was entertaining reading in a frontier community that had little else but newspapers to read; and the witty

version, it was bought in 1855 by Jeremiah Russell, who took it to Sauk Rapids to publish the *Sauk Rapids Frontierman;* from Sauk Rapids it traveled to St. Cloud, thence to Osakis, thence to Lindstrom, and, finally, to the museum of the Minnesota Historical Society. Claims have been made also that the old hand press now owned by the *Burnett County Journal* in Grantsburg, Wisconsin, is the original Goodhue press. In the *Publications* of the Canadian North-West Historical Society for 1928, a pamphlet on "The Story of the Press," it is stated that at one time the *Nor'Wester,* a newspaper of the Red River Settlement, was printed on Goodhue's press. C. E. Foote, publisher of the *Inter Ocean* at Superior, Wisconsin, in a letter of February 14, 1885, to the Minnesota Historical Society, stated that at that time he had the press in his shop. The fact that as early as August, 1849, Goodhue had two presses in his shop may be the basis for some of the confusion. It has been fairly well established that Goodhue's original press was bought in Cincinnati in 1836 by John King, who used it to print the *Dubuque Visitor;* that it printed the *Herald* at Lancaster; and that Goodhue brought it to St. Paul to print the *Pioneer.* The various claims as to the later history of the press may be found in the *Daily Argus-Leader* (Sioux Falls), November 8, 17, 1919; the *St. Paul Pioneer Press,* November 9, 1899; the *Monthly South Dakotan,* 1:56, 116 (August, November, 1898); Willoughby M. Babcock, "The Goodhue Press," in *Minnesota History Bulletin,* 3:291-294 (February, 1920); John C. Parish, "Three Men and a Press," in the *Palimpsest,* 1:56-60 (July, 1920); and S. Melby, "The Goodhue Press," a manuscript in the possession of the Minnesota Historical Society.

[4] *St. Paul Pioneer Press,* November 9, 1899. James M. Goodhue, Jr., in the *St. Paul Pioneer* of January 28, 1868, stated that his father brought with him to Minnesota two journeymen. On February 10, 1851, Goodhue wrote to Sibley that he had "9 or 10 men employed whose pay probably exceeds $20. each per week." The letter is in the Sibley Papers.

[5] Stevens, in *Minnesota Historical Collections,* 6:498; *Pioneer,* December 5, 1849.

remarks and endless humor of its overgrown editor-newsboy must have been a source of delight to subscribers as he made his rounds.

Unlike most frontier newspapers of the time, which as a rule simply rehashed matter from eastern papers, the *Pioneer* was predominantly local in tone. The keynote of Goodhue's editorial policy, sounded in the first issue of his paper and recurrent again and again in succeeding issues, is well expressed in an editorial in the *Pioneer* of April 17, 1851, headed "The Uses of the Press":

"The most important purpose of the newspaper press, especially on the frontier, is to mirror back to the world, the events, the peculiarities and the whole features of the new world by which it is surrounded. It necessarily has, or should have, a provincial character. Its radius of observation, is rather confined to the sphere around it. — The great news centres, the mammoth presses of the Atlantic cities, derive intelligence from all quarters and radiate news over the whole continent. They are the grand reflectors of intelligence. The frontier press, is more influential indirectly than directly; by being copied and multiplied in the enormous city papers, which penetrate every corner of the world. Can we make Minnesota known abroad, by filling our sheet with nothing but reprints from other papers, so that, for anything contained in it, the paper might as well be printed in London or New York? For general intelligence, the news of the world at large, we expect our readers to look into the journals of the great cities. An important or interesting item of intelligence from Minnesota, copied into the N. Y. Tribune, or the Herald, or the Sun, or the North American, or Pennsylvanian, will do more to make our Territory known abroad, than the issue of a whole edition of the press from which the article emanated.[6]

"As a citizen of the Territory, rather than the editor of a

[6] The *Herald* and the *Sun* were New York newspapers. The *Pennsylvanian* and the *North American* were daily papers published at Philadelphia.

paper here, we feel gratified therefore, by seeing in those and in other influential journals, so many quotations from our humble journal. When a bookseller has inquiry made in his store, for a map of Minnesota, he would hardly expect to satisfy his customer by saying, 'I have it not, sir; but here is a pocket map of the world, which of course includes Minnesota.' So neither should we expect to satisfy our readers, with a weekly issue here of a paper, which is not essentially a Minnesota paper. We would rather, now, present a daguerreotype of Saint Paul, sitting now in our office, as we see it springing up fresh and vigorous, like the skeleton of a great city, where but yesterday stood a forest, filled with wild Indians — we would rather represent to the world abroad, the sounds of the hammer and the saw and the axe, which greet our ears now from every quarter of the town, or paint the shining river that flows under the bluff, one hundred feet below Bench street, from which a stone may be thrown into it, or describe the tumultuous joy with which the multitudes of our people, old and young, flocked down to the levee, to greet the landing on Friday week, of the first boat of the season, the Nominee, than to write a political homily as long as the Mississippi river, and twice as turbid.

"Of all the news that relates to Minnesota, of every event here which is calculated to excite the attention and the interest of the world, we take special note; and we never have been and never will be outdone here in this, which we consider the paramount business of a frontier editor; we will not, though politics should 'go to the dogs.' We are for all the details, particulars and items of intelligence that we can glean, concerning our town and our Territory. Special news, is the life and soul of a newspaper here, if it has any."

To this course Goodhue adhered throughout his editorship of the *Pioneer*. Near the close of his career, in the issue of April 22, 1852, he reiterated his policy:

"When Saint Paul becomes a large news centre, justifying

the publication of a large newspaper, then our readers may expect more interesting miscellany and more of the general news of the world. *Then*, the primary object of this press will be, to make the world known to Minnesota; *now*, the primary object is to make Minnesota known to the world. . . . Our people must at present, rely mainly upon papers taken by them abroad, to learn the details of the history of the world. But unquestionably the first duty of every Minnesotian, is to sustain and to force forward a press in Minnesota, that shall have *magnitude, elevation,* and internal, inherent power enough, to throw its flashing rays across the whole continent."

The *Minnesota Pioneer* was a four-page, six-column sheet until October 4, 1849, when it was enlarged to seven columns. "Sound Principles, Safe Men and Moderate Measures," printed at the top of the first page, was its motto until October 25, 1849, when it became "Democratic Principles, Democratic Men, and Democratic Measures." For a year beginning in October, 1849, Goodhue's younger brother, Isaac, was co-editor.

While much of the subject matter of the first page was similar to that of the *Wisconsin Herald* —articles on a variety of subjects clipped from other newspapers and periodicals, poetry, "melancholy" and "dreadful" accidents, "terrible" murders, jokes, anecdotes, and foreign and domestic news items — articles descriptive of Minnesota or on some phase of Minnesota history frequently found a place on this page. The third and fourth pages were devoted to legal and other notices and to cards of professional men and advertisements of business houses not only in St. Paul and neighboring communities, but also in Dubuque, Galena, St. Louis, and other river towns. When there were not enough advertisements to cover the two pages, foreign and domestic news items and other matters of the sort found on page one were used as fillers. During legislative sessions the laws and the journals of the two houses crowded out exchanges.

The second page was Goodhue's own, to a far greater degree than the editorial page of the *Wisconsin Herald* had been. It was devoted to articles and paragraphs, varying in length from several columns to a sentence or two, and concerned for the most part with local matters. The editor discussed local politics; recounted social events; reported on the progress of building and the growth of trade and industry in St. Paul, Stillwater, and St. Anthony; described the territory in general and its various localities in particular; pointed out the advantages and potentialities of Minnesota for agriculture, industry, and commerce; specified the needs of the territory, and suggested ways to fulfill them; glorified the beauty and the climate of Minnesota; prophesied about the future of the territory; lectured the citizens on their manners and their morals; hounded and ridiculed his adversaries; perpetrated hoaxes; and castigated purveyors of nostrums.

Goodhue's personality — his vigorous intellect, rich imagination, unusual perceptive powers, his amazing energy, wide range of interests, wit and humor, and fundamental sincerity — dominated the editorial page of the *Pioneer* and made it a colorful and vital newspaper. His descriptive articles and paragraphs, with their wealth and variety of detail, and his lively accounts of local events and progress, make it an invaluable historical document for the Minnesota of his day. His writing was informal and uneven, often evincing the haste demanded of a newspaper reporter. Sometimes, impatient of the slow medium for the torrent of ideas rushing through his mind, he poured words from his pen in long, breath-taking sentences, piling adjective on adjective with fantastic effect; but he knew, too, the uses of simplicity, and many of his most devastating paragraphs were arresting in their brevity. His political articles had more force and logic and less wind and bombast than those written by his adversaries, despite the correspondent in a rival paper who referred to him as "this Bombastus Furioso of the press." [7] His humor, at times rowdy

[7] *Minnesota Democat*, September 2, 1851.

and irreverent, his tall stories, his puns and his hoaxes, were typical of the frontier, but they were generally spontaneous and original.

Original, too, and often picturesque, were his figures of speech. A suggestion of the emotions of Minnesotans as they faced the long winter with the closing of the river, which cut them off completely from the rest of the world, is given in his mention of the departure of the steamboat "Nominee" for the season. "She went off," he wrote, "with a tear in her eye, and disappeared around the bend, Mr. Neill's church steeple standing on tiptoe to catch the last glimpse of her." St. Paul at winter's end he described as "impatient as a young widow waiting for her nuptials, for the hour that shall unite her again with the world." Many of his figures of speech were decidedly earthy in flavor. The "nasty corruption" of a certain political faction, he wrote on one occasion, was "more loathsome than the remembrance of a putrid carcass, *stirring* with maggots under an August sun"; and another time he likened the same group to "a bale of odoriferous Winnebago furs — less offensive as it is, than it would be unpacked." Of a St. Paul newspaper he wrote: "Like a steaming, unwashed tripe, this journal again comes out, and it becomes the duty of the Pioneer, to throw chlorine over it, for the sake of the public health." [8]

Goodhue's savage diatribes against his enemies, political and other, could hardly have been printed had present libel laws been in effect. Nor was he above name-calling, for such epithets as "a sorry sore-lipped puppy," "a church-burning Whig outcast," "an ass, stuffed with arrogance," "a miserable drunkard," were by no means uncommon in the *Pioneer*. But it was not the part of an editor to deal gently with error, in his opinion; rather, let him "slash away — anything, but *salve*, salve, when the dissecting knife is needed. A journal that does noth-

[8] *Pioneer,* March 27, November 21, 1850, June 26, October 9, 1851; Goodhue to Sibley, September 14, 1850, in the Sibley Papers.

ing but paddle along with public opinion, without breasting the current of popular errors, is of no value — none whatever." [9]

Most obvious in every issue of the *Pioneer* was Goodhue's sincere and enthusiastic love of Minnesota and his great faith in its future. He made it evident that when he arrived in St. Paul on that "raw, cloudy day" in April, 1849, he came to stay, to devote all his energy and talent to furthering the interests of the territory and its people. If from his efforts he hoped to reap financial gain, he was no different from any other pioneer who cast his lot upon the frontier. While he did not win riches in Minnesota, he must have made at least a respectable living. There were times, it is true, when he found himself in financial straits, hard pressed to find money for paper and other printing supplies, especially when the government was slow in paying him for his share of the territorial printing. [10] The *Pioneer* was undoubtedly sustained mainly by its large number of advertisements and legal notices, as well as by job printing, for the population of the region did not provide a large subscription list. In 1851 the editor wrote that he printed a thousand copies of the *Pioneer* each week, "which is many more than our subscription list requires; yet so great is the transient sale of the paper, that we have not a single copy left, a week after publication." [11] In common with all frontier newspaper publishers, he found it difficult to collect from subscribers. Frequent evidence of this is found in the *Pioneer*, as, for example, a paragraph in the issue of June 20, 1850:

"A young fellow named J. H. Bowman, from Boston, lately living near St. Anthony, slipped off down the river, the other

[9] *Pioneer*, February 6, August 28, 1851, June 3, 1852.
[10] On April 22, 1850, Goodhue wrote to Sibley that he owed six hundred dollars for paper and had "not a dollar to pay"; and "worse than that," he was entirely out of paper. He continued: "The cost of supporting my printing establishment here, has been enormous; altho' I have managed my business with the strictest economy, living poor and laboring very hard." The letter is in the Sibley Papers.
[11] *Pioneer*, August 14, 1851.

night, without paying his subscription to the Pioneer. Publishers of newspapers will please remember his name; as he is a fair representative of a large class of newspaper patrons, who only require to be known to be properly appreciated."

Besides the office of territorial printer, Goodhue held only one other public office in Minnesota — that of overseer of the poor of Ramsey County, at a salary of twenty dollars a year. But he engaged in other ventures. An advertisement in the *Pioneer* of February 6, 1850, announced that he would "attend promptly to the business of preparing papers and forwarding the requisite proofs to obtain land warrants for soldiers who are entitled thereto, by discharge." The St. Paul *Minnesotian* of December 6, 1851, noted that Goodhue had bought a lot on the corner of Sibley and Water streets, with the intention of building there a large warehouse. In 1850 he and his brother Isaac obtained from the Ramsey County commissioners a license to maintain a ferry across the Mississippi River at the Lower Landing, and two years later the territorial legislature granted the two men the exclusive right to maintain a ferry there for ten years. Evidence that there was a larger purpose behind this enterprise than the collection of ferriage is contained in a letter written by Goodhue to Henry H. Sibley on February 6, 1850: "Mine and my brother's ferry goes into operation in April. We shall at least expect to *share* in the benefits of preoccupancy on the other side." Goodhue had in mind the contemplated treaties with the Sioux Indians, by which their lands on the west side of the Mississippi would be opened to settlement. When the Goodhue ferry bill was under consideration in the Council, Lorenzo A. Babcock offered a substitute for the title: "A bill granting to James M. Goodhue and Isaac N. Goodhue, the right to secure a valuable claim on the west side of the Mississippi river, to the exclusion of all other citizens of the Territory, and St. Paul in particular." [12]

[12] *Pioneer*, January 9, 1850; Minnesota Territory, *Laws*, 1852, p. 55; *Council Journal*, 1852, p. 68. The letter is in the Sibley Papers.

But these various enterprises were subordinate interests that served the purpose of absorbing whatever of the man's abundant energy was unexpended on his real vocation — the conduct of the *Pioneer* in such a way as to serve best the interests of his adopted territory. That his success in this purpose was appreciated by his contemporaries is indicated in the statement by one of them that "he was the individual above all others, who had promoted the general welfare of Minnesota"; that "his most bitter opponents were convinced, whatever might be his course toward them, that he loved Minnesota with all his heart, all his mind, and all his might." [13]

[13] Edward D. Neill, "Obituary of James M. Goodhue," in *Minnesota Historical Collections*, 1:245 (1872).

4. Old Settlers Versus New

IF GOODHUE HAD HOPED TO HOLD THE JOURNALISTIC FIELD IN Minnesota without rivals, he was soon disappointed. At about the same time that the first issue of the *Pioneer* appeared, another paper, the *Minnesota Register*, was circulated in the territory. It had been printed in Cincinnati, but it was dated St. Paul, Minnesota Territory, April 27, 1849, and "A. Randall & Co." were named as publishers. Associated with Randall was John P. Owens, who brought the press of the *Register* to St. Paul in May; but it was not until July 14 that the second number of the paper was published. Randall meantime had sold his interest to Nathaniel McLean of Cincinnati, who did not come to Minnesota until the following August. Meanwhile another press had arrived in the territory, that of the *Minnesota Chronicle*, the first number of which was published by James Hughes on May 31. That all three papers could survive in the small community was hardly to be expected; the goal of each was, of course, the public printing.[1]

While the territorial officers were all Whig appointees under President Taylor, there was as yet no party organization in Minnesota of either Whigs or Democrats, and party politics had played no part in the affairs of the region. Henry H.

[1] Newson, *Pen Pictures*, 100; Williams, in Minnesota Editors and Publishers Association, *Proceedings*, 1870, pp. 33, 39; *Galena Daily Advertiser*, May 8, 21, 22, 1849. Goodhue, on his way to Lancaster to get his family and complete his removal to Minnesota, wrote to Sibley from Galena on May 6, 1849: "I learn that Dr. Randall of Cincinnati, being in ill health, has sold the press which he designed to establish in Saint Paul. *Another* press, belonging to Dr. Hughes of Ohio, is on the way to St. Paul and will reach that *grand focus* of printing presses, by the boat which carries this letter." The letter is in the Sibley Papers. A prospectus for still another St. Paul paper, the "Minnesota Standard," to be published by W. W. Wyman, former editor and proprietor of the *Madison* (Wisconsin) *Express*, was issued in the spring of 1849. The "Standard," however, failed to materialize. *Prairie du Chien Patriot*, April 4, 1849; *Galena Daily Advertiser*, March 30, 1849; *Pioneer*, July 19, 1849; Wyman to Sibley, February 18, 1849, Sibley Papers.

Sibley, who had long been the chief representative in the Minnesota country of the American Fur Company and its successor, Pierre Chouteau Jr. and Company, had been elected, the previous year, delegate in Congress from "Wisconsin Territory," on the novel theory that that part of the old territory which had been excluded from the new state of Wisconsin existed as a territory until Congress should make some other provision for its government. Party politics had not entered into his election, although his sympathies were with the Democrat party, as was the case with most of the earlier settlers in the region. Sibley had found his political neutrality an advantage in securing the passage of the bill to organize Minnesota Territory. A rival candidate for the delegacy had been Henry M. Rice, also a Democrat and a partner in the fur company, whose defeat had in no way stifled his political ambitions. Rice increased his following by courting newcomers to the territory and by making gifts and sales of lots in upper St. Paul, where he had acquired considerable property. The rivalry between Sibley and Rice, aggravated by business differences, gave rise to two political factions, and the constant warfare between them was the chief factor in territorial politics for some time to come.[2]

In this state of political affairs the three newspapers felt the need of moving with caution. Each coveted the territorial printing, and in whose gift it would be no one would know until after the election of members of the legislature in August. The *Pioneer* had the advantage of priority; it was well established when the *Chronicle* first issued, and the *Register*,

[2] Folwell, *Minnesota*, 1:236-241, 367; Wilson P. Shortridge, *The Transition of a Typical Frontier, with Illustrations from the Life of Henry Hastings Sibley*, 61-63 (n.p., 1922); William Anderson and Albert J. Lobb, *A History of the Constitution of Minnesota*, 21-28 (Minneapolis, 1921); "Address of Henry H. Sibley, of Minnesota, to the People of Minnesota Territory," in the *Pioneer*, May 5, 1849; letters to Sibley from David Lambert, January 13, 1849, from Dr. Thomas R. Potts, January 24, 1849, and from Jacob W. Bass, January 28, 1849, in the Sibley Papers; Sibley to Charles T. Cavileer, February 15, 1849, in the Cavileer Papers, in the possession of the Minnesota Historical Society.

as has been stated, had temporarily suspended publication after the first number. Goodhue had had an opportunity to take soundings and mark his course before the arrival of the other papers; and it became more and more apparent with each successive issue of his paper that he had cast his lot with Sibley. In the first number of the *Pioneer* he took a neutral stand in politics, assuming the position that party politics had no place in a territory. The *Register* and the *Chronicle*, whose editors were Whigs, also professed themselves against drawing party lines. The political stand that Goodhue maintained throughout that summer was expressed in an editorial in the *Pioneer* of June 14, 1849, entitled "Party Warfare":

"There is a time and a place, for every thing; an appropriate sphere. Women shine least in the political circles. Boys had better be in the school-room than in the camp. It is more appropriate for those who have the control of public affairs, to agitate political measures, than for those who are 'only passengers.' What would be thought of the wisdom of our neighbors in the Selkirk Settlement if they should divide into parties and wrangle and hate each other, as whigs and tories? [3] If they should get into a fever heat on the question of repealing the Irish Union? or quarrel like cats and dogs about the English corn laws? or interest themselves so deeply in a contested election in the House of Commons, or become so bitterly opposed in the array of party on some disputed question of Parliamentary privilege that they could scarcely address each other with civility? Would such a state of things as this further the interests of that settlement? There, where concert of

[3] The Selkirk Settlement, or Red River Colony, was founded by the Earl of Selkirk in 1812, on a land grant along the Red River of the North obtained by him from the Hudson's Bay Company. The settlers were a mixture of European nationalities — Scotch, English, Swiss, French, and others, and Indians with whom they had intermarried. During the 1820's floods, poor harvests, and grasshopper plagues drove many from the colony. Some of them settled near the protective walls of Fort Snelling, and formed the nucleus of St. Paul. The trade with the Selkirk Settlement for many years was of great importance to St. Paul. Theodore C. Blegen, *Building Minnesota*, 77, 120 (New York, 1938); Folwell, *Minnesota*, 1: 213–220.

action is indispensable, where union alone can afford any respectable show of strength, how is any measure to be con-
certed or any scheme for the general welfare, consummated
without union? For let it be remembered that where partyism
plants its foot, there is no recess too private and no sanctuary
too holy for it to violate. It is omnipresent. It is not only in
the election, but it is in the town meeting, the school meeting,
the road meeting, in the church, in the highway, at the fireside, at the table, at the very altar of God; like the lice of
Egypt,[4] it is in the very kneading troughs, coloring, defiling,
poisoning every thing it touches.

"There is but one condition of things that makes partyism
tolerable, anywhere; that condition, thank God, we are not
in. It is where the people who take part in politics, have to
decide political measures by their *votes*, and where there is
sufficient population and strength to warrant a division of the
people into parties, without inducing great feebleness and
insufficiency of action. The effect of two opposing forces is
to neutralize both forces. Therefore, a division into parties,
naturally induces a weakness of the whole. A division of a
small State into parties is like separating two sticks which if
bound together could barely support each other; while a
division of a large State, is more like separating a bundle of
sticks into two parcels, either of which still retains much
strength.

"Does Minnesota fill the first of these conditions? Have our
people any vote to cast on the question of a tariff? Have they
anything to do with a sub-treasury? Can they thrust their
fingers into our foreign relations? Have they to decide
whether or not negroes shall be subject to slavery in New
Mexico or California? Let us not forget our true relation to

[4] The "lice of Egypt" held a peculiar fascination for Goodhue. In the
Pioneer of November 8, 1849, referring to Whig office-holders, he wrote:
"No nation has been so cruelly infested since the plague of vermin upon
Egypt"; and again, on January 16, 1850, he likened those same office-holders
to "a plague, unequalled since the hour when Egypt went lousy."

the Federal Government. We are not a State. We have no
vote in the Senate, none in the House; we have nothing to do
with making Presidents or cabinets. Sometime we may have;
so may Canada; so may Cuba; so may Yucatan! but now, in
our callow Territorial condition, almost without a Territorial
pin-feather upon our back, without a vote, we had almost said
without *anybody to vote*, with everything to *ask* of Congress
and with no power to *command* anything – for Minnesota in
this condition, to attempt to launch out upon the dirty sea of
National Politics, would be as disastrous as it would be for a
chicken with the shell on its head, to try to swim out into the
lake with a flock of swans. What have we to do with Congress? To ask and obtain all the favors we can. Do we want
to carry up our applications for appropriations as a *Whig*
Territory to a Democratic Senate? or as a Democratic Territory to a Whig House of Representatives? Fools! What we
want let us ask for. 'Ask and you shall receive'; but to hold
out one hand to receive a gift and the other to strike the giver,
is the conduct of a madman.

"... This press is friendly to the present Administration.
No press is more so; but we want it distinctly understood,
that we will not, either secretly or openly attempt to defeat
the election in this Territory, of men who have acted with
either or any of the political parties in the States they came
from, provided they are such as will be guilty of the gross
folly of attempting to draw party lines and organize a senseless opposition in advance, to an Administration from which
we have every thing to gain by minding our own Territorial
business and by which we have every thing to lose if we
provoke useless quarrels about measures of a national character
which we have no sort of legislative control over."

The first territorial election was held on August 1, 1849.
There was no contest over the election of delegate to Congress. No one cared to challenge Sibley's popularity, and he
was given a unanimous vote. But the election of members of

the legislature occasioned great excitement. Both Sibley and Rice wanted their friends in the legislature, and both worked, although quietly, toward that end. Whigs and Democrats also were active during the campaign, but no open attempt was made to draw party lines, except at Stillwater, where an "Independent" ticket, composed of Whigs, and a Democratic ticket were submitted to the people.[5]

In the St. Paul district two Council and four House members were to be elected. On July 10 the voters of the district, in answer to a call posted anonymously, held a caucus to nominate candidates. Minnesota's organic act provided that none but those who were inhabitants of the territory on March 3, 1849, could vote at the first election. To a motion that the meeting adjourn until July 14, Rice moved an amendment to the effect that settlers who had come to Minnesota after March 3 be invited to attend the adjourned meeting and voice their preferences for candidates, which was adopted. At the adjourned meeting candidates were nominated for the legislature.[6]

The inclusion of newcomers in the caucus was resented by many of the preterritorial settlers, who saw in it an attempt to dictate to the electors; and the resulting antagonism between old and new settlers was not lessened by the attitude of the newspapers. The conflict centered about two candidates for the Council, David Lambert and James M. Boal, the latter the nominee of the caucus. While the *Pioneer* in general assumed a neutral and conciliatory tone, admonishing the voters against "local division, the distinctions resulting from diversity of occupation . . . classification of our people as old settlers and new settlers," nevertheless it lost no opportunity to men-

[5] Shortridge, *Transition of a Typical Frontier*, 65; letters to Sibley from Potts, January 24, 1849, from Henry L. Moss, July 14, 1849, from Gideon H. Pond, July 16, 1849, and from Joseph R. Brown, July 20, 1849, and a letter from Rice to John H. McKenny, July 13, 1849, in the Sibley Papers.

[6] *Chronicle*, July 12, 19, 1849; *Pioneer*, July 19, 1849. The organic act may be found in any issue of the Minnesota *Legislative Manual*.

tion old settlers and pay them tribute; and no great insight
was needed to know who were the *Pioneer's* favorites. It took
the stand that, while it was "not wrong" for newcomers to
attend the caucus, it was "injudicious," for "it had a tendency
to create an antagonism to no purpose." The "secret" of the
"whole matter" was that *"there were aspirants who relied upon
new influences to bring them forward; and there were other*

FORBES'S TRADING POST, ST. PAUL

aspirants who relied upon the ballot box." The *Pioneer* published the proceedings of the caucus, with the ticket nominated, and announced the candidacy of two other aspirants
to the legislature. These two, Lambert and Joseph R. Brown,
and one of the caucus' nominees for the Council, William H.
Forbes, were mentioned as old settlers of Minnesota, and high
tribute was paid to their qualifications. All were friends of
Sibley. Of the other candidates, the *Pioneer* said merely that
it was needless "to write complimentary words. They are all
known to every one of your electors, and are already before
the people as candidates." [7]

[7] *Pioneer*, July 19, 26, 1849.

The *Chronicle* published the caucus ticket under the heading "Regular People's Ticket" and decried the "illiberal effort . . . to raise prejudice against it . . . because the new settlers participated in the selection." Both the *Chronicle* and the *Register* came out strongly for Boal and against Lambert, whom the *Register* called the *Pioneer's* "pet candidate." "Wasn't it all fixed long ago," said the *Register*, "that it was absolutely essential that he [*Lambert*] be helped to a seat in the Council, and that he help the *Pioneer* to something nice after he gets there?" The *Pioneer* ignored such outbursts. Lambert was defeated; but after the election Goodhue was able to say with truth, "Our readers will bear witness, that we have admitted nothing abusive or indecent into our columns." [8]

Late in August the *Chronicle* and the *Register*, by uniting as the *Minnesota Chronicle and Register*, gave the *Pioneer* a more powerful rival, one that Goodhue was to find difficulty in treating "with manly forbearance and courtesy," as he described his attitude toward its predecessors. [9] The new journal gave as reasons for the union "partly . . . business considerations, but mainly . . . a desire, nearly unanimously expressed by friends of both establishments, to have published at the Capital of our Territory *one* journal occupying high moral and conservative grounds." Goodhue's rejoinder was characteristic: "We extend to this new journal the hand of fellowship; hoping that they may have the same success that attended the Chronicle and the Register; and that we may indeed 'have published at the capital of our Territory *one* journal, occupying high moral and conservative grounds.' " [10]

On August 27, Goodhue's younger brother Isaac, whose name was soon to appear on the *Pioneer* as co-editor, wrote to Sibley in regard to the public printing:

[8] *Chronicle*, July 19, 1849; *Register*, July 28, 1849; *Pioneer*, August 2, 1849.
[9] See below, p. 46.
[10] *Chronicle and Register*, August 25, September 1, 1849; *Pioneer*, August 30, 1849. A day or two after the union of the two papers, McLean, the owner

"The indications now are that the contest will take party grounds. The Whigs in St. Paul seem determined upon it. The support we have received from the Democrats has arrayed many of the Whigs against us. We think we now see that our private interests would have been better insured, had the division taken place before the election. We now have only to say, that we feel ourselves entitled to the most active efforts of our friends to help us in turn. . . .

"We feel that you are the man to save us. Your security from all harm, your popularity it seems to us, with all deference, will render it safe for you to see and fix almost every member."

Sibley replied on the following day that he had "left no step untaken to render you service." He had told his friends "that your having commenced the first publication in the Territory of a regular print, as well as the proper & respectable manner in which it has been conducted, give you a prior and undoubted claim to support by the people as well as in the Legislature." He felt that the "answering position of the 'Pioneer' in opposing the drawing of party lines, has not only met the concurrence of the people, but should ensure to it, a firm and cordial return in the way of substantial patronage." [11]

In the *Pioneer* of August 30 appeared Goodhue's "claims" for the office of territorial printer, addressed "To the Public of Minnesota":

"The publication of the Pioneer, was commenced in April last — about one month after the passage of the organic act.

of the *Register*, bought Hughes's interest in the *Chronicle*. Associated with McLean were Owens of the *Register* and S. A. Quay. In the *Pioneer* of August 30, Goodhue announced that "in the course of two or three weeks, the *Pioneer* will be enlarged to the size of a full double medium sheet, and will appear in a new dress of beautiful new type"; and that it was his "intention soon, to issue a prospectus for an agricultural journal, to be published as early as practicable next spring." The *Pioneer* first appeared in its enlarged form and "new dress" on October 4, 1849. The agricultural journal failed to materialize.

[11] Both of these letters are in the Sibley Papers.

Having been a citizen of the Northwest for the last eighteen years, living under the same laws by which we are governed, and knowing tolerably well the history, condition, and resources of Minnesota, my sympathies were early enlisted here; and regardless of high inducements offered to publish a daily journal elsewhere, I determined to make my home amongst you, and to commence the publication here of a journal, there being then no press within several hundred miles of Minnesota. Commencing under embarrassments that seemed then almost insurmountable, our first number was issued. Every person assured us, that a party print was not wanted, and that by pursuing the course we have taken, we might rely upon the approbation and patronage of the whole Territory. We have never swerved one inch from a line of strict impartiality. This is not the print that has assumed to be a Whig paper, a party paper, to catch Whig favor and has since jumped onto the platform of neutrality. We have never changed drag ropes.

"Anxious at first, to direct the attention of the world toward Minnesota, we published and distributed gratuitously, in the months of April and May last, over two thousand copies of the Pioneer. The approval I have received from candid men of all parties, as well as the result of the late election, prove that I have taken the course which the people prefer. They have confidence in the fairness and integrity of the Pioneer. — They, too, can judge, whether or not the Pioneer has awakened abroad an interest in Minnesota. All will agree that its columns have been very fully devoted to descriptions of the various parts of our Territory, both in the form of editorial articles and of well written communications from others. No one will deny, who has glanced at the papers for the past few months, that the Pioneer has been more extensively copied than any other newspaper, far or near. This fact we attribute mainly to the spirit of inquiry about our Territory, which the Pioneer has certainly contributed its share in awakening, and to which *no other print has manifested any capacity to respond*. Towards one and all, the Pioneer has been invariably courteous, dignified and respectful.

"Fully aware that no more than one paper could be decently sustained here, we have treated with manly forbearance and courtesy, both of the other prints which have since been commenced here; having an abiding confidence that our people would see and judge, and sustain us, although an hundred clamorous presses might rush in and sponge an existence until the meeting of the Legislature, for the mere chance of the public printing. Entertaining this confidence, the proprietor of the Pioneer has invested his money in real estate here; and having no intention in any event, to decamp on the first boat after choice of a territorial printer, cannot be regarded as a mere adventurer following in the train of political victors. — We have made arrangements to remain here and shall be prepared to do all the printing that is to be done, as well as it can be done anywhere. In addition to our former printing materials, we have procured a new press of the largest size, and every material necessary for every variety of State printing.[12] . . .

"With this brief recital I submit my claims to the Legislature for the office of Territorial Printer.

JAMES M. GOODHUE

The legislature convened on September 3, and on the next day Goodhue was elected to do the incidental printing of both houses by a vote of 5 to 4 in the Council and 11 to 4 in the House. On September 5 Gideon H. Pond offered in the House a resolution that Goodhue be elected territorial printer for the ensuing year. Substitutes to the effect that the printing be given to the *Chronicle and Register* in equal proportion, under direction of the secretary of the territory, were offered and

[12] The remainder of the paragraph is a quotation from the letter which accompanied the bills for the *Pioneer's* new type, praising the quality and the quantity of the type.

rejected. Another substitute that the secretary be authorized to contract for the public printing, except that already disposed of, and assign it to the lowest bidder, was laid on the table; and the House postponed the election of printer until September 18.[13]

On September 6 Pond wrote to Sibley that the "excitement was so great *out* of the House as well as in it that although we could have carried the question yesterday by about a two third majority I did not feel willing to do it then." He mentioned the objections that were urged against the resolution, among them that it was unjust to give all the printing to one man; that it was "drawing a line between old and new settlers and supporting the former at the expense of the latter"; that it was illegal; that if carried it would "force up political party standards"; that Goodhue had "pledged himself to the democratic party and that this is the only reason why they vote for him"; and, finally, that Congress would not sanction such an act.[14]

When the resolution was taken up on September 18, it was postponed indefinitely. Meantime both houses had appointed committees to consider and report on the public printing; and bills were introduced in both houses to regulate the printing. The bill that passed, the Council bill, which was approved on November 1, required that "hereafter" in each legislative session, the Council and House in convention should, immediately after hearing the governor's message, elect a person or persons to do all the incidental printing and the printing of the laws and journals. The size, form, type, and paper were specified, as well as the price. The incidental printing was to be paid as other expenses of the session; the laws and the journals were to be paid for out of the Congressional appropriation for territorial expenses. The Council journal for 1849 was to be printed by McLean, and the House journal by Good-

[13] *House Journal*, 1849, pp. 18, 19, 20, 21, 22, 29; *Council Journal*, 1849, p. 18.
[14] The letter, erroneously dated "August 6," is in the Sibley Papers.

hue; the laws were to be printed by McLean and Goodhue jointly.[15]

There appears to have been some dissatisfaction with the incidental printing, particularly in the House. That body, on October 11, appointed a committee "to examine into the causes of the delay of the printing of bills . . . and to report to the House such arrangements as they may deem necessary, with regard to obviating this inconvenience." The committee reported that Goodhue had been delayed by alterations made by a committee chairman in a long bill while it was in process of printing, and that further delay was not expected. A few days later the House appointed another committee to investigate the delay in printing bills, and to engage the *Chronicle* office to print bills "which are likely to be delayed under the existing arrangement with Mr. Goodhue." The Council on October 17 passed a resolution directing its secretary to have the daily slips printed by the *Chronicle* for the rest of the week, "in order to give the printer to the Council an opportunity to furnish the bills which have accumulated at his office." A motion to amend by striking out all after the word "Resolved" and inserting "That Messrs. McLean and Owens be employed to do the incidental printing for the Council, for the remainder of the session" was lost.[16]

The appropriation bill of 1849 allowed Goodhue $2,260 for the incidental printing and $235 for newspapers furnished to members of the legislature, a sum with which he was by no means satisfied. McLean and Owens were allowed $332. A committee appointed by the House to measure the printing done for the legislature reported that it had been unable to complete the measurement of the printing done by Goodhue, but that it was "satisfied to the extent of one million ems of composition; and referred the remainder of the amount for

[15] *Council Journal*, 1849, pp. 33, 40, 42, 93; *House Journal*, 1849, pp. 36, 66; *Laws*, 1849, p. 47.
[16] *House Journal*, 1849, pp. 96, 99, 113; *Council Journal*, pp. 90, 91.

adjustment, to the next . . . Legislature." The Council passed an amendment to the appropriation bill to allow Goodhue an additional $238 for publishing the governor's proclamation and other documents in the *Pioneer* before the legislature met, but the House refused to pass it. Thereupon the Council passed "A bill for the relief of James M. Goodhue," which was negatived by the House.[17]

Goodhue was sorely disappointed with his treatment by the legislature. Not only had it failed to give him *all* the territorial printing, but it also, he felt, had set too low a price for the printing. For this he placed much of the blame on the "meddlesome interference in legislation" of Charles K. Smith, the secretary of the territory. Moreover, Smith had told Goodhue that he would not pay him "one dollar for incidental printing." [18] Goodhue's vengeance was thorough. In the *Pioneer* of November 8 appeared an editorial headed "Licensed Thieving," which was the opening barrage in a campaign of abuse so bitter and violent that it ultimately drove Smith from Minnesota:

"When, long after his official duties required him to be here, Secretary Ewing's [19] Secretary of the Territory of Minnesota, stole into Saint Paul, last summer, we supposed, not only from the influences which secured his appointment, but also from the hang-dog looks of the fellow, that he would steal *in* Saint Paul. That he was snappish, unmannerly and mean, as unfit to occupy a public post as a sore-headed dog is to occupy a parlor, he has daily demonstrated since his arrival. The record of his meanness, in all private transactions, would fill a volume; and can be substantiated by all who have dealt with him.

"His meddlesome interference in legislation secured him the contempt of both Houses of the Legislature, with the excep-

[17] *Laws*, 1849, p. 88; *House Journal*, p. 178; *Council Journal*, pp. 156, 158, 159.
[18] Goodhue to Sibley, January 22, 1850, Sibley Papers.
[19] Thomas Ewing was secretary of the Department of the Interior.

tion of a few lick-spittles who profited by their fawning. One of these persons advocated the bare-faced villainy of appropriating to the Secretary five hundred dollars extra pay, for superintending inkstands, putting the members benches out of doors at the end of the session, dealing out to the members a stick of red tape at a time &c.; and actually got the appropriation made. That member was Mr. Wilkinson of Stillwater. Some other smaller toadies of the Secretary, did some things for his benefit which we feel bound to notice hereafter. Would it — *will* it be believed that beside this five hundred dollars, a bill of seven hundred dollars was brought in for stationery furnished to the 29 members of the Assembly during sixty days, being about thirty dollars for each member? and that this was a bill of stationery in which the Secretary furnished fire wood for the Capitol at an allowance of four dollars, if not six dollars per cord, ready for the stove? We could add to this list, other instances of gouging — such unblushing frauds as ought to be the subject of indictment. The pocketing of picayune on each sovereign is too small an item to mention.[20]

"After paying off the members, at least such as had been subservient to his purposes, what has he done with the remaining portion of the $13,500?[21] We do not know of a clerk or laborer who is able to get his pay, or if such instances *do* occur, it is a matter of special favor. For the incidental printing as well as for a large amount of advertising done for the Executive Department before the Secretary had yet arrived in Minnesota — printing done at an enormous expense and

[20] *Laws*, 1849, pp. 87, 88. The appropriation act of 1849 included a paragraph allowing five hundred dollars to Smith for "indexing . . . and distributing the laws, superintending the public property of the Territory, superintending generally, and purchasing various articles for the use of the Legislative Assembly . . . renting rooms; for extra labor and service done in transcribing and furnishing extra copies of the laws, memorials, and resolutions . . . not provided for by the organic law, but directed by the Legislature." Morton S. Wilkinson settled in Stillwater in 1847. From 1859 to 1865 he represented Minnesota in the United States Senate.

[21] This was the amount of the Congressional appropriation to the territory.

amounting to more than $2,700, we have received only six hundred dollars — an amount insufficient to cover our bills now due in Saint Louis, for stationery.

"As it does not appear, by all we can ascertain, that the Secretary has paid out more than five or six thousand dollars, and he does not condescend to explain what he has done with the rest of the $13,500, nor deny that he has received it, we feel constrained to believe that he intends to make a *clean grab* of all that remains, or else that he has invested the money in some *private speculation*. We are ready to bet that he will prove a defaulter; and that he has given mere straw security in his bond; and that this poor pettifogger, who was raked out of the kennel in Ohio by Secretary Ewing, on purpose to plunder the Treasury, and with the absolute certainty that he could touch nothing valuable that would not stick to his fingers, after stealing *in* the territory, will steal *out* of it with all he can plunder and with the united execration of all honest men."[22]

Thereafter nearly every issue of the *Pioneer* contained a caustic reference to Smith. He was lashed unmercifully in editorials, and taunted and ridiculed in shorter items. When Goodhue reported a December thaw, he described it as "producing mud as tenacious as — the fingers of the Secretary." He announced that he intended "to apply the curry-comb" to Smith, "if it *does* start the hair a little." And when later he received an anonymous gift of a currycomb, he remarked that he "must have *tools to work with*, if the rest of the Augean stable proves as foul as the stall of the Secretary." "God never suffered so great a thief to live," he wrote, "that we dare not

[22] Smith's defense against Goodhue's charges of embezzlement appeared in an extra edition of the *Chronicle and Register*, dated December 20, 1849, a copy of which is in the Ramsey Papers, in the possession of the Minnesota Historical Society. In this document Smith stated that he did not receive the sum appropriated by Congress until after the adjournment of the legislature; that he had advanced sums due to various persons from money that he had borrowed in St. Louis; and that the Congressional appropriation did not cover the territorial expenses.

rebuke him for stealing. — Where the *penitentiary* cannot do justice, something remains for the *pen* to do." He suggested that the county in which the Pillager Indians lived be named "Smith County." He threatened, "if the Secretary's official life continues much longer," to "keep up the record of his misdeeds, by issuing it in a weekly Appendix to the Pioneer." He drew up charges of embezzlement against Smith which he published in the *Pioneer* and sent to Sibley in Washington, urging him to place them in the hands of the secretary of the treasury. And when Smith was removed from office in the fall of 1851, Goodhue's parting shot was the remark that his prophecy made two years earlier that "secretary Smith had stolen *into* the Territory, and stolen *in* the Territory, and would in the end, steal *out* of the Territory, with whatever plunder he could abstract from it," had been verified.[23]

[23] *Pioneer*, November 1, 15, December 5, 12, 1849, January 22, 1850, June 12, 19, October 30, November 13, 1851; Goodhue to Sibley, December 11, 1849, Sibley Papers.

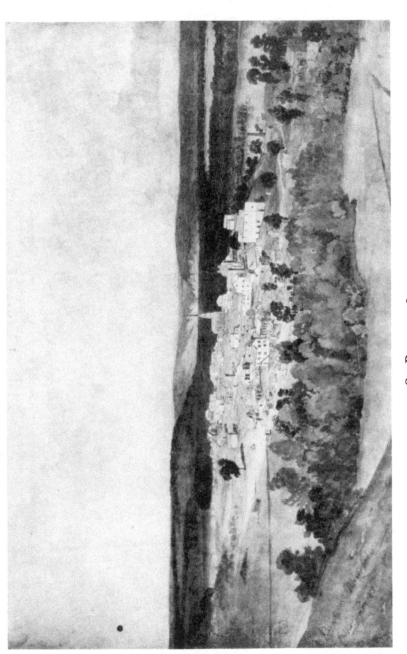

St. Paul in 1851

[From a photograph, owned by the State Historical Society of Wisconsin; of a water color by Jean Baptist Wengler. The original is in Linz, Austria.]

St. Anthony in 1851

[From a photograph, owned by the State Historical Society of Wisconsin, of a water color by Jean Baptist Wengler. The original is in Linz, Austria.]

5. Fur and Anti-Fur

THE MOVEMENT BY THE DEMOCRATS TO DRAW PARTY LINES WAS brought into the open on September 24, 1849, when a number of them organized as a caucus at Rice's house in St. Paul and issued a call for a Democratic convention. The *Chronicle* declared that the caucus owed "its paternity to a well known individual in this community, an unsuccessful candidate for Congress at a late election" — that it was a result of Rice's political ambitions. "We want no better name under which to rally," said the *Chronicle*, "than '*The Territorial Party*,' a union of all honest men, for the best interests of Minnesota, irrespective of all other party names."[1]

The Democratic convention was held at the American House in St. Paul on October 20. It adopted a platform and named the *Pioneer* the party organ. A letter from Sibley was read, in which he declared himself a Democrat, but announced his intention of remaining neutral, since he had been elected delegate without regard to party politics. The next issue of the *Pioneer* contained the following notice: "OBITUARY. Died suddenly, in Minnesota, on the 20th inst. at 9 o'clock P. M. The 'Territorial Party.' Disease, delirium tremens, induced by a secret habit of imbibing Whig spirits."[2]

A bitter campaign preceded the election of county officers on November 26. The *Pioneer* supported the Democratic candidates, although Goodhue wrote to Sibley in confidence that too many of them were Rice adherents. It "would not have received my support," he wrote, "but that it was 'regular' and as the 'organ' I was *bound* to support it." The *Chronicle* supported the "Peoples' Ticket," composed mainly of Whigs. The "Peoples' Ticket," as a result of the disaffection of many

[1] *Pioneer*, October 4, 1849; *Chronicle and Register*, October 13, 1849.
[2] *Pioneer*, October 25, 1849; *Chronicle and Register*, November 3, 1849.

53

of Sibley's friends who disliked the Rice complexion of the Democratic ticket, was elected, with the exception of one candidate. "I only regret the result," wrote Goodhue to Sibley, "on account of the *impression* that will go abroad, that this Territory is Whig. . . . The Whigs here are more bitter against you than against any one else, not excepting myself — alleging that you made my politics — which is rather too true for a pleasant joke. . . . Against my wishes and judgment, we are precipitated into the torrent of politics — and together. . . . You are the pilot." [3]

During the winter and spring of 1850 the Minnesota newspapers were generally silent as to politics; but the politicians — Goodhue among them — were working quietly but diligently toward the election of a delegate to Congress, which was to take place the next fall. The election in November, 1849, had placed Goodhue in a dubious position. The Rice faction considered him too friendly to Sibley for their purposes; and many of Sibley's friends found it hard to forgive him for supporting the Rice-concocted ticket. In letters to Sibley, who was in Washington, Goodhue was accused of being "leagued with the Rice faction," and of forgetting "the true interests of the party — in his main object *the printing*." [4] One correspondent wrote that many of Sibley's friends felt that, because of Goodhue's "known and avowed selfishness," he was "only waiting for an opportunity to throw" Sibley "off." "If Rice gets here before you do," he continued, "and offers him a

[3] Goodhue to Sibley, November 26, 1849, Sibley Papers; *Chronicle and Register*, December 1, 1849. Goodhue wrote to John H. Stevens on November 29, 1849: "As the *organ*, I have tried to grind for the *organization*, whatever it may be. . . . whatever comes up as *regular* I have to *conjugate* through all modes and tenses — and class everything else as 'irregular, defective, or redundant — *until after election*.'" The letter is in the Stevens Papers, in the possession of the Minnesota Historical Society. The heated campaign waged by the newspapers may be followed through the October and November issues of both papers.

[4] Many letters written to Sibley during this period, in particular those from Potts, January 15, from Lambert, January 26, from James S. Norris, April 14, and from Forbes, March 12, in the Sibley Papers.

consideration for his services he will get them. He will try
and pick a quarrel with some one connected with you in business and make that an excuse for dropping you." [5]

Whether or not there was any real foundation for the sus-
picions of Sibley's friends, Goodhue's letters to the delegate
and the attitude of the *Pioneer* gave no indication of any
weakening in his allegiance to Sibley. Sibley apparently was
not especially desirous of a renomination, but he was reluctant
to give up his office to Rice or to one of Rice's followers.
Goodhue wished to maintain the *Pioneer* as the organ of the
Democratic party, but not as the organ of a faction of that
party. He wrote Sibley that he would support the nominations
only of a convention of representatives form "every portion"
of the territory. "We must have a new Democratic organization," he wrote. "The moment you return, it must be attended
to, so as to unite the whole party." He had no preferences in
the selection of candidates, "aside from a consideration of the
success and welfare of the party." "I agree with you," he
continued, "that any pledges now given, with reference to
your successor after the next term, if you should then decline,
would be altogether impolitic. A pledge to do all that is fair
and support all fair nominations, is all that can with propriety
be given." [6]

Meanwhile the Rice forces were preparing the way for the
nomination of Alexander M. Mitchell, the Whig marshal of
the territory, whom they hoped to elect by a coalition of
Whigs and Rice Democrats. The "Territorial Convention"
which nominated Mitchell on July 31 sounded the keynote
of his campaign in the following resolution: "That we have in
our midst a dangerous monopoly known as the 'American
Fur Company,' wielding a powerful influence, injurious to
and destructive of the interests of the community at large,
prepared by any means to retain their baneful influence at the

[5] Potts to Sibley, April 17, 1850, Sibley Papers.
[6] Goodhue to Sibley, February 6, 19, 1850, Sibley Papers.

sacrifice of the welfare and independence of our people; and we do therefore, pledge ourselves, and call upon our constituents to assist in checking its power." [7]

On July 30 Goodhue wrote to Sibley: "If you do not come back before next week, we shall nominate you as an Independent candidate for Delegate. Party organization, now, is out of the question." He announced in the *Pioneer* of August 8 that he had been "requested to say" that Sibley would be a candidate, and followed the announcement with an editorial in which he said that he had long waited for the Democratic central committee to call a party convention, and that if a call was not made within a week he would "feel at liberty to nominate a good, staunch, unflinching Democrat"; and his description of the man whom he would nominate left no doubt as to his identity.

No call was made for a Democratic convention as such, but on August 10 a second "Territorial Convention" nominated David Olmsted, a Democrat, and passed resolutions describing Olmsted as "standing aloof and disconnected from all the local parties or factions, now so numerous all around us"; approving Governor Ramsey's administration; and declaring that "the nomination of Col. A. M. Mitchell . . . was brought about through the agency of a faction . . . for the gratification of individual, private and selfish interests." Olmsted had the support of the *Chronicle and Register*, which was at that time owned by him and edited by Lorenzo A. Babcock.[8]

Goodhue had no sympathy with the "mongrel" nomina-

[7] *Pioneer*, August 8, 1850. On March 18, 1850, Goodhue wrote to Sibley: "There is a disposition here . . . to stir up odium against the Fur Company, which I regret, on account of your connection with the Company. . . . It is impossible for me — for any press — to maintain itself as the avowed champion of the Company. The most I can do — the most you can do, is to make it distinctly understood that Mr. Sibley is not the Fur Company — and to allay as much as possible, this unreasonable sort of hostility — a thing to be done by *adroit indirectness* rather than by any active measures of defense." Sibley Papers.

[8] *Chronicle and Register*, August 12, 1850.

tions made by the two conventions, and in the *Pioneer* of August 15 he announced that he would support Sibley, whom he lauded extravagantly in a long editorial. He wrote Sibley that Olmsted's backers had "basely attempted to seize an advantage by pre-arranging a Convention, which they packed with Olmsted delegates. . . . I refused to submit your claims to any convention — brought your name out at the head of my columns and denied that any person was authorized in your absence to put your name in the convention; so it was withdrawn. . . . all your friends here, are working hard up in the Collar. . . . We are spending all our time and as much money as seems needful." Of his conduct of the campaign, he wrote: "We have aimed all our artillery at Mitchell & Rice; and raised so much 'noise & confusion' that Olmsted's friends were dumb foundered and *forgot* that they had a candidate." Olmsted withdrew from the campaign a week before the election.[9]

The election was held on September 2, and Sibley was elected, but by fewer than a hundred votes. After it was over Goodhue wrote in the *Pioneer* of September 5: "Never have we before witnessed an election, as hotly contested, as our election of last Monday. . . . Hope, fear, avarice, ambition, personal obligations, money, whiskey, oysters, champagne, loans, the promise of favors, jealousy, personal prejudice, envy, every thing that could be tortured into a motive, has been pressed into the canvass."

With the election of delegate out of the way, the Minnesota publishers were free to devote their attention to the contest for the public printing, which would be decided by the second territorial legislature when it met in January. Rice had recently built a three-story brick building in upper St. Paul, and into it the *Chronicle and Register* moved with a new editor, Charles J. Henniss. Henniss announced that his paper would advocate Whig principles and would "recognize and favor as candidates for office only those whom the Territorial

---

[9] Goodhue to Sibley, August 28, 1850, Sibley Papers.

party shall, by their regularly appointed delegates, place in that position." On December 10 appeared the first number of a new paper, the *Minnesota Democrat*, which also was issued from the Rice building. Its editor, Daniel A. Robertson, announced that the *Democrat* would be "a zealous and unwavering advocate of the principles and organization of the Democratic party."

RICE'S BUILDINGS
The one at the left housed the *Chronicle* and the *Democrat*.

Goodhue and other Sibley men were convinced, in spite of the loud denials of the *Chronicle* and the *Democrat*, that both papers were controlled and influenced by Rice. Goodhue reported the situation to Sibley in a letter of December 10: "Robinson [*Robertson*] of Ohio is here with a new press, which our friends all understand to be in Rice's interest, while it will profess to aim at harmonizing the party. Hennis of phila has also got into the Chronicle — and both presses are in Rice's 3 story brick — and are starting off, unquestionably, under the auspices of that great man; but the Whigs have taken hold of Hennis and pushed one leg of the Chronicle onto the Territorial platform, while the other stands upon Whiggery. . . . There will be a strong rally of Rice folks and Mitchell Whigs to give all the printing to the Chronicle and the Democrat. I am after them, consenting to give the

Chronicle half the incidental printing, but the Democrat nothing." [10]

In an editorial entitled "Party Organization," the *Pioneer* of December 19 announced its political position. It would stand "firm and upright upon the solid platform of Jefferson Democracy," and whenever the Democratic party should re-organize "upon principle" instead of upon "personal jealousy or ambition," it would support the organization.

The legislature convened on January 1, 1851. The two houses met in joint convention to elect a territorial printer on January 7, but postponed the election one week. On January 10, Edmund Rice, a brother of Henry, offered the following resolution in the House, which was adopted: "That a committee of three be appointed to enquire and report, whether any newspaper publisher, or other person has offered or made any gift of money, or other valuable thing, to members of this House, since their election, with intent to influence the act or vote of such members in favor of the appointment of such publisher to do the whole, or any portion of the Public Printing, and that said committee be authorized to send for persons and papers." Rice headed the committee appointed by the speaker. On the next day a resolution was offered that the committee be instructed "to inquire whether any newspaper publisher or other person, has made threats of personal violence to members of this House, or threats of any kind, with intent to influence the action of such members in their Legislative capacity," which was adopted with this facetious amendment tacked on: "And that said committee be authorized to take

[10] *Chronicle and Register*, December 2, 1850; *Democrat*, December 10, 1850; *Pioneer*, January 9, 1851; letters to Sibley from Goodhue, December 10, 1850, January 10, 1851, from Forbes, December 17, 1850, and from Ramsey, January 28, 1851, Sibley Papers. Stevens wrote to Sibley on January 6, 1851: "Rice bought up the '*Chronicle & Register*'; he also owns the '*Democrat*' — both of which are his organs, the two filthy sheets galling the public — but the cloven foot stuck out too much. . . . Rice sticks out all around, every column and every line shows it, while Goodhue works for money — dollars are his asylum — he dreams by them at night and is ready to work by day — provided he can get well paid for the work."

into consideration any words of a threatening character, that were uttered by Hole-in-the-Day [*the Chippewa chief*], in his speech of last Friday." [11]

The committee made its report to the House on January 13. From the testimony taken before the committee it appeared that Goodhue had written a letter to William W. Warren, a member of the House, stating that Mrs. Goodhue had found the Warrens "uncomfortably situated" at the American House, and offering them quarters at the Goodhue home "without any reference to profit on my part, say, at a venture, at one half the price they charge you at the American House"; that Warren had shown the letter to Edmund Rice; that when Goodhue heard of the appointment of the legislative committee to investigate the letter, he had threatened to "whip the whole God damned Rice fraternity"; and that he had promised the St. Anthony delegation that if they would give him their votes he would furnish a press for their town. The testimony brought out further that Goodhue had not directly offered money to any member of the legislature, although he had conveyed "the idea of personal advantage" in conversations with members. The report of the committee was accepted and the House passed a motion to postpone "the whole matter" indefinitely. [12]

On the day after the bribery committee reported, Goodhue, by a union of Whigs and Sibley Democrats, was elected to do all the territorial printing. "This," Governor Ramsey wrote to Sibley, "is one of the greatest victories that your friends have yet achieved." To gain this victory, however, Goodhue was forced to promise the printing of the volume of laws and of one of the journals to a Whig paper soon to be established. [13]

[11] *Council Journal,* 1851, p. 21; *House Journal,* 25, 26, 31, 34.
[12] *House Journal,* 1851, p. 39.
[13] *Council Journal,* 1851, pp. 36, 37; *House Journal,* 40; Ramsey to Sibley, January 14, 1851, Sibley Papers. Ramsey wrote in his diary on January 14, 1851, that the Whigs had "an arrangement whereby they are to have half the printing for Stevens or whoever else they may agree upon." Ramsey's manuscript diary is in the possession of the Minnesota Historical Society. On April

The elation of Goodhue and his friends over the election was matched in degree by the bitter disappointment of their opponents. "Faces may now be seen a yard long," wrote Joseph R. Brown to Sibley. The *Democrat* was content with the remark that *"under all the circumstances,* the ill success of friends in electing us Printer, is a great moral triumph, of

GOVERNOR RAMSEY'S FIRST HOUSE, 1849
It later became a hotel, the New England House.

which we may well be proud"; but so violent was the abuse heaped on the Whig members of the legislature by the *Chronicle,* that they felt constrained to publish a circular defending their vote. Three candidates, stated the circular, had appeared for the printing: the *Pioneer,* "professing attachment to the

23, 1851, Allen Pierse, a St. Paul lawyer, wrote to Ramsey: "Goodhue does not yield up that public printing with good grace. I understand all his democratic friends, *Mr. Sibley among them* told him the thing *must* be done." The letter is in the Ramsey Papers. See also H. L. Tilden to Stevens, March 9, 1851, in the Stevens Papers, and Goodhue to Sibley, February 6, 1851, in the Sibley Papers.

interests of the Territory, and indifference to national politics"; the *Democrat*, "a journal which had been established but
a few weeks, edited and published by . . . a stranger in the
Territory, and a partisan of an ultra and stereotyped stamp";
and the *Chronicle*, which claimed to be a Whig organ, but
whose "special champions" were Democrats, and whose editor, although "but a short time a resident of Minnesota," had
"exhibited a marked distaste and disrelish for Whig associa-
tions," and had "never advised with the Whigs in the legislature or out of it." The Whig members "preferred to rebuke
factious interests, diametrically opposed and deadly hostile
to Whig policy, by the election of Col. Goodhue secured by
an arrangement which they know will be satisfactory to the
Whigs of the Territory, for some Whig press, which, without
fear, favour or influence, shall advocate Whig principles, a
share of the public printing." [14]

[14] Brown to Sibley, January 14, 1851, Sibley Papers; *Democrat*, January 21,
1851; *Chronicle and Register*, January 20, 27, 1851. A copy of the circular,
dated January 30, 1851, is in the Ramsey Papers. It was reprinted in the *Pioneer*
of February 13.

6. Bowie Knife and Pistol

DURING THE FALL OF 1850 A MOVEMENT HAD BEEN CARRIED along by the Mitchell-Rice forces to remove certain territorial officials who had stood in their way and to replace them with friends. Their main target was Chief Justice Aaron Goodrich, in whose place they hoped to establish David Cooper, an associate justice of the territorial Supreme Court. A petition was circulated in Minnesota for the removal of the chief justice, and an article entitled "Administration of Justice in Minnesota," in which Goodrich was maligned and ridiculed, was contributed to the New York *Spirit of the Times.*[1] Goodhue retaliated by publishing in the *Pioneer* of January 16, 1851, an editorial on "Absentee Office Holders," in which he assailed the personal and official conduct of Mitchell and Cooper in language that for pure venom could hardly be matched:

"While we regret the continued absence of a U. S. Marshal, and a judge of the 2d district, from Minnesota, we would not be understood to lament the absence of A. M. Mitchell and David Cooper, the incumbents (oftener *re*cumbents) of those two offices. — It would be a blessing if the absence of two such men were prolonged to eternity. In the present scarcity and high price of whiskey, their absence may be con-

[1] The article, signed "Panama," was published in the *Spirit of the Times* on December 14, 1850. It was written by Benjamin Thompson, a resident of St. Paul, according to a letter from Potts to Sibley, dated January 21, 1851, in the Sibley Papers. Goodhue wrote to Sibley on January 10, 1851: "I feel constrained to write you . . . in regard to the infamous conspiracy of Rice, Mitchell and Cooper, to destroy the character of Chief Justice Goodrich and to place Cooper on the Bench. . . . After paving the way . . . by the circulation of the most vile slanders against him . . . they are now making an onset to remove him." The letter is in the Sibley Papers. Judge Goodrich was removed from office in November, 1851. William G. Le Duc, *Minnesota Year Book for 1852*, 96 (St. Paul, 1852).

sidered a blessing. The loss by these men, of poor washer-women, laundresses, barbers, tailors, printers, shoemakers and all persons, with whom that sort of men make accounts, is quite as large already, as ought to fall to the share of the poor people in one Territory. We never knew an instance of a debt being paid by either of them, unless it were a gambling debt — and we never knew an act performed by either of them, which might not have been quite as well done by a fool or a knave. We never knew either of them, even to blunder into the truth, or to appear disguised, except when accidentally sober, or to do anything right, unless through ignorance how to do anything wrong, nor to seek companionship with gentlemen as long as they could receive the countenance of rowdies.

"Since the organization of the Territory, Mitchell has not been in it, long enough by a continued residence, to be entitled to vote; yet he has been long enough here to be known as a man utterly destitute of moral principle, manly bearing, or even physical courage. His mileage and per diem as the witness for Henry M. Rice, in perpetrating the Winnebago contract fraud, at Washington, has given him some funds, enough to enable him to obtain credit, in various parts of our Territory.[2] Like Judge Cooper, he lacks in Minnesota, a legal residence, so that creditors can have no service of process upon him to collect their debts. They are a brace of very independent gentlemen.

"As for Judge Cooper, besides lacking a residence at Stillwater, at least ever since last May, he has neither there nor any where else, any attachable property, that the officers can find.

[2] The United States commissioner of Indian affairs contracted with Rice in April, 1850, to remove to their reservation at Long Prairie, Minnesota, several hundred Winnebago Indians scattered over Wisconsin, Iowa, and Minnesota. Because of the compensation allowed Rice, among other things, the contract received much criticism in Minnesota, especially by the *Pioneer*, and Sibley officially protested against it. It was made the subject of an investigation by the House committee on Indian affairs, which completely exonerated Rice. Folwell, *Minnesota*, 1:311–318.

He has land claims, to be sure, which he has some way got in possession, on one of which he has obtained the construction of a cabin, for building which, he yet owes. He left Stillwater, owing a large amount for postage, owing stores, groceries and tradesmen of every description. He is not only a miserable drunkard, who habitually gets so drunk as to *feel upward* for the ground, but he also spends days and nights and Sundays playing cards in groceries.[3] He is lost to all sense of decency and self respect. *Off* the Bench he is a beast, and *on* the Bench he is an ass, stuffed with arrogance, self conceit and ridiculous affectation of dignity. The law requires him to reside in his own judicial district; but he not only does not reside there, but in Minnesota, he dates, his correspondence at St. Paul, and affects to belong here — an unspeakable indignity to our town. On his passage up the Minnesota river last summer, paying such attentions to a certain California widow on board, as a sot well could pay, he not only kept drunk, but when the boat returned to Fort Snelling, and the news there met him, of the death of his wife in Pennsylvania, he was so shamefully inebriated, that the awful intelligence scarcely aroused him.

"Such is the man, aided by Mitchell, (whose least fault is drunkenness, and whose very name is a bye word for contempt in Minnesota,) these we say, are the men who are now attempting to make this Judge Cooper, the Chief Justice of Minnesota! We did think that by the appointment of two such men to *any* office in Minnesota, we had drained the cup of degradation to its dregs. If any punishment deeper and more damned than this, awaits us, we can only say, may God have mercy upon Minnesota!

"We have uttered *truths* here, good wholesome truths; for the proof of which we stand responsible. It is our habit to tell facts and nothing else; and we have some *more* facts, 'a

[3] In Goodhue's day the term "groceries" was used for barrooms, as well as for intoxicating liquors.

few more of the same sort left.' *Will* the administration keep infamy upon stilts here? clothe drunkards blacklegs, and unprincipled rowdies, with political power? put a premium on vice by placing profligate vagabonds in office? — Again we say, we do not complain that A. M. Mitchell and David Cooper, are habitually absent at Washington, doing the dirty work of Henry M. Rice, but we *do* complain that we have not a marshal and a judge of the 2d. district, whose absence is not a blessing to Minnesota. We have had enough officers, who are daily liable to arrest under the vagabond Act — who never set a good example, perform an honest act, or pay an honest debt. We can endure much without complaint. It is less the need of a marshal and a judge that we complain of, than of the infliction of *such* incumbents. Feeling some resentment for the wrongs our territory has so long suffered by these men, pressing upon us like a dispensation of wrath, a judgment, a curse, a plague, unequalled since the hour when Egypt went lousy, we sat down to write this article with some bitterness; but our very gall is honey, to what they deserve." [4]

Public excitement was intense when the *Pioneer* with this article appeared on January 14, two days before the regular publication day. The following morning a handbill was circulated calling on "all the lovers of decency and all of those who feel any interest in the reputation of our Territory" to gather at Mazourka Hall in St. Paul that evening for "a public expression of the sentiments of the community, in regard to the subject and the writer" of the article. [5]

On that same day, January 15, Goodhue and Joseph

---

[4] Mitchell resigned early in 1851. Cooper remained on the bench in Minnesota until 1853. *Democrat*, February 11, 1851; W. E. Ames to Sibley, February 11, 1851, Sibley Papers; Sibley to Stevens, January 1, March 4, 1851, Stevens Papers; Warren Upham and Rose B. Dunlap, *Minnesota Biographies, 1655–1912* (*Minnesota Historical Collections*, volume 14 — St. Paul, 1912).

[5] The contents of the handbill were reprinted in the *Chronicle and Register* for January 20, 1851.

Cooper, a brother of the judge, met on a St. Paul street. An exchange of angry words was followed by a struggle in which Goodhue was stabbed twice and Cooper was shot before they could be separated. The wounds of both were serious, but not fatal. Goodhue was confined to his room for about two weeks, and Cooper somewhat longer. The *Chronicle's* account of the "deadly affray" implied that Goodhue was the assailant; according to the account in the *Pioneer*, which was written by Goodhue's friends and supported by the statements of eyewitnesses, Cooper first attacked Goodhue, and Goodhue shot Cooper in self defense. It was the *Chronicle* account that was published in papers abroad.[6]

Contemporary comments on the fight indicate the state of the public mind in St. Paul. The newspapers were full of it. Governor Ramsey wrote in his diary on January 17: "Much excitement prevailing in town in regard to the affair between Goodhue and Cooper"; and the following Sunday he noted that the sermon preached by the Reverend Edward D. Neill at the Presbyterian Church "was mostly in reference to the affray of Wednesday the 15 inst." Sibley's friends hastened to write him their various versions of the affair.[7] David Fuller, a St. Paul merchant, gave his brother George the following account in a letter written on January 19:

"Have had Mobs Street fighting and a friend of mine Joe Cooper, a brother of Judge Cooper received I am afraid a mortal wound. He had three shots fired at him, only one took effect. In return he gave his opponent which is the Editor of the Pioneer three very bad stabs with a bowie knife. . . . It

---

[6] *Chronicle and Register,* January 20, 1851; *Pioneer,* January 23, February 13, 1851; *Galena Daily Advertiser,* January 25, February 17, 1851; *Democrat,* February 25, 1851.

[7] Many letters to Sibley in January and February, 1851, in the Sibley Papers; letters to Ramsey from James Cooper, February 8, from Sibley, February 9, from Thomas Foster, February 10, and from David Cooper, February 15, 1851, Ramsey Papers; Ramsey Diary, January 15, 16, 17, 19, 1851. Sibley wrote that "Goodhue's article . . . was entirely too abusive and severe, however much of truth there may be in the charges."

originated from an article published in the Pioneer against the Judge his Brother. The attack was made in the Legislative Hall, but they soon found their way into the street and then it was fun. Every man was armed with something. A man had better not show himself without his pocket full of rocks which was my situation exactly and I made them count too, you would have laughed to have seen me spread myself." [8]

FULLER'S STORE IN UPPER ST. PAUL

An "indignation meeting" was held that evening at Ma-zourka Hall, which passed resolutions denouncing Goodhue as "a man who disregards the most sacred relations of life, and violates the sanctity of the grave — who devotes the columns of a newspaper, fostered by the patronage of the government, to the publication of scandalous falsehoods"; labeling the editorial in the *Pioneer* "an infamous, malicious and unjustifiable libel"; and praising the past conduct of Cooper and Mitchell. A correspondent wrote Sibley that the "number who participated in the meeting were very few, and if Goodhue's friends

[8] The letter is in the Fuller Papers, in the possession of the Minnesota Historical Society.

had chosen they could have voted down the whole of their proceedings"; and another described the meeting as "a perfect farce." "It is true," he wrote, "the meeting was large, but the cause was that during the day threats had been made that Goodhue would never issue another paper in St. Paul, and there was many threats of attacking his office in circulation, — two thirds of the meeting was composed of men who attended with a determination to take no part . . . unless there should be a demonstration of violence." [9]

To counteract the effects of the Mazourka Hall meeting and the *Chronicle's* report of the affray, Goodhue's friends arranged a second meeting, which was held in the Methodist Church two weeks later. This meeting, Goodhue reported to Sibley, "was badly managed on the part of our friends. . . . Rice's folks got their own officers and although our friends were more than two to their one, we accomplished nothing but to pass a string of lop-lolly resolutions, not half up to the mark." A resolution sanctioning the proceedings of the Mazourka Hall meeting was voted down. Among the resolutions adopted was one offered by a Goodhue supporter deprecating attempts of any person "to forestall the law and take into his own hands the revenge of his own wrongs," and one submitted by a friend of Cooper denouncing attacks of the press on the personal character of individuals "as tending to personal violence and breaches of the peace." In his account of the meeting in the *Pioneer*, Goodhue interpreted the latter resolution as a reference "to the outrageous and abominable attacks made by the *Chronicle* of last week, upon the private character of the editor of the Pioneer." [10]

In the *Pioneer* of February 6, Goodhue, who by that time

[9] *Chronicle and Register*, January 20, 1851; Potts to Sibley, January 21, 1851, Brown to Sibley, January 24, 1851, Sibley Papers.

[10] Goodhue to Sibley, February 6, 1851, Sibley Papers; *Pioneer*, February 6, 1851; *Chronicle and Register*, February 10, 1851. The *Chronicle's* attack on Goodhue was published under the title "The Whig Party in Minnesota" and signed "A Whig," in the issue of January 27, 1851.

was back at his desk, took matters into his own hands in a
column and a half headed "Base Forgery of Public Sentiment."
The Cooper affair, he wrote, was the result of a conspiracy
to murder him, "and thus prepare for electing another territorial printer." It was "deliberately planned on the 14th ult.,
the weapons provided, the assistants stationed, and the whole
bloody transaction attempted on the 15th." But that was
"only one of a series of crimes" committed by the conspira-
tors. They had taken advantage "of the helpless condition in
which they had thrown us, by the infliction of wounds which
they hoped were fatal," and had "drummed up an indignation meeting at Mazourka Hall, a little handful of the minions
of Henry M. Rice, who run at his whistle, and who are ready
at his bidding, to stab a man or his reputation." He had been
told that most of those at the meeting were his friends, "who
were there to see that the Pioneer received no detriment at
the hands of those outlaws"; and that fewer than a dozen persons voted for the resolutions or took any part in the meeting.
He declared that the sentiments expressed by the resolutions
were not those of the meeting, nor of the people of Minnesota,
who "do maintain, defend and uphold, the manly, fearless and
independent character of the Pioneer — a paper which utters
the truth fearlessly, and is for that reason alone a terror to the
wicked." Appended to the editorial were statements of persons whom the *Chronicle* account had "made to figure in the
indignation meeting . . . without their knowledge or consent."

The *Chronicle and Register* expired with the issue of February 10, 1851, but the *Democrat* remained to carry on the warfare against the *Pioneer* and the coalition of Sibley Democrats
and Ramsey Whigs — a warfare characterized by name-calling
and bitter recriminations on the part of both papers. The
Democrat represented the *Pioneer* as the organ of "the Monopoly," that is, "the Fur Company," and the *Pioneer* retaliated by calling the *Democrat* "the Rice Organ" and "the

Winnebago Fur Company organ," referring to Rice's connection with the Winnebago Indian trade; and each paper accused the other of being unduly influenced by "Federal," or Whig, interests.

The *Pioneer* maintained its stand that the people of Minnesota were not yet ready for party organization — that past attempts to organize had only increased "the partizan and factional tendency of things" and had "proved the utter fallacy of attempting to cloak either faction with the name of Whig or Democrat." Goodhue did not care to see the Democrat party *"organize Rice end foremost"*; but, he declared, "the Pioneer is Democratic . . . and when the majority say, now is the time — we want to place you again in that post, which you have never abandoned, as the organ of the Democratic party, to the largest fragment of which you adhered, when its unity was destroyed — the *Pioneer is there.*" [11]

The *Democrat*, on the other hand, clamored for organization, and accused the *Pioneer* of "corrupt efforts . . . to provoke and embitter division in the democratic ranks." Robertson, the editor, was convinced that "the Pioneer is now the whig organ of the Territory." "It is now manifest," he wrote, "that it is the policy of the Whigs to divide the Democracy into two parties, and the appointed and paid employment of the Pioneer, to aggravate and foster that division." [12]

The question of the public printing for 1852, strangely enough, was not fought over in the newspapers. On January 17 the legislature, by a large majority vote, elected Goodhue and John P. Owens and George W. Moore of the *Minnesotian*, a Whig paper which had been established in September, 1851, to do all the incidental printing of the legislature, as well as the printing of the laws and the journals. The *Democrat* made only a brief comment on the matter: "As we asked no favors, and expected none, we are not disappointed

[11] *Pioneer*, February 27, March 13, 1851.
[12] *Democrat*, February 18, March 4, 11, 1851.

in the manner in which the printing patronage was disposed
of." [13]

While the hostilities between the *Democrat* and the *Pioneer*
continued throughout 1851 and 1852, they were less violent
as time went on, and they occupied less space in the columns
of the papers, particularly in the *Pioneer*. Relations between
the *Pioneer* and the *Minnesotian* were in the main cordial. All
three papers reflected the prevailing political excitement over
the location of the capitol and the penitentiary, the legislative
apportionment bill of 1851, and the fall elections of that year.
But those matters were greatly overshadowed by the Sioux
treaties in the summer of 1851 and their ratification a year
later, a subject over which there was no real controversy in
the newspapers, for on it all Minnesotans were of one mind. [14]

[13] *House Journal*, 1852, p. 46; *Democrat*, January 21, 1852.
[14] See below, pp. 201–216.

THE EDITOR

7. Minnesota Booster

GOODHUE ONCE WROTE IN THE PIONEER: "I DWELL UPON MIN-
nesota and St. Paul; for they are ever in my thoughts and a
part of my very existence. There is not a party tie or political association, that I would not instantly sever, to promote
their welfare."[1] The columns of his paper bear ample witness
to the truth of this declaration. His role in local politics was
necessitated by the dependence of the *Pioneer* on the public
printing, involved as it was in the bitter personal and factional
quarrels that make the story of early Minnesota politics so
complex. Even if his personal ambition — a dominant characteristic according to his enemies and many of his friends —
had not been involved, it is hard to imagine a man of his temperament remaining aloof from the excitement of the battle.
But politics was by no means his major interest, and the
columns of his paper, except during the heat of partisan contests, were concerned more with matters that were closer
to his heart: to make Minnesota, its advantages and possibilities, known to the world, thereby attracting immigrants to
increase its meager population; and to point the way to its
physical, industrial, agricultural, and social development. He
considered it his most important duty as a frontier editor to
"hold a faithful mirror up to Minnesota, to reflect its true
impress and image upon the world."[2] On the whole the mirror
was faithful; if at times it flattered, it served its purpose by increasing the population that the young territory needed above
all else for its development and prosperity.

A large proportion of Goodhue's editorials were written
to attract settlers to Minnesota. Some of them were addressed
frankly and directly to prospective immigrants; others took

[1] *Pioneer*, October 31, 1851.
[2] *Pioneer*, April 15, 1852.

the form of descriptive articles in which the purpose was less
obvious. In nearly every mail the editor received letters asking for information about Minnesota. Most of them he answered in detail, either privately or in the *Pioneer*. Sometimes
his answers took the form of editorials inspired by these inquiries. Again, he printed selections from a number of letters,
and gave the answers "in one covey." And now and then he
printed an entire letter, and answered it fully, question by
question, in his paper. He published large editions of the
Pioneer for distribution abroad, and his articles were widely
quoted in newspapers in the river towns and in eastern states.
There is no doubt that these editorials were responsible for
many of the immigrants who flocked into the territory in the
early days.[3] Typical of his answers to questions about Minnesota is an article in the *Pioneer* of May 19, 1849, written
while he was absent from Minnesota to bring his family to St.
Paul:

"It is always interesting to notice the leading topics of
conversation in every place we visit: What do you suppose
the text is in Galena? Cholera?[4] Not at all. California? No.
That name has lost its tinsel and glitter; and has become associated with death and disaster. You hear nothing but Minnesota, the St. Croix, St. Anthony and St. Paul. One would
suppose that all the Saints in the calendar had broken loose
up above. Where is that dray load of goods going? To St.
Croix. Where is this furniture going? To St. James.[5] Where

[3] In the *Pioneer* of May 5, 1849, Goodhue wrote: "We are printing a large
edition of the Pioneer, and shall continue to issue large numbers without reference to the number of our subscribers; believing that at this juncture, our
young Territory stands in that interesting attitude to the world, which requires a liberal *disbursement* of intelligence." The editor frequently quoted
from exchanges items about Minnesota that presumably had their source in
his paper.

[4] In 1849 and the two years following, cholera was epidemic throughout
the United States. There were a few deaths from the disease in St. Paul. John
W. Armstrong, "The Asiatic Cholera in St. Paul," in *Minnesota History*,
14:288–302 (September, 1933).

[5] St. Croix was the settlement at the Falls of St. Croix, now Taylors Falls.
So far as the present editor knows, there was no place in Minnesota called

are they taking all these bales and packages? To St. Paul. Where are these saws and mill irons going? To St. Anthony. What is the destination of these cattle and horses? Why, they are to be let down, as it were in a sheet by the four corners, before St. Peters.[6] Every man you meet wants to hear from St. Paul. How old is it? how long is it? how does it look? what are wages? what are rents? what will sustain the business of the town? what are town lots worth, won't there be a

SEVEN CORNERS, ST. PAUL, IN 1852

revulsion — won't the great town be at the Falls? how many presses are there? what will they do for eatables in that cold country? is there any *land* up there?

"Our answers are — St. Paul, except as a little old French trading post, is *no* year old — the town is about as large as a mob on the increase — it looks as if the seed for a multitude of tenements had been scattered yesterday upon a bed of guano, and had sprouted up into cabins, and stores and sheds and warehouses, fresh from the saw mill, since the last sun

"St. James" at the time that Goodhue wrote. The present city of St. James in Watonwan County was not settled until 1869. Warren Upham, *Minnesota Geographic Names*, 575 (*Minnesota Historical Collections*, volume 17 — St. Paul, 1920).

[6] St. Peters was the early name of Mendota.

shone — it looks just as St. Louis did within our remembrance, when the germinating principle of Yankee enterprises first infused into it.

"As for wages, why at St. Paul as everywhere else, the employer hires as cheap as possible, and the laborer gets all he can — being an amount probably bearing some proportion to the amount of labor performed. Any man who is really in earnest about it, except a grave-digger, can find plenty of work to do in St. Paul, and a chance to invest all his earnings in real estate which will soon double in value. As for rents, like Rachael's children, they *are not.* Let no man who wants a shelter over his head, think of staying in St. Paul beyond the time of a visit, without being prepared to build something of a house, if it be nothing but a dry goods box with a roof over it. Pine lumber delivered, will cost from $13 to $15 per thousand.

"As for the question, what is to sustain the business of St. Paul, we answer, it must sustain itself, as all towns have had to do. It creates itself, naturally and necessarily from its geographical position. The enquirer says he can see what St. Louis has to sustain it; true, my friend, but when St. Louis was what St. Paul now is, there was a class of men like yourself, who could not tell what resources St. Louis had — because they were not yet developed in the upper and surrounding country; there were others who looked with an eye of faith upon the destiny of St. Louis, who could see what resources that town would have in a few years, and their faith is now rich fruition.

"What are town lots worth? Well, in our humble judgment, they are worth all they can be sold for. The price varies from $25 to $500 per lot, of fifty feet by one hundred and fifty. If you do not think they are worth that, there are those who do; and we can show you town lots in other villages — and perhaps larger villages, larger lots and richer soil — which can be bought for less money. We should be glad to sell some of that sort to any gentleman who has a taste for gardening, and who wants such resources as horticulture will supply 'to sustain the business' of a village.

"As to whether there will be a revulsion some time in St. Paul, we can only say, we have no doubt of it. We should expect nothing else of any town which has in it the essential elements of a vigorous growth; but we would not recommend the cultivation of dwarf apple trees, for fear that thrifty trees might have the tips of their limbs nipped by the frosts of winter; would you? If so, why *go it*, and see which will succeed the better in orcharding.

"Won't the great town be at the Falls? There will be a great town at the Falls, no doubt; but whether it will be *the* great town, is another question. The Falls will very soon be connected with St. Paul by a railroad eight miles long, almost before the people in general begin to talk about it;[7] because it will pay, and because there are men interested in both those places, of great capital and capable of planning and executing as comprehensive plans for the growth and advancement of Minnesota, as the longest headed of those shrewd Bostonians who spread their net of railroads over the eastern end of this continent, and ensnared in it the trade of the St. Lawrence and the trade of the great lakes, while New York was quietly snoozing on the banks of the Hudson, and glorifying the great Dewitt Clinton, whose ditch is now enriching the city of Notions.

"When we left St. Paul the other day, there was only one paper there — the *Pioneer;* perhaps there are twenty there now — the farther off we get, the more St. Paul newspapers we hear of. No doubt presses will come as fast as they are needed. The press in our time, keeps on the very foremost wave of

[7] It was not until 1862 that St. Paul and St. Anthony were connected by railroad. The road was built by the St. Paul and Pacific Railroad Company and later became part of the Great Northern system. William Crooks, "The First Railroad in Minnesota," in *Minnesota Historical Collections*, 10:445, 448.

advancing population, or rather, it sometimes falls down on the fore-side of the foremost wave. The Pioneer, when she issued in April last, was the northernmost paper printed in the United States — all the population west of St. Paul being Sioux Indians. Before those two great engines of civilization, the whiskey shop and the printing office, the poor Indians stand no more chance than so many Mexicans before two batteries of grape and canister.

"What will Minnesotians do for eatables? Ha! ha! That is funny. Time was, when the miner at Galena wondered if, after all, it would not be worth while, by way of experiment, to try to raise potatoes and some kind of small corn, in the mines. How is it now? Is it not admitted on all hands, that there is not a more prolific soil in the world, than that of the mines? Let it once for all then be stated as a fact long established, that all crops raised in Wisconsin, can be raised in Minnesota — that the second dent corn, which does not ripen even in New York or in New England, is a sure crop in Minnesota — that the soil generally contains more sand than the soil of Wisconsin or Illinois; but it is very warm and eminently productive and exhaustless. — Such is the character of lands subject to entry between St. Paul and Stillwater. Of the western part of the Territory, still Indian lands, Mr. Bay,[8] a gentleman familiarly acquainted with every portion of the North West, says that the region west of the Mississippi to the ridge dividing its waters from the Missouri, is *the* Minnesota — a country unsurpassed for natural wealth in the whole world — compared with which, the eastern side of Minnesota is a mere waste.

"We have thus rambled on, regardless of method, to answer some of the inquiries made about Minnesota. In conclusion, we will *advise* no person to go. Men of the right stamp will always find the right spots; and men of the right *nerve* will

[8] The reference may be to either of two prominent St. Louis lawyers, Samuel M. Bay or his brother, William V. N. Bay.

stay in them and flourish, regardless of all temporary inconvenience."

Goodhue's faith in the "glorious destiny" of Minnesota was unbounded. Seldom could be resist an opportunity to prophesy, and his predictions of the future greatness of the territory recur again and again, throughout his writings, in a paragraph here or a sentence there, and now and then they are the subject of whole editorials. He predicted for Minnesota "a rapidity of growth unparalleled even in the annals of Western progress," and pictured its lands covered with farms, with "fences and white cottages, and waving wheat fields, and vast jungles of rustling maize, and villages and cities crowned with spires, and railroads with trains of cars rumbling afar off." Agriculture would be a leading industry, "more profitable here than any where in the whole west," and Minnesota would one day be "the *Dairy land* of the West." He foresaw the state's great summer resort industry when he wrote: "We confidently look to see the time, when hundreds of the opulent" from the South "will build delightful cottages on the borders of our ten thousand lakes and ornament their grounds with all that is tasteful in shrubbery and horticulture, for a summer retreat." [9]

Not so happily inspired were his prophecies concerning Minnesota's forests and minerals. "*Centuries*," he wrote, "will hardly exhaust the pineries above us." He was convinced that there were large coal fields in the Blue Earth and Minnesota valleys, and that there were copper mines west of Lake Superior "as rich as the richest" of the mines on the southern shore of that lake. He had heard that iron ore had been found in the territory, but had "never thought the discovery of it, of any particular importance." [10]

In an article in the *Pioneer* of July 5, 1849, headed "Minnesota — Her Destiny," he sees the future state as "the New

[9] See below, pp. 86, 98, 111, 205.
[10] *Pioneer*, April 8, 1852.

England of the West," supplying to the surrounding states the inspiration for their education, laws, and religion, as well as industrial products:

"We regard this Territory as destined, to become the New England of the West. — We infer this from various considerations. In the first place *old* New England is becoming every year farther removed from the centre of the States with respect to territory and influence. 'The march of empire is westward.' Time was when she supplied the old States with their education, their laws, and their religion; but these things she now does at a comparatively less extent than she has; and her supplies in these respects must continue to diminish in the same ratio that they have heretofore. — Whence shall come the demanded supply of these moral wants? We think they must come from some other meridian so constituted by nature as to produce it. — Again, New England has heretofore supplied the old States with certain *wares* that cannot be expected from any foreign source. She is now becoming too remote from the Western States and Territories, to warrant their carting the heavy products of their soil from one to two thousand miles to make an exchange for articles to be carted back again the same distance. She must look for these supplies in some other quarter.

"Where shall that quarter be? It must be in a meridian where the arts will naturally flourish. Now survey the map of our country over the space west and south of the Hudson river, and what country will you find so similar to New England as Minnesota? It is situated in about the latitude of the State of Maine; but considering the fact, that this climate is shorn of the influences of the sea, our latitude, virtually corresponds with that of Massachusetts as near as we can estimate. It is the universal testimony of immigrants from the New England States, that the climate seems here almost precisely as it does there. If there is any difference, it is in favor of Minnesota. But in respect to soil, it is superfluous to say that this Territory is incomparably superior to Massachusetts.

"Will the New England character find the elements of its subsistence in the South? No! It dies out upon the savannahs of the South. It can no more prosper there than the orange or the sugar cane can flourish on New England's gravelly hills. The leaven of New England intelligence, morals, commercial and mechanical enterprise, requires to be constantly renewed by new supplies from the original source. The professional talent of the South can generally be traced back to a Northern origin. And, as to mechanics, who believes that Lowells and Manchesters and Lawrences can grow up, on her low, champaign soil: in her languid sultry climes? But these towns must arise — the teeming millions of the West must have a supply for their moral wants and their physical necessities. Whence shall this supply come? We answer emphatically from the North-west — the region west of the great lakes.

"Minnesota we foresee will be the destination of the largest current of immigration from the Eastern States, until its lands and its water privileges are occupied. Here they will find, an unqualifiedly healthy climate, fertile and well drained lands, and upon the Mississippi the best market for mechanical products in the Union. With such a population will come not only the arts but science and morals. Our Falls of St. Anthony with hundreds of water powers upon other streams will be turned to manufacturing purposes. Thrifty towns will arise upon them. Our undulating prairies will rejoice under the hand of husbandry; these hills and valleys will be jocund with the voices of school children, and churches shall mark the moral progress of our land."

St. Paul, Goodhue was confident, would "with more inevitable certainty become a large city, than any other town that is now budding into existence on the Continent of North America." He visioned it as "one great city" covering all the ground "from Pig's Eye to the Falls," its levee lined with steamboats, and trains "thundering across the bridge" into the city, fifteen hours from St. Louis, on their way to Lake Superior. St. Anthony would undoubtedly have "extensive mills and manufactories"; but, in his opinion, "the ultimate hope of the town for a large population, rests upon that class of retired people of substance, as well as invalids and people of fortune, desiring literary privileges in a retired, beautiful town, who will certainly be more strongly attracted there than to any place we know of in the Great Valley." "All Saints," Goodhue's name for the incipient village on the west side of the river that was to become Minneapolis, was "in all respects as pleasantly and advantageously situated as St. Anthony, for mill purposes," and would "soon be a flourishing village." Traverse des Sioux, he predicted, would be the principal town in the Minnesota Valley, and Itasca "with its fine harbor and natural advantages for trade, would not be distanced in the race of improvement." These two towns of great prospects in the 1850's have long since been abandoned. And another prophecy, unexpressed, was doubtless in the back of his mind: that the *Pioneer*, under his editorship, some day would be a great metropolitan daily.[11]

In the *Pioneer* of March 27, 1850, Goodhue foresees the influx of immigrants that were to pour into Minnesota during that spring and summer "like locusts," establishing farms and swelling village populations:

"In a few days more, the boats will be here, with their thronging multitudes of immigrants. In a few months, hundreds of new buildings will leap into existence in Saint Paul, and hundreds of new faces will greet us, all strangers now, and we who are here now, shall be comparatively lost sight of and forgotten; there will be new enterprises, new fashions, new morals here. Let us treat them hospitably, frankly, kindly;

[11] Traverse des Sioux was on the Minnesota River near the present city of St. Peter, and Itasca was on the Mississippi near the site of Elk River. See below, pp. 85, 110, 162, 205; *Pioneer*, April 8, 1852.

taking them in, though strangers, as we were ourselves taken in, last year.

"Saint Anthony, Saint Croix, and Stillwater, will also receive their share of immigration. They are all places deserving the attention of immigrants, having their various advantages to suit the different tastes, habits and pursuits of different persons. The settlement of lands and opening of farms through that fine region of country between the Saint Croix and the Mississippi, must also inevitably give an impulse to the growth of a fine village at Douglass' Point. — Wabashaw, the commercial focus of the trade of Minnesota on the half-breed lands south of us, will have a rapid growth this season — very likely may be as large in a year as Saint Paul is now; for immigrants will pour into that tract this spring, like locusts, and open farms all over it.[12]

"Nor will that beautiful belt of land up the Mississippi, be lost sight of by the keen eye of the immigrant. — Itasca, with its fine harbor and natural advantages for trade, undoubtedly the head of navigation, at least for the most of the season, for boats plying upward from Saint Anthony; Itasca will not be distanced in the race for improvement. — Upon the Saint Croix, Osceola, and Marine Mills, will both receive a new impulse this season; while Stillwater, with her trade extending into the pineries of the St. Croix, stands upon a permanent basis of prosperity, with interests so independent of ours, that no reasonable rivalry can exist between that and any town on the Mississippi, unless it be a strife whether Saint Anthony or the mills of the Saint Croix, shall get the larger share of the pine mill-logs found between the Saint Croix and the Mississippi.

"West and north of Saint Paul and Saint Anthony for a great distance, we do not know how far, into the region of

[12] The Wabasha Reservation on Lake Pepin was reserved by treaty in 1830 for the Sioux half-breeds, who never occupied the tract. It was not until 1854 that it was surveyed and opened to settlement. Folwell, *Minnesota*, 1:321–325.

the lakes — and in all directions around White-bear lake, Speculation is turning its eager eye — a beautiful region, of rich land, diversified with meadows, hills, valleys, oak-openings, lakes, timber and partial prairies. We predict a very rapid multiplication of farms all through that section, especially north of Saint Paul. The excellent crops and high prices of the past year, have convinced the most skeptical amongst us, that Agriculture will be a leading interest in Minnesota; and that its immediate connection with an adequate home market for the supply of garrisons, the Indian consumption, and the pineries, will make Agriculture more profitable here than anywhere else in the whole west."

Throughout the East and the South the belief prevailed that the climate of Minnesota was too frigid, the growing season too short, and the soil too barren for man to live in comfort and produce crops. To combat these prejudices Goodhue filled his columns with praises of the healthful and bracing qualities of Minnesota's climate, and the fertility and productivity of its soil. His comparisons of the "salubrious" climate of the territory with that of "the bilious south" and California, "afflicted with that lingering, living death, the fever and ague," [13] would have brought down upon his head the wrath of chambers of commerce in those sections, had they existed then. Such a comparison is found in the *Pioneer* of June 5, 1851:

"Although we have in Minnesota, immense tracts of land, as rich as the best soils in which the victims of agues and bilious fevers find sure and early graves along the sluggish streams of Iowa and Illinois, we have, universally, a pure, bracing, wholesome atmosphere, and *Health* standing up manfully under the burden of daily toil — sound livers and firm muscles. In Minnesota, honest Toil is not compelled to hobble about through harvest time upon such miserable crutches as calomel and quinine. . . . Never has a case of fever and

[13] See below, p. 96.

ague originated here; and except for the use of invalids who come up, pale as a procession of the ghost of Banquo and its attendants, from the damp plains of the South, which like cemeteries open their black jaws and swallow, in their very youth, the generations of livid wretches who have been lured there by the *one idea* of fertility; except for these invalids, who fly from those charnel-houses to recruit their health in this land of cataracts and pine forests, and dry, wholesome atmosphere, there is no use for quinine, or Morrison's pills,[14] or Rowand's Tonic mixture, or any of the antibilious nostrums of our times, the sale of which, in some of the towns south of us, constitutes a large share of their commerce."

Typical of Goodhue's editorials in praise of Minnesota's climate and agricultural advantages is an article in the *Pioneer* of September 26, 1850, addressed "To the Farmers of the United States and Europe:

"We design now, to give those of you who are desirous of removing to a new country, some of the reasons why you ought to prefer Minnesota for the business of farming. To begin with, if you are of that incorrigible class of persons who have taken it into their brains, that no part of this great globe is habitable, by reason of the cold, to a higher degree of latitude than about forty degrees north, we have no use for you. Stay in your doorless cabins and go shivering about in your thin slazy garments of jeans, through the mingled frost and mud, and the icy sleet and chilling fogs of that most execrable of all climates — an hermaphrodite region, half tropical and half frigid — a cross of the North Pole upon the Equator. Stay where you are. We want here a race of men, of higher physical and mental powers, of more meat and muscle, of more force and energy. The whole of the British Islands, the nursery of that vigorous stock of the human fam-

[14] An advertisement of "Morrison's Compound Sarsaparilla, or blood pills — the great renovator of the system" appears in the *Minnesota Register* of April 27, 1849.

ily, which first taking root on the rocky shore of the Atlantic, has, in two hundred years, uprooted the forests filled with barbarous Indians, and like the prolific locust tree, spread wider and wider its annual shoots, until its shadows are reflected from the Pacific — those British Islands lie more than five degrees north of St. Paul. The whole of England, Ireland, Scotland, Belgium, Holland, and a part of France, *lie north of the extreme northern boundary of Minnesota.*

. . . .

"The human family, never has accomplished anything worthy of note, beside the erection of the pyramids, those milestones of ancient centuries, south of latitude 40 degrees north. The history of the *world,* is written chiefly above that parallel. South of it, existed slavery, in one or another form, always, to a great extent, both in ancient and modern times, and wherever consumption contrives to place a saddle upon the back of production, and rides, there will be want and wretchedness; for Nature has ordained it for the true welfare of man, that every human being shall labor, in some honest and useful vocation.

"But there are prejudices against our climate. Some insist upon it, that we cannot raise Indian corn. Show them prolific fields of it, as we now can hundreds, the naked ears glittering like gold in the mellow sunshine of autumn, and the ground beneath almost paved with yellow pumpkins, and yet they look incredulous, and shake their heads, and say 'It won't do. I was here last June, and your Springs are too late. You can't make a *cawn crap y'here,* no how you can fix it, stranger.' These wise people have a theory — that maize is adapted solely to the latitude they came from; and they are as stubborn in maintaining it, as the geologists are in their theory that there can be no mineral coal north of the Illinois coal beds; although it is actually found here, in various localities, ranging south from Crow Wing river as far as the mouth of the Blue Earth, of the most admirable quality. If we could not raise Indian corn, we should remember, that with the exception of a part of Italy and Spain, all populous Europe, subsists very well without it. But maize, we admit, is *the* Cereal crop of America. We subscribe to all Mr. Clay's beautiful eulogium upon it;[15] and perhaps the most valuable quality of this grain, is, its adaption to longitudes, rather than *latitudes. There is not an Esquimaux Indian* basking by his lake side in the sunshine of his brief, hot summer, who cannot raise and ripen one variety or another of maize. From the delta of the Mississippi, to the remotest spring branch that supplies Lake Itasca, the head of the river, this crop can be raised, and *is* raised and ripened every year. What folly then, to contradict these palpable facts!

"The same reasoning applies to wheat; yet in fact, we live even too far *south* for sure crops of winter wheat. Those choice wheat lands of Europe, on the shores of the Baltic, are far north of us. At Red River, many hundred miles north of St. Paul, they raise better wheat than ever goes into the markets of Milwaukee or Chicago. There is not a plant of any description, raised in Wisconsin, that does not ripen here. We have tomatoes here abundant and ripe, in a garden which was not fenced until June. We have had no frost yet. All our crops are ripe. Last season, we gathered cucumbers in November, which were planted very late, for pickles.

"Our soil is generally productive — on this side of the river, although much of it is sandy, it is a very productive soil; not as compared with the Middle or Eastern States, but as compared with Wisconsin or Illinois. There are fields here, which the French have cultivated, without manuring, for twenty years, which produce good crops, barren as the soil may look to a Sucker, from the bottoms of the Eel river or the

[15] In a speech delivered at New Orleans in 1847, Clay said: "America [has] . . . a never-failing and abundant supply of Indian corn — that great supporter of animal life, for which we are not half grateful enough to a bountiful and merciful Providence." Calvin Colton, ed., *The Works of Henry Clay,* 3:48 (New York, 1904).

Big Muddy. The farmers here, in the average, get *larger crops* per acre, than we have ever seen raised in any other part of the West. We do not say that all Minnesota is fertile; but that it will compare favorably, in fertility, with any portion of the world.

"Consider then, our advantages here in regard to health. No bilious fevers, no shaking with ague in the harvest field; no loss of crops by sickness. Is this nothing? Why, we have seen thousands of acres of grain in Illinois, 'going back into the ground,' literally rotting, unharvested, because every body was sick, and labor could not be hired at any price.

"Of the extent and value of our home market for produce, it is needless for us to repeat what we have so often written — that in no other part of the West, is there anything like an equal demand for agricultural products; to supply the Indian tribes on the Minnesota and Mississippi rivers, to supply the forts, and to supply the great and increasing business of the pineries and the manufacture of lumber. Every farmer has a natural tariff to protect him, equal to the cost of shipping the same kinds of produce which he offers in market, from several hundred miles below, by steamboat; added to the insurance, and the profits of the produce dealer — all which, is more than fifty per cent premium in his favor, over the farmer who lives down the river, and who has no such home markets as ours, at his door. Add to this, the cheapness of choice lands in Minnesota, our freedom from the burden of State Government, and the moral, intelligent, and industrious character of our people, and the immigrant, if he *is* a man, and expects to live by *exertion*, will find more inducements to make his home in Minnesota, than in any of the bilious regions south of it."

In much the same vein, with emphasis on the rewards of honest toil, is an article in the *Pioneer* of May 30, 1850, headed "Agriculture in Minnesota":

"Besides trees, cranberries, wild rice, and grass, we have

never represented that Minnesota could boast of any spontaneous productions of the soil. We have never said that wheat could be cradled, fifty bushels to the acre, where no wheat had been sown, that *volunteer* crops of corn could be harvested, and that Irish potatoes could be found growing wild here, three hundred bushels to the acre, and whole sections of land covered with garden sauce, prairies yellow with wild pumpkins, and that ten thousand roasted pigs with carving knives and forks stuck in their haunches were running about squealing to be eaten. We have never represented that people who have houses to build in our village, were sitting amongst their piles of lumber, anxiously looking for the arrival of an army of men, professing to be carpenters, strangers from afar, whom they might set instantly at work here at house building, at $2 per day and roast beef; or that we were a band of communists, who would undertake to feed the whole hungry world; nor that proprietors of village property would hurry down to the boats and say to every stranger, 'my dear sir, come up with me and take your choice of my corner town lots at your own price, to be paid for at your own convenience; and if you want any assistance call upon me; labor is plenty here, work is light and wages high; or if you prefer to hold an office, name what office you would prefer.'

"Our encouragement to come has always been predicated upon the idea that those who came here, are willing and able to work. Have we ever described Minnesota as a paradise for loafers, a retreat for pensioners upon the toil of others? On the contrary, we always represented that men, here, would get enough of the primeval curse, enough of thorns and briars, enough of cold, and enough of heat; but with honest toil, enough of bread, of clothing, and of the comforts of life; and of that richest of blessings that ever Heaven bestowed upon man, good, vigorous health, such as all the coined and uncoined gold of California cannot buy.

"We have said and do say that our territory richly yields, if cultivated, all the products of the north temperate zone; that our second rate lands are much superior to the best lands of the middle and eastern states; that in the production of all that is usually cultivated in gardens, including melons, the soil of our village or of St. Anthony, is not surpassed by the most luxuriant gardens of Long Island; that any given number of men, of equal strength and skill, can go to work upon our prairies and produce in any given year, not only greater cash results, but even a greater number of bushels of any produce suited to the temperate zone, or a greater number of tons of hay than the same number of men can produce upon the fattest plains of the Wabash or in the very kidneys of the American bottoms.

"To accomplish this takes some capital and much labor. What that is valuable is accomplished without labor? Who levelled the forests of Ohio, tree by tree? Men, men, we want men; we want producers who expect to labor. We have plenty of land, good land, within half a day's ride of any of our villages, at government prices; and land even nearer, by paying the first purchaser a profit for it. And why quarrel with the man who came before you and made a choice location, if he does want to make something by selling his land? Would not you, or you, have done the same thing? If you see a horse worth $100 offered in market for $50, and buy the horse, has your neighbor who wants to buy that horse to work, a right to insist upon your selling him for $50, so that *he* and not *you* shall have all the profits of a good bargain?

"What is $3.00 or $4.00 an acre for a beautiful piece of ground lying between our flourishing town and the equally prosperous village of St. Anthony? You may buy 40 acres of such land for $5 per acre, and hire it plowed, hire it fenced, seed it, and pay for all of the expense of cultivating and harvesting upon it, a single crop of potatoes; and with a medium crop, you will clear the purchase-money, the seed, all the labor, and have a handsome sum left for profit besides.

"We have much more to say upon this subject, but our limited space prohibits it."

To choose between the American Bottom and Minnesota could hardly have been difficult for the prospective settler

THIRD AND BENCH STREETS, ST. PAUL, 1852
The *Pioneer* office is at the left, facing Third. The house in the middle, once Vital Guerin's, was Le Duc's residence, adjoining his book store.

who read in the *Pioneer* of April 24, 1851, of the sad plight of the farmer on the Mississippi flood plain in southern Illinois:

"Every good thing, has its alloy. The perpetual summer of the tropics, produces inactivity in man, as well as a super-abundance of spontaneous fruits to supply his wants. — The herdsman upon the pampas of South America, with his innumerable cattle that are reared without the expense of feeding or shelter, with all his apparent resources of wealth, is poor — but little better than the savage. The farmer upon the

American bottoms, who turns over his hundred acres of black furrows in one field, which presently becomes, as it were a young forest of maize, waving and rustling in the sultry breezes of August, as he sits in the open space between his two log cabins, at noonday, feeble and enervated, and his little pale children, shaking with ague, gather around him, and he listens to the shrill cry of the locust, and sees afar off upon the Mississippi river, the steamboat, even the steamboat, hot, panting, exhausted, smiting the sluggish waters with feeble strokes, his very heart sinks within him; and he sighs for the cool, bracing mountain air, or the stimulating sea breeze and the sparkling spring water; and would exchange all his corn fields and his acres, for a garden amongst the sterile rocks of the north, with its rigors, its snow banks, and its little painted school houses. So California, has its alloy; ah! much more alloy than gold. It may be considered an axiom, that the richest lands are not found in the most healthful climates. — Nature delights in making an equitable average in the distribution of her favors; although her equivalents at first thought may not all seem quite fair.

"What shall it profit a man, to choose lands, watered by creeks full of fever and ague and horn pouts and lily pads, producing 100 bushels of corn to the acre, and worth 20 cents per bushel, rather than lands watered by trout brooks, and mossy springs, producing only 50 bushels of corn per acre, worth 75 cents per bushel? But 'we say no more; God knows what we mean.'

"Now we have plenty of land in Minnesota that is good enough without looking up the Minnesota river after it, upon Indian Territory; (where, if we are not mistaken, there will be some ague found.) Settlers! What do you want? Will it satisfy you to get land as good as there is in New York, or New England, where the climate is even better and the market, all you please to ask? Such lands you can find. We have warm, sandy loams, rich argillaceous soils, clay lands, precisely like the barrens of Michigan — all — all productive lands — far better than they look; and in fact such as will soon make an industrious farmer rich. Or will you be satisfied with nothing but the flat, unctuous prairies of Illinois, extending in unbroken plains, and watered by stagnant creeks? If so, in God's name go there and settle, and when the great blazing sun sets and leaves you there upon the chill, naked prairie, your children sick and uneducated, and without one hope or aspiration rising above the dead level that will surround you there — remember — remember, that we told you of these things!"

That the immigrant hordes who passed Minnesota by in their rush to California for gold gave the editor mighty concern is evident in an article in the *Pioneer* of June 7, 1849:

"For years, the tendency of emigration, throughout the world, has been westward. The discovery of a continent by Columbus, almost uninhabited, a continent abounding in mineral wealth, a soil of luxuriant fertility, forests stirring with game, vast lakes and multitudes of rivers alive with fish, opened a natural avenue for the outflow of the pent-up population of Europe. But the stream of westward emigration has been greatly widened, deepened and quickened, since the establishment on this continent, of a free government; and especially since that government has demonstrated its inherent elasticity and power of self-extension, to the area, if need be, of a whole continent, nurturing into vigorous vitality, State after State, where stood the ancient wilderness and broad oceans of prairie. Within the past year, a *great gulf stream* of emigration has set out westward across the whole width of our continent, flowing to California on the Pacific. That broad stream carries with it, not only men and women and children, but has swept away multitudes of cattle and wagons and every description of property, to the value of millions of dollars.

"That stream is now subsiding. The world has never be-

fore witnessed, and probably never will again witness, a movement so vast, so expensive, and we fear it must be added — so
visionary, foolish, ruinous! In no possible event, can this
movement fail to ruin most of the participators in it. It is
melancholy to see old men and young men yea, and delicate
women and children, hurried into this miserable maelstrom
— hazarding health, life, all comfort, all social and religious
privileges — every thing — for the vague chance of standing
up to their arm-pits in the unwholesome water of the Sacra-
mento or its tributaries, and washing out a few ounces of
gold dust, which when obtained will scarcely buy for them
the commonest comforts of life. — Truly ''tis distance lends
enchantment to the view.' How else could it be, that so many
persons in the pursuit of happiness, could have passed by
unnoticed, the wide blooming plains and hills of Minnesota,
of *virgin* Minnesota — with her lands as fertile as the banks
of the Nile — her forests of ancient pines, her noble rivers,
leaping over their rocky barriers in wild majesty — her thousand lakes of crystal waters — and above all her fresh, bracing
climate, which fills everything animate within her borders,
with youthful vigor — to wander away and die upon the arid
plains of California!

"Contrast the two regions. California, is on the western
verge of the continent, while Minnesota is in the very heart
of it. The former, is afflicted with that lingering, living death,
the fever and ague; while to the latter, the whole family of
bilious ailments is unknown. To go to the former requires the
greater part of a year and much expense; while to reach the
latter, you have but to take a pleasant, cheap and short excursion by steamboat, up the Mississippi, to place you within the
sound of the falls of St. Anthony, the very roar of which is
enough to cure an invalid. In the former, you cannot find
what you want, to live comfortably, and what you do get,
costs all you have got; while in the latter, you can have if you
want it, at a moderate charge for freight, a parlor and even

almost a house, translated by steamboat from Galena, Saint Louis or New Orleans, and landed for you at Stillwater or Saint Paul. There you may look for speculation, gambling, vice; here, you will find industry, morality and virtue. There you will find no government and a people too intent upon gain to establish a government; here you will find a government as well organized as in any of the States. California is in a latitude which has never proved favorable to the highest development of human greatness; while Minnesota, embraces the latitude of those nations of the earth which in all ages have produced the most vigorous minds and the greatest aggregate of intellectual and moral force.

"We do not complain that Minnesota is forgotten. Not at all. Our Government at Washington has not forgotten it. — The eyes of half the Continent are turned upon it — the weary emigrant on his way to California turns his tearful eye back to the North-East, and curses the folly which induced him to pass it by. The vigorous growth of Stillwater, the bustling stir up the St. Croix, the 'noise and confusion' at the falls of St. Anthony, the fresh opening farms in every direction around us, the hundreds of tenements at St. Paul, leaping into sudden existence, remind us that Minnesota is not forgotten; but the wonder to us is, that any could have started on a fool's errand to California, while so much, even of the rich delta between the Saint Croix and the Mississippi, is yet even unclaimed."

The allure of Minnesota as a summer-vacation land is set forth in the *Pioneer* of July 22, 1852:

"Who that is idle would be caged up between walls of burning brick and mortar, in dog-days, down the river, if at less daily expense, he could be hurried along through the valley of the Mississippi, its shores studded with towns, and farms, flying by islands, prairies, woodlands, bluffs — an ever varied scene of beauty, away up into the land of the wild Dakota, and of cascades and pine forests, and cooling breezes?

— Why it is an exhilarating luxury, compared with which, all the fashion and tinsel and parade of your Newports and Saratogas, are utterly insipid.

"Reflect a moment. The planter in his cotton fields that bloom along the shores of the lower Mississippi, a vast plantation on which the girdled trees yet stand, beholds his luxuriant crops; he looks in through the latticed windows of his house, shaded with vines, not a leaf lifted by the breeze, his debilitated wife and pale children, almost gasping for breath, brazen summer burning like an oven, no sound of life but the shrill scream of the summer locust upon the trees. What is such a life to him and those he loves, but death prolonged? Afar down the sluggish river, he sees approaching a steamboat, the mighty engine that heat cannot enervate. Boldly it dashes its arms into the sparkling water. 'Wife and children; be ready in fifteen minutes. Pack your trunks, your band-boxes. We will fly northward.'

"Amid changing scenes, surrounded with luxuries, and delighted with new acquaintance, hour after hour flies away. Cities and villages fly along apparently past them, a grand moving panorama. In little more than a week, during which they have experienced more of life, more events, more to mark the progress of time, than in a year of plantation life, they are lionizing in St. Paul, St. Anthony or Sauk Rapids, romping over the lands of the wild Sioux, riding, fishing, hunting, filled with new life and energy, by breathing the fresh, exhilarating breezes of the North.

"A month in Minnesota, in dog-days, is worth a whole year anywhere else; and we confidently look to see the time, when all families of leisure down South, from the Gulf of Mexico along up, will make their regular summer hegira to our Territory; and when hundreds of the opulent from those regions, will build delightful cottages on the borders of our ten thousand lakes and ornament their grounds with all that is tasteful in shrubbery and horticulture, for a summer retreat."

8. The St. Croix-Mississippi Delta

IN THE ARTICLES BELOW GOODHUE REFLECTS IN HIS "FAITHFUL mirror" the regions near St. Paul — Pig's Eye, Red Rock, Cottage Grove, Little Canada, and White Bear and Bald Eagle lakes; Stillwater and the St. Croix; and St. Anthony and the Mississippi River above the falls. To write them he traveled about the regions on horseback and by stage, carriage, and steamboat over rough trails, across virgin fields, and up and down rivers, alert always for agricultural and commercial possibilities — examining the soil, observing the contours of the land, noting the advantages of location and the physical appearance of villages, the natural resources of their environs, and their transportation facilities — in short, gathering for prospective settlers the specific facts that he knew they wanted.

Most obvious to the reader of these descriptions is the editor's determination to convince the world of Minnesota's great agricultural resources. As he traveled up the St. Croix and the Mississippi; as he rode across the delta between the two rivers and over unclaimed and untouched fields to St. Anthony and White Bear Lake; and as he stood on the bluff above Pig's Eye, looking over the "magnificent scene" to the south, he saw first of all the "rich meadows," the "fertile table lands," a "country designed by nature for the most profitable employment of Agriculture."

Stillwater, at the time of Goodhue's visit in the spring of 1849, was a village of six hundred inhabitants, only some two hundred less than the population of St. Paul. It had been the seat of St. Croix County, Wisconsin Territory, and, under the provisions of the Minnesota organic act, it continued as the seat of that county until Washington County was established by the legislature in October, 1849, with Stillwater as the county seat.[1] The village, well located on the St. Croix River, with the great northern pineries back of it, owed its existence to the lumber industry. Goodhue visited Minnesota soon after his arrival in Minnesota, and in the *Pioneer* of May 5, 1849, he described that "delightful village":

"This charming village nestles in the lap of an amphitheatre of hills, on the western shore of St. Croix lake — which is not exactly a lake, but rather an estuary of the river St. Croix, about one mile wide and extending upward from its confluence with the Mississippi river, about twenty-five miles. Stillwater, near the head of the lake is always accessible to steamboats from the Mississippi and is a place of much commercial importance to the extensive lumber regions up the St. Croix and its tributaries. Why the village is called *Stillwater*, we do not know; for its waters when we saw it last Sunday, were pitching and tumbling in the lake like a school of porpoises on a holiday, and quite a sea-like surf came foaming and roaring to the shore. It is perhaps called Stillwater on the principle of nomenclature mentioned by Virgil — 'lucus a non lucendo' — *Still*water because of the *roaring* of its waters.

"But whatever it may be called, there is not a more delightful village from the frozen source of the Mississippi down to the burning delta. It has a fresh, vigorous appearance — youthful and robust. The buildings are new and mostly substantial — some of them really elegant. Few better finished buildings can be found than the Minnesota House. Nothing so readily prepossesses the favorable opinion of a traveler in favor of a village, as the excellence of its hotel. Men are rare who are proof against the seductions of good fare and fine accommodations. So much for the stage house; and we have heard

---

[1] The results of the territorial census taken in June, 1849, are given in the *Council Journal*, 1849, pp. 165–184. The census credited St. Paul with 840 inhabitants. The act establishing Washington County is in Minnesota Territory, *Laws*, 1849, p. 7. The Minnesota organic act may be found in any issue of the Minnesota *Legislative Manual*.

the Stillwater House spoken of by others who have tarried there, in terms of equal commendation.[2]

"A number of cool, delightful springs burst out of the semi-circle of hills in the rear of Stillwater, sufficiently copious and elevated to furnish the very chambers of the village with streams of running water, by the aid of aqueducts. One of the most striking features of Stillwater, is the viaduct from the hill in the rear, which spans the village, and carries a copious supply of water over the town, to propel a saw mill or a grist mill built upon the shore of the lake. A road will soon be opened from Stillwater to lake Superior. This is a work of truly national importance, and demands the immediate attention of Congress. This road, when completed, will be likely to increase the business of Stillwater very sensibly, if that village should become the place [*line omitted in the* Pioneer] merchandize from below in its transit to lake Superior.[3]

"In a notice of this fine village it would be improper to omit to mention its unrivalled resources in building materials. Besides boundless supplies of pine lumber, Stillwater has ample quarries of rock, extremely convenient for use, and of the choicest quality, also lime and sand; and what is more, Stillwater can boast of as good builders as any other town, as they make abundantly evident by their works. If any one desires to know whether or not Stillwater is a place of business, let him look at the column of business cards from Stillwater in this number of the Pioneer — and that column does

---

[2] Both hotels were on Main Street. The Minnesota House was built by Elam Greeley in 1846 for a private residence, and the Stillwater House was built by Anson Northup in 1845. William H. C. Folsom, *Fifty Years in the Northwest*, 400 (St. Paul, 1888); George E. Warner and Charles M. Foote, eds., *History of Washington County and the St. Croix Valley*, 526 (Minneapolis, 1881).

[3] Congress made appropriations for the construction of this road in 1850 and in following years, but it was not until after the end of the territorial period that the road was completed. Arthur J. Larsen, "The Development of the Minnesota Road System," 55, 60, 63, 109, a manuscript doctoral dissertation, a typewritten copy of which is owned by the Minnesota Historical Society.

not, by any means contain a complete list of their business men, although we are perfectly willing it should. One of the most reliable business men of Stillwater informed us that the annual lumber transactions alone of that town, were to be computed by hundreds of thousands of dollars. Such is a slight picture of Stillwater — a town, after seeing which, no traveler would think of leaving Minnesota.

"It will be recollected that Stillwater is the county seat of St. Croix county; also that a land office has been established there by an act of Congress.[4] The soil in St. Croix county is generally good, not exactly the rich black loam found in the fertile districts of Wisconsin and Illinois, but good warm, reddish soil, mingled with sand, with a substratum of clay — a soil which very promptly responds to sunshine and manure. Stillwater, then, is not without Agricultural resources, which, when developed, will greatly benefit the town. Success to Stillwater!"

Late in the summer of the same year Goodhue was one of a party of excursionists who made a pleasure trip up the St. Croix on the steamboat "Highland Mary," when he again visited Stillwater. In the next issue of the *Pioneer*, that of August 16, he described "The River St. Croix and Its Towns." While there is ample evidence of the man's sensitivity to natural beauty elsewhere in his writings, one may wonder that he could travel up one of the most picturesque rivers in America and devote so few words to its rare loveliness:

"This stream, celebrated for the manufacture of pine lumber, forms the boundary line on the East side of the Mississippi river, between Wisconsin and Minnesota. The sources of the St. Croix and of its tributaries, penetrate the wide expanse of swamps and plains covered with pine forests, extending from

---

[4] The land office for the sale of the public lands in the Chippewa land district was removed from the Falls of St. Croix to Stillwater on March 2, 1849. *Laws of the United States . . . Exhibiting the . . . Legislation of Congress upon which the Public Land Titles Have Depended, December 1, 1880,* 266 (46 Congress, 3 session, *House Executive Documents,* no. 47 — serial 1976).

the western shore of lake Superior to the ridge of highlands dividing its waters from the tributaries of the Mississippi on the West. These vast solitudes, are yet mostly in the undisturbed possession of the savages; but have been imperfectly explored by hunters and voyageurs.

"We shall now describe more particularly than we yet have described, the lower St. Croix. On the morning of the 10th of August, the steamboat Highland Mary No. 2, John Atchison, master, entered the mouth of the St. Croix, with, probably, one hundred passengers on board, nearly all of whom were making the excursion, for the sake of seeing the wonders of the St. Croix river.[5] . . .

"Passing rapidly through the lake, thirty miles, we reached Stillwater, near the head of the lake. The country is surpassingly beautiful on both sides, being prairie along the shores, while at a greater distance, the land rises in gradual slopes and is covered with a scattering growth of oaks. Here and there a farm is seen; but the most of the lands are not yet even claimed.

"On the Wisconsin shore, a few miles below Stillwater, is Willow River, the county seat of St. Croix county, Wisconsin.[6] It is a charming spot for a town, upon a beautiful sloping bench, overlooking the lake. — The lands in the rear of the village for an extent of forty miles and for many miles up and down the St. Croix, are equal to the choicest lands in Wisconsin or Illinois, and are nearly all subject to entry. No spot offers greater inducements for the immigration of farmers. Or where can more productive lands be found than the whole of that rich peninsula between the St. Croix and the Mississippi river? Here is this very Highland Mary with 1500 bushels of Indian corn on board from below to supply lumbermen on the St. Croix at, say 50 cents per bushel, when corn can be raised at least as cheap, along the shores of this

[5] Here Goodhue gives a partial list of the passengers.
[6] Willow River was an earlier name of Hudson.

river, as any where else in the world — yes, *cheaper;* for those
who raise corn here, have no sickness to combat and no doctors' bills to pay. Here is Stillwater, as fresh as a rose in a
flower pot. Here is the salient point of lumbering operations
on the St. Croix, and the county seat of St. Croix county,
Minnesota. — Here are McCusick's mills, propelled by an overshot wheel, thirty feet in diameter, by a small stream from
the bluff.[7] From here to St. Paul on the Mississippi river, by
land, it is eighteen miles — by the rivers, sixty miles.

"Our boat is off again from Stillwater. Pass a mile and we
are at the head of the lake. — Here enters the St. Croix river,
by several mouths; through one of these, in a narrow channel
we pass up. Steamboats seldom try navigation here. The river
is every where divided by islands into a number of streams.
Now we pass a batteaux, navigated by a lumberman bound up
stream. — In the night, we pass the Arcola mills, owned by
Moore and brother.[8] Four miles higher up, we come to the
Marine mills, under the direction of Mr. Orange Walker, one
of the proprietors. These mills and the houses and property
thereunto appurtenant, were built by five enterprising men,
with no capital but their own untiring industry. The property
is considered to be worth $50,000. The mills are propelled
by a small stream falling upon a large overshot wheel. The
buildings here, include several good houses, extending up the
ravine made by the mill stream; and begins to look like quite
a smart village.[9]

[7] The sawmill was built by John McKusick and his associates in 1844. William H. C. Folsom, "History of Lumbering in the St. Croix Valley," in *Minnesota Historical Collections,* 9:301.

[8] Goodhue misunderstood the name of the mill owner at Arcola. According to Warner and Foote, eds., *St. Croix Valley,* 476, the sawmill at Arcola
was built in 1847 by Martin Mower and three associates. Mower continued
the operation of the mill for many years.

[9] The Marine Lumber Company, which constructed the mills at Marine,
consisted of thirteen partners. All the partners except Walker and George B.
Judd later sold their interests, and in 1850 the name was changed to Judd,
Walker, and Company. Folsom, *Fifty Years in the Northwest,* 375, 376, 379;
Warner and Foote, eds., *St. Croix Valley,* 470.

"Having discharged a few hundred bushels of corn, we left again, for the falls of St. Croix; but soon found the Highland Mary struggling upon a sand bar; which she crossed over after many struggles. Here the shores are abrupt and are covered with forest trees — on we go — creation here considerably tumbled up — quite a primitive looking country. Another sand bar. The Highland Mary has danced upon it now, until she is tired. Several hundred bags of corn, destined for the falls, are landed upon the shore, piled up and covered with barge blankets. On we go. Another sand bar. — Capt. Atchison used every persuasion to coax Mary to jump over it; but although Mary can do up the Highland fling in good style, it was not in her knees to leap over such bars. Night was approaching; and with much chagrin, Capt. Atchison discharged the remainder of his freight on the shore in the midst of a pouring rain storm and turned the head of the Highland Mary down stream. A boat of lighter draught can navigate the St. Croix, beyond all doubt."

St. Anthony, with its splendid water power, like Stillwater was a lumber manufacturing town, though somewhat smaller. According to a census taken in the summer of 1849, the population of St. Anthony and Little Canada together was 571. The following description of St. Anthony was written for the *Pioneer* of August 9, 1849. Considering the Falls of St. Anthony as they now exist, one may well question when Goodhue speaks of "the sublimity of the Falls . . . but little less wonderful . . . than Niagara." Even early pictures, made before the changes, both natural and artificial, that have occurred in the falls during the past century, fail to give the impression of "sublimity":

"The importance of the subject, and our want of full and definite information about it, is the only reason we have not yet attempted to describe the Falls and to set forth the unrivalled advantages of that locality for business. Here it is, that after a progress of four hundred miles from above, through a channel in which no obstruction occurs to steam-boat navigation worth mentioning, that the whole volume of the Mississippi pours down in a precipitous sheet from a bench of limestone rock, to the depth of eighteen or twenty feet. Of the sublimity of the Falls we will not now speak; although in this respect the cataract of St. Anthony is but little less wonderful than that of Niagara. The roar of this immense volume of falling water is often distinctly audible at St. Paul, a distance of eight miles.

"*The Water Power.* At a distance of more than half a mile above the Falls, the stream becomes very rapid, and is divided by an island planted upon a base of rock and crowned with trees. This island runs parallel to the east shore at a distance from that shore of about fifteen rods, and extends below the Falls. It is by extending a strong dam fastened into the ledge at the bottom with immense iron bolts, from the foot of this island to the east shore, that the hydraulic power of the river is controlled—a power which has no limit that an engineer would ever have occasion to compute, and which may still be doubled by constructing another slight dam a few rods below the upper dam, across the brow of another bench of rocks over which the water, after being once used, falls to the perpendicular depth of about twelve or fifteen feet. From the upper end of the island a boom is constructed to near the opposite shore, so as to turn the mill logs when driven, into the mill pond, on the east side of the island. Near the head of this island, will be the landing for steamboats in the trade above the Falls, and of course, the point for terminating a railroad to connect with the navigable waters of the river below.

"A very large saw mill is erected, capable of making two millions [of feet] of lumber per annum; and another mill of the most substantial and thorough description is in the process of erection.[10] It is the plan of the proprietors to erect mills

[10] The two sawmills were erected by Franklin Steele and his associates,

enough to employ eighteen or twenty saws, beside using all the water that may be wanted for other machinery. Lumber, for the present, will be the leading interest. The saws went into operation last autumn, and have had no rest since, night or day, except Sundays, and the demand for lumber at the Falls and at St. Paul, has not nearly been supplied. There will not be a supply for years, however many mills may be built, to keep pace with the growth of Minnesota, and our wants for building and fencing materials.

"*The Pinery.* Nor is there any ground to apprehend a want of mill logs; for between the Falls of St. Anthony and the Pokagomon [*Pokegama*] Falls — another St. Anthony, 400 miles north — is a vast body of pine timber, perhaps the most extensive in the world, into which the axe has yet made no inroads. This region of pines is watered by the Crow Wing river, The Rabbit, The Pine, Leech Lake, and many other streams, and enbosoms in its sombre shades of evergreen trees, Winnipic [*Winnibigoshish*] Lake, Cass Lake, Leech Lake, Pokagomon [*Pokegama*] Lake, and many other fine sheets of water; and is interspersed with many tracts of fine rich lands which are destined to be cultivated and inhabited by our countrymen.

"*Navigation above the Falls.* From the Falls of St. Anthony to Sauk Rapids, the Fur Company have already opened navigation. Boats have been constructed this season, under the direction of Mr. Rice, for towing. A tow path has been prepared, and a boat towed by two horses, has made several trips, loaded each time with 100 barrels of flour. Mr. Rice thinks that the steamboat Senator could run even as far as Pokagomon Falls. At any rate, the only obstruction is a few boulders at Sauk Rapids, which could easily be removed in low water. If the experiment which is about to be made of running boats above the St. Peters [*Minnesota River*] to the foot of the

Caleb Cushing and Robert Rantoul, in 1848 and 1849. Daniel Stanchfield, "History of Pioneer Lumbering on the Upper Mississippi and Its Tributaries, in *Minnesota Historical Collections*, 9:340.

Falls should succeed, there will be only an interruption of a mile or two then, to Pokagomon Falls.[11]

"*Scenery, &c.* The beauty of scenery at St. Anthony cannot be exaggerated. We are particularly delighted with that bench of table land back of Water street, some 30 feet high parallel to the river, which overlooks the island and the Falls. Along the bench, a row of houses has sprung into existence since our last visit. A healthier spot than St. Anthony cannot be found this side of the White hills. Most of its inhabitants are from the lumber regions of Maine — people of industry, energy and enterprize. Those who are loafers and tipplers by trade, will find no encouragement at St. Anthony. — Every person there works for a living. — There is not a grog shop in town. They go in for water, and they won't have anything else.

"*Proprietorship of the Falls.* This water power was first claimed by Mr. Franklin Steele, 12 years ago. Mr. Steele is the Sutler at Ft. Snelling, a most worthy officer, and a man who has done not a little for Minnesota. He built the first house ever built in Minnesota. He built the first mills on the St. Croix River. He is emphatically a pioneer. Laboring under disadvantages which no man can imagine, in obtaining labor and tools and materials for the work, he succeeded in time in building the dam and getting things in motion. He has expended at the Falls over fifty thousand dollars. A few months since, Cushing and Company of Massachusetts, having failed to comply with the conditions of their purchase of a part of this property from Mr. Steele, he sold one half of the water power to Mr. A. W. Taylor, of Boston, a gentleman who seems to have had a keen perception of the capabilities of the place.[12]

[11] It was the next summer before the experiment was made. See below, p. 181.

[12] Steele made a pre-emption claim on the east side of the Falls of St. Anthony in 1837, immediately after the negotiation of the treaties which opened up the lands between the St. Croix and the Mississippi rivers to settle-

"Mr. Godfrey [13] who is also one of the mill proprietors, is the operating agent of the mills, under whose thorough and efficient management the business of the concern now seems to be abundantly profitable, with high promise of still greater and better things for St. Anthony — a place of which we are constrained to say, in all sincerity, that one more inviting to the invalid, the laborer, or the capitalist, cannot be found East or West, North or South; nor can a more beautiful town site be found anywhere than Saint Anthony, commencing at Mr. Cheever's landing, [14] the head of navigation for the river below the Falls, and extending to the head of the Island, where navigation above the Falls commences. Amongst the gentlemen interested in St. Anthony, beside those who reside there, we will mention the names of Franklin Steele, Hon. Mr. Sibley, Mr. Rice, Mr. [James B.] Gilbert, Capt. Paul R. George, and several others whose names do not now occur to us — all of them amongst the last men in the world to let St. Anthony stand still for want of capital, energy and enter-

ment. His extensive improvements at the Falls were described by Goodhue in the *Lancaster Herald* of June 24, 1848. In July, 1849, Steele sold part of the water power to Robert Rantoul, Caleb Cushing, and their associates for $12,000, with the result indicated by Goodhue. He then sold half the water power to Arnold W. Taylor in 1849, but in 1852 he bought back Taylor's share. Steele made a claim at the falls of the St. Croix also in 1837. The next year he organized the St. Croix Falls Lumber Company, but the company's mill was not completed until 1840, some months after the Marine mills began operation; so his mill just missed being "the first mills on the St. Croix." Steele could hardly have built "the first house ever built in Minnesota," for by the time of his arrival in Minnesota in 1837, squatters, fur traders, and missionaries were settled in the region, and living in dwellings of one kind or another. Sibley built his stone house at Mendota in 1835. Folwell, *Minnesota*, 1:227, 228; Folsom, in *Minnesota Historical Collections*, 9:293; Warner and Foote, eds., *St. Croix Valley*, 191, 192; Stevens, *Recollections*, 120, 166; Isaac Atwater and John H. Stevens, eds., *History of Minneapolis and Hennepin County*, 1:30 (New York, 1895).

[13] Ard Godfrey, a millwright from Maine, arrived in St. Anthony in 1847 and aided in the construction of Steele's sawmill there. Rodney C. Loehr, "Caleb D. Dorr and the Early Minnesota Lumber Industry," in *Minnesota History*, 24:127 (June, 1943).

[14] William A. Cheever in 1847 settled on a claim on the site of the University of Minnesota. Stevens, *Recollections*, 120.

prize, to develop those mighty resources which God has lavished there.

"*Surrounding Country.* A finer agricultural region than that which surrounds St. Anthony, cannot be found. On the east side of the river, down to the junction of the St. Croix and the Mississippi, is a wide expanse of prairie and oak openings, diversified with lakes and patches of natural mowing. On the west side, the eye extends over a vast expanse of fertile table lands of surpassing beauty, extending to the St. Peters river on the south, and as far west in the wide range of the buffalo as you may choose to go. In fact, whichever way you may travel from the Falls, you will pass over a region of country designed by nature for the most profitable employment of Agriculture. Farmers must and will turn their attention this way. There is certainly no spot in our country where farming is likely to be so well rewarded as here. To say nothing of the payment of Indian annuities and the demand for produce for the lumber trade, it is plain that extensive mills and manufactories must soon be built at St. Anthony, which will employ multitudes of hands in the manufacture of all articles of heavy transportation, and build up that most valuable of all trade, the trade of exchanges between the town and the country.

"Considering the bracing climate of this region as well as the prolific soil, it is very doubtful whether as many bushels can be produced per annum by the labor of one man in any other part of our continent. All crops do well. Corn is a sure and an abundant crop. If we were to specify the crop that is most excellent and abundant, however, it would be the potato crop. Farmers, especially of New England, if they could but once see our lands, would never think of settling on the bilious bottoms and the enervating prairies south of us. What is fertility, what is wealth, without vigorous health and activity of body and of mind? These are considerations that will weigh more in the future with the immigrants, than they hitherto have; a clear, bracing air, an invigorating winter to give elasticity to the system — and water as pure and soft as the dews of heaven, gushing from hill and valley.

"*Connection with the Atlantic.* When we consider how soon the upper Mississippi will be placed in direct communication with the Atlantic by railroad extending east from Galena and by steamboat through the Wisconsin and Fox rivers and the lakes — a work already well in progress [15] — is it too much to predict for this young Territory and for the manufacturing interest of St. Anthony, a rapidity of growth unparalleled even in the annals of western progress?"

Two years later Goodhue again described St. Anthony in the *Pioneer,* and the article, in the issue of June 12, 1851, gives some indication of the rapid growth of the village during that brief period. The editor, ever ready to prophesy, foresaw the "extensive mills and manufactories" to be built at St. Anthony, employing "multitudes of hands"; less fortunate, however, was his vision of the town as "a famous and fashionable watering-place," although for a time it attracted many summer visitors from the South. At St. Anthony Goodhue boarded the steamboat "Governor Ramsey" for a trip up the river:

"Although taking an enthusiastic interest in the growth and prosperity of Minnesota, the Editor of the Pioneer has never found time, until the past week, to visit the Mississippi river above the Falls of St. Anthony. That we have so long neglected to see and describe that region, certainly the most delightful picture — the most charming landscape we have ever beheld, in the whole extent of the Great Valley south

[15] The Galena and Chicago Union Railroad was completed to Galena in 1854. In 1864 it was merged with the Chicago and Northwestern. The canal uniting the Fox and Wisconsin rivers was completed in 1851. During the next twenty-five years millions of dollars were spent on the improvement of the two rivers, but navigation of the route proved impracticable except for light boats. Frederic L. Paxson, "The Railroads of the 'Old Northwest' before the Civil War," in Wisconsin Academy of Sciences, Arts, and Letters, *Transactions,* vol. 17, part 1 (Madison, 1912); Reuben G. Thwaites, *Wisconsin; the Americanization of a French Settlement,* 277–279 (Boston, 1908).

of it, to Louisiana, we much regret; and we now earnestly recommend to *every* person visiting Minnesota, to go *up the river;* without which, he can have but a very, very inadequate idea of the beauty, fertility and native agricultural wealth of our Territory.

"Two lines of convenient stages, make, each, two trips a day, from Saint Paul to St. Anthony and back.[16] We left on

BENSON'S STAGE OFFICE, ST. PAUL

Thursday morning; and were delighted to see farming operations progressing, plowing, fencing, planting, every where, on that charming prairie which is spread out between the two towns, a distance of 9 miles. This alone, inspired us with

[16] The two stage lines were the "Red Line," operated by Willoughby and Powers, and the "Yellow Line," run by Pattison and Benson. They took their names from the color of their coaches. The rivalry between the two lines was intense, according to Stevens in his *Recollections*, 112. Of the Yellow Line, Goodhue wrote in the *Pioneer* of March 25, 1852: "Messrs. Pattison & Benson, have ordered two new coaches, large elegant carriages, the best that can be manufactured in Concord, N. H., to run as stages between St. Paul and St. Anthony. Travellers will find Benson a right clever, obliging man, who performs all that he promises. There is no quibbling, cheating, lying and gouging, about Benson. His livery horses, are none of your lank, spavined, ring-boned, foundered, half-hipped, wheezing, hoof-bound, knock-kneed, gambrel-legged, sore-headed, shadowy animals, that look as if they had just come limping out of the Apocalypse — the progeny of the Pale horse described in Revelations, which "Death and Hell followed after'."

fresh hope, to see so great a change wrought in so short a
time — so many hundreds of acres under tillage, which were
covered, last year, only with the wild grass and flowers of
the prairie.

"A mile before we reached Saint Anthony, we saw its
bright, fresh-painted houses, shining amongst the distant trees,
and saw the water-fall glistening in the sunshine, and seeming
more like a picture than the original of a picture; but as we
approach nearer, and listen to its sullen roar, and see the spray
and examine more closely the material of the exhibition, the
cataract becomes a grand reality, filling the beholder with
mingled emotions of beauty and of sublimity, the proportions
of which, depend upon the constitution or present disposition
of his own mind. Far away, down the steep rocky channel,
below the falls, sweeps the angry current; but now, we begin
to see the pleasant, fresh-painted houses of the village, on our
right hand, here a cottage, and there a substantial two-story
house and there again a cheap building, without cornice or
ornament, peculiar to the West, a building which is neither a
one-story house nor two-story — (a detestable style of architecture) and away upon the sloping hillside, various houses in
the process of erection, and piles of fresh-sawed lumber away
off amongst the tall prairie grass of last year's growth, be-
tokening that buildings will soon be there and streets of Saint
Anthony, now known only by reference to the town plat.

"Here are stores — new law-office — more new houses —
more piles of fresh-sawed lumber — new cellars commenced
— and now we come to the saw-mills, active as ever, shingle
machines, lath factory, lathes, and the bustling industry of
men and teams in and around the mills — like a big heart, sending active pulsations of business all over the town, and into
the neighboring country and far off, into the pineries. Here
is a company of gentlemen, officers, from Fort Snelling, taking a survey of the village and the water-fall, from the terrace
back of Main street. They think, and truly think, that Saint

Anthony is destined to be a famous and fashionable watering-place — that neither Saratoga, nor Newport, nor Niagara, can offer equal inducements for a summer residence, to invalids and people of leisure. Now we pass along Main street, and here seems to be an unimproved space intervening between the upper and lower part of the town — to the upper town — which certainly shines with prosperity — everything looking new and clean. Here we come to the Saint Charles Hotel — a fine, spacious building, full of strangers.[17] What a contrast within a few months! What a change since a year ago, when the stranger who visited Saint Anthony could not obtain a dinner, unless through the compassion of some citizen, here were invited to dine at some private house. After dinner at the Saint Charles, the whistle of the steamboat is heard, and we hurry down to

"*The Governor Ramsey.* This boat, the first that ever rode in the waters of the Mississippi above the falls, was built by Capt. John Rollins and others; who for this enterprise deserve the lasting gratitude of Minnesota. In the hands of such men, a comparatively small sum of money, would be so expended, as to open the navigation of the river, many hundreds of miles further. This boat, differs from all other boats, in having locomotive boilers, the boilers consisting of a great number of small cylinders, all of which, coming in contact with the fire, present a large extent of boiler surface within a small compass, for the generation of steam. Contrary to the predictions of many, the boilers do not become crusted with lime, but are kept, with proper care, entirely clean. The engines are also different from any that we see elsewhere in the West; and are very perfect in their way; so is their management by the engineers; for the stern paddle wheel responds to their touch, quick as thought.[18]

[17] The St. Charles Hotel was built by Anson Northup in 1849–50 to accommodate seventy-five guests. Stevens, *Recollections,* 119.

[18] Rollins, convinced that the Mississippi above the Falls of St. Anthony could be navigated by boats similar to those which accomplished the difficult

"The boat being small, of course does not afford very complete arrangements for passengers. There is a small cabin, which sleeps perhaps a dozen, and a still smaller cabin for ladies. Freight, of course, is a very important part of the business of this boat; and especially the transportation of Indian and garrison supplies. Whatever was wanting in extent of accommodations, was compensated by the polite and obliging attentions of Capt. Rollins. Amongst the passengers, were the Rev. Mr. Chase, of Natchez, Miss., and several gentlemen and ladies from the State of New York — three ladies, all in the bloom of health, and particularly fine looking women, who stood in the relation to each other, of grandmother, daughter, and grand-daughter. Now the boat, with some difficulty, passes out between two islands, into the main channel and heads up stream, the water swift, oh, how swift! being just at the head of the falls. A feeble boat could not stem the current. Fire up, boys! Dry wood this season; last season they had to burn green wood. It takes half a cord an hour, to run the boat.

"For a long distance on our right, extends a boom, parallel to the shore, by which mill logs from above are turned down between the island and the east shore, into the mill-pond.[19] The river looks much smaller than at Saint Paul, and seems to be lifted up, out of the chasm through which it runs below the falls, to a level with the shores; — or rather, which is the fact, there is no chasm until the river finds one, after breaking over the apron of rock at Saint Anthony.

"*Shores of the Upper Mississippi.* There are none of the

navigation of the Penobscot in his native Maine, had the boiler, engine, and iron work for the "Governor Ramsey" made in Bangor and shipped by sea to New Orleans and thence up the Mississippi to St. Paul. There the hull and wood work were made, under the supervision of experienced ship carpenters from Maine. The dimensions of the boat were 120 feet keel, 26 feet beam, and 19 feet deep. Stevens, *Recollections*, 113; Le Duc, *Minnesota Year Book for 1851*, 48.

[19] On the building of the boom, see Loehr, in *Minnesota History*, 24:128–131 (June, 1943).

abrupt bluffs, such as are seen down the river; but the land comes down, by an easy, gradual slope, to the very edge of the water, and as you look away far back, and see the smooth land, now covered with green, gradually rising as the view recedes from the river — far — far away — the remotest object is a swelling ridge of prairie land, or of oak openings, on the right hand; & on the left, a forest — nothing short of a dense forest of vigorous young trees, as far as can be seen — and in the channel, islands, some of them large, covered invariably with a heavy growth of elm, hackberry, maple and cotton-wood; and whenever, as an exception to the general appear-ance of the shores, there is anything assuming the form of an abrupt bluff, it is crowned with pine trees. Occasionally a spot of unusual beauty, bursts upon the view; such as the landscape at the mouth of Rice Creek — or Itasca prairie, or the eastern shore near Swan river.[20]

"The land is evidently very rich — at Itasca,[21] we noticed the formation to be, a bed of gravel, upon which rested a body of marl, supporting a rich sandy loam, not less than 18

[20] Swan River is considerably north of the most northern point reached by the "Governor Ramsey" on this trip. Early Minnesota maps show no other Swan River. Goodhue may refer to the Crow River, which enters the Mis-sissippi near the former village of Itasca. Le Duc, in the *Minnesota Year Book for 1851*, 28, gives the following information about the settlement at the mouth of Swan River: "Swan River, or Aitkin's Ferry, 25 miles above Watab, is a well-known trading post and ferry, held by one of the oldest traders and pioneers of Minnesota, Mr. Aitkins [*William A. Aitkin*]. There are 70 white inhabitants at this point." The settlement was also known as Aitkinsville. William W. Warren, "History of the Ojibways," in *Minnesota Historical Collections*, 5:384.

[21] Le Duc, in the *Minnesota Year Book for 1851*, 28, writes: "Seven miles above the mouth of the St. Francis, or Rum River, [we] find Itasca, a town laid out by Messrs. Beattie and Holmes, which as yet contains but two houses." In 1852 a postoffice was established there, and later a station on the Northern Pacific Railroad near the village site was known as Itasca. That station, as well as the village, was abandoned, giving way to the village and station of Dayton on the opposite, or western, side of the Mississippi. James Beatty and Thomas A. Holmes were engaged in the Indian trade. Both were members of the territorial legislature, Holmes in 1849 and Beatty in 1852 and 1855. Holmes founded the town of Shakopee in 1851 as a trading post. Upham, *Minnesota Geographic Names*, 24; Upham and Dunlap, *Minnesota Biogra-phies*.

inches or two feet deep. At various points, we saw extensive fields under cultivation, crops of oats, potatoes, every thing that had been sowed or planted, giving rich promise and all with whom we conversed bearing full testimony to the excellence of every kind of crop that has been tried there. The land — the fields, the crops, speak for themselves, and there is no room for argument about it. *There is no better land in the whole valley of the Mississippi*, than the whole region extending from the falls of St. Anthony to Sauk Rapids; above which, we have not been. We are informed, that the land is much the same, above Sauk Rapids; which place is northwest of St. Paul, nearly one hundred miles, and north, less than forty miles. At a distance of from three miles to fifteen miles, from the east shore of the river, extends a tamarac swamp, for an immense distance, between St. Anthony and Sauk Rapids, designed by nature, it would seem, expressly to furnish farmers with rails without splitting them; a hint from Providence, which the settlers up there, are not slow to comprehend.

"At various intervals along the river, the trees, &c., in this tamarac swamp, are visible, far in the back-ground, picturesque as a distant forest of tapering masts. What lies east beyond that swamp, we do [not] know; but Benton county[22] may well be content with the vast extent of fine arable lands, that are in sight of the river — sufficient for 10,000 farmers, and as yet unclaimed. The soil is *exactly* like that of Rock River — quite as little waste land, much more timber, & with a landscape which we can recollect nothing down the river, to compare with, unless it be the shores of the Mississippi at the Lower Rapids, including the back ground of Nauvoo and Montrose.

"The first night, we passed on board the boat, at the mouth of Swan river. (The Ramsey does not run nights.) The next

[22] Benton County, as established in 1849, included the present Benton and Sherburne counties, and parts of Morrison, Mille Lacs, Crow Wing, and Aitkin. Folwell, *Minnesota*, 1:247, map.

morning we moved onward, every mile attracting our attention to new beauties of scenery. All seemed surprised, we certainly were, at the vast extent of forests on the west bank of the river. Every few rods, we met a canoe full of Winnebagoes, returning with their goods from the payment. There, in a huge bark canoe filled with squaws and papooses and bales of goods, comes their head chief, Winnishik, himself sitting in the stern and steering.

"Most of the canoes, on the approach of the steamboat, slide out into some little nook or eddy near the shore, until our boat has passed. At short intervals we find farms, some of them large, and all giving good promise.

"*The Thousand Islands.* This is an exaggeration; but then the islands are so many and so large, that they seem to have taken resolute possession of the channel, as if to drive the stream back, which however, swiftly glides between them, giving the boat good warm exercise to brave the current. We come to the granite formation, at the foot of the rapids, striking out boldly across the river, to bar the channel. Useless. What obstacle will not the power of steam overcome? The boat dashes across, through ripple and eddy, then tacking suddenly takes another course, buffeting the stream, escaping the rocks, and riding in triumph, above and beyond the chain of rock. Good, old, primitive granite, how familiar you look! The very material of those cragged mountains amongst which we were born; how like the familiar faces of the old men, does it seem, who tottered to the church where we worshipped in infancy!

"*Sauk Rapids.* And here the boat lies panting and cooling herself in the swift water, like a weary beast. Let her rest; while we walk along the shore of the rapids, about three miles, to the head thereof. We leave the boat and the warehouse and the few teams that are busy there, with freight and passengers. — How wide the river is! Spreading out, over a vast expanse of granite fragments — swift but no where precipitous, and evidently impassable for steamboats. But what excellent water-power, all along the rapids, without need of so much as a dam, unless perhaps a short wing dam? Here we come to a row of deserted trading houses, formerly occupied by Merrick [*Nathan Myrick*], [Thomas A.] Holmes, [Henry] Jackson & [Curtis] Bellows. — Well; the traders *ought* to make money. Next beyond is Roberts [*Louis Robert's*] trading house, which seems to be at present a tavern.²³ — The Indian trade is now mostly concentrated at Watab, which is on a delightful prairie, three or four miles further up the river.²⁴

"But here is Russell's — at the 'head of the rapids.' Here is a good comfortable house, stables, oxen, fat swine, large enclosures, fields of oats, and every thing to indicate thrift and good living. Here resides the Judge and Clerk of the Court; and Courts *must* and *will* have things comfortable. Here is Counsellor Phillips of Saint Paul, District Attorney of Benton County, preparing his prosecutions. The Sioux who killed poor Swartz, are to be prosecuted.²⁵ The people of Benton

²³ Jackson and Robert were among the more prominent of the early traders. Their names will be met again in the following pages. Jackson settled in St. Paul in 1842. He erected a log cabin on what was then a high bluff overlooking the Mississippi River at the foot of Jackson Street, where he sold goods to the Indians. He was a member of the Wisconsin territorial legislature for two years, the first justice of the peace and the first postmaster of St. Paul, and a member of the first legislature of Minnesota Territory. He was one of the founders of Mankato, where he settled in 1853. Louis Robert (pronounced Robaí) was of French-American ancestry. He settled in St. Paul in 1844 and engaged in the Indian trade. His store was east of Jackson's, on the river bank at the Lower Landing. Robert was one of the original proprietors of the town, and he took a prominent part in the Stillwater convention of 1848 which memorialized Congress for the organization of Minnesota Territory. He later engaged in steamboating on the Mississippi, being owner and captain of several steamboats at various times. Robert Street in St. Paul was named for him. *Pioneer*, April 15, 1852; Williams, *Saint Paul*, 118, 140–143; Christopher C. Andrews, *History of St. Paul*, part 2, pp. 133–135 (Syracuse, 1890).

²⁴ According to Le Duc, in the *Minnesota Year Book for 1851*, 28, Watab was laid out as a town in 1850, and in 1851 there were "four trading establishments, with the necessary out buildings."

²⁵ Jeremiah Russell was in the Minnesota country as early as 1837. In 1849 he opened a farm two miles above Sauk Rapids. The judge mentioned was Bradley B. Meeker. William D. Phillips settled in St. Paul in 1848. The murder

talk like rational, law-abiding men, who desire to see law and justice take effect and nothing more. The next morning, Saturday, we returned to the boat, which cast off her ropes at 8 o'clock, and we swept swiftly back, through the enchanting scene which we have above hastily sketched, reached St. Anthony at 4 P. M., took stage back to our own delightful Saint Paul, and the labors of the press, highly delighted, and more confident than ever, of the glorious destiny of Minnesota."

In "A Ride to Red Rock and Cottage Grove" in the *Pioneer* of August 30, 1849, Goodhue describes the oldest settled farming region in Minnesota, which he pronounced "emphatically the best section of country in all the West":

"The best portion of the delta lying between the Mississippi and St. Croix rivers, is known under the name of Red Rock and Cottage Grove. In company with a resident of the latter locality, who was well qualified to point out the many features of those sections which are most interesting to the stranger, we last week took a hasty tour around that way. From the limited time we had to spend abroad, we were unable to take more than cursory glances at the numerous objects worthy of observation, nor had we time to note the improvements only of a part of the settlers. We came home again reluctantly, but promising ourself the pleasure of revisiting that region on an early occasion.

"On horseback, we descended the steep bluff in the rear of Pig's Eye, and came nearly upon a level with the Mississippi bottoms, probably in an air line, some two or three miles from St. Paul. Here, on the first ascent from the bottoms, are wide fields of heavy and excellent grasses, which we presume to be free to such as may desire to lay in their winter's stock of hay. It would be an easy matter to draw the hay in the winter season, by way of the river to St. Paul. We continued along the grade for some five miles, passing by good mowing

of Aaron Schwartz is reported in the *Pioneer* of May 22, 1851. Folsom, *Fifty Years in the Northwest,* 466; Upham and Dunlap, *Minnesota Biographies.*

grounds, of which the people in the neighborhood have availed themselves considerably by already having put up many stacks of hay.

"At a distance of some ten miles, in an air line from St. Paul, we emerge from the oak openings which are principally on our left and the meadows upon our right, into a clear, dry prairie called Red Rock. In a pleasant little thicket of various kinds of trees, we arrive at the house of Mr. John Holton, who, after a residence of some five or ten years, has made himself and family almost as comfortable as they could be in an older country. His lands extend back from his house among the oak openings, and in front reach the river.[26]

"Almost a mile beyond, upon the river's bank, is the residence, store, and wood-yard of Mr. J. A. Ford. He is an old settler. Within ten rods of his house and close by the river, is the rock from which the place derives its name. This rock is nearly round in shape, of about the size of a hogshead, and lying upon the surface of the ground. It is red — having been painted by the Indians, and made an object of worship.[27] Within a quarter of a mile of Mr. Ford's are two blockhouses, which were formerly occupied as a Mission school for the Indians. The Rev. gentleman who had charge of the school resides there still in the quiet pursuit of agriculture.[28]

[26] John Holton arrived in Minnesota in 1837 with a missionary party led by Alfred Brunson, who established a Methodist mission at the Sioux village of Kaposia on the site of South St. Paul in that year. Holton later settled on a claim across the river at Red Rock. See Folsom, *Fifty Years in the Northwest*, 384, 385. On the mission, see Folwell, *Minnesota*, 1:204–207.

[27] John A. Ford, who had been the blacksmith for the Indians at Kaposia, kept a store at Red Rock and continued to do blacksmith work for the settlers in the neighborhood. Later he engaged in farming. The rock, an oval granite boulder about five feet long, was later removed from its original site on the bank of the Mississippi to the west side of the railroad at Red Rock station. The Indians frequently repainted the rock with vermillion paint. Folsom, *Fifty Years in the Northwest*, 384, 385, 386; Upham, *Minnesota Geographic Names*, 570.

[28] In 1841 the reduced Methodist mission was removed from Kaposia to Red Rock, across the Mississippi on the east side, and placed under the superintendency of Benjamin T. Kavanaugh. A school was opened for the children of whites and mixed-bloods. Folwell, *Minnesota*, 1:20.

"Farther along, the prairie becomes wider between the timber upon the river and the bluffs which majestically sweep up on the left to a height of at least 100 feet. The prairie is here from one to two miles in width. Here is the improvement of Mr. Charles Cavileer, of St. Paul. The location well commends his taste and judgment. Farther along is the field of Mr. W. R. Brown, comprising some fifty acres, in an excellent state of cultivation. Upon the left, high up the ascent, amid a colonnade of large oaks, is his home; a cheerful scene.[29] We pass on some two miles over a wide expanse of gently undulating prairie to the farm of Mr. [John] Atkinson, who is said to have been very successful during the few years he has lived here.

"Now bearing away to the left, over a prairie as wide, apparently, and as beautiful as we ever saw, we arrive in the course of some three miles at Mr. [Lewis] Hill's, whose house shelters itself from the winds of the west and north, under the point of a tall oak forest. His fields lie in front. Looking east, across a clear and swaying prairie, we see 'Cottage Grove.' Entering the west side of this grove, we pass down a gradual descent, in a southeasterly direction by a small pond, and through diversified scenes of knolls and dells, over an extent of some three miles, when we emerge upon another wide, and to our eye limitless, prairie, until we arrive at the house of Mr. R. Kennedy.[30]

"Our course has now bent around to this point, until we are brought within a mile and a half of the Mississippi. This is another of these beautiful spots which are invested with the

[29] Charles T. Cavileer and William R. Brown came to Minnesota in 1841 with the missionary, Kavanaugh. Brown, a carpenter, erected the mission buildings at Red Rock. About 1846 Cavileer made St. Paul his headquarters. Brown's diary, covering the period from October 25, 1845, through June 14, 1846, is published in Rodney C. Loehr, ed., *Minnesota Farmers' Diaries*, 37–82 (St. Paul, 1939). The diary mentions many of the persons in the vicinity of Red Rock and Cottage Grove referred to by Goodhue. Facing page 62 in the *Farmers' Diaries* is a map showing the locations of the various settlers.

[30] Robert Kennedy at that time was the proprietor of the Central House in St. Paul.

charms of home. The house stands back in the edge of the timber, securely entrenched from the storm in every direction but the one which opens upon the fields. At noon in the interim of the hospitalities which we here received, and which to our taste were an earnest of there 'being a few more left' for their guests, when Mr. and Mrs. K. take the direction of the Central House of St. Paul, we walked easterly through a spur of the grove to the estate of Messrs. [William] Ferguson

THE CENTRAL HOUSE

& [Jacob] Mosher. It is 'carried on' by Mr. J. Bassett, with marked evidences of economy and thrift. We entered the field through a high slide-gate, of a commendable pattern, which, with several other objects about the premises, evince the mechanical ingenuity of Mr. Mosher.[31]

"In their field of corn and oats, were left, upon the leafless stocks, the marks of the devastating progress of the worm, which has made such havoc this season. Probably this is not

[31] Mosher was a carpenter as well as a farmer. A John and a Joseph Bassett are both listed in the 1849 census under the Lake St. Croix precinct, which covered this area. *Council Journal*, 1849, pp. 167, 168.

the army-worm, but the name has been applied for want of the true name. Not being able to extend our tour any farther in this direction, which would conduct us to Point Douglass, at the confluence of the Mississippi and the St. Croix, four miles below, we return on the back track a mile or so, passing the field of Mr. J[ames] S. Davis, which is laden with abundant crops. When Mr. D. takes home his better half we shall probably be disposed to dwell longer upon his premises. We leave his place, and bearing to the right of the grove, we take the direction towards Stillwater for about a mile and arrive at the hospitable residence of Mr. J. W. Furbur. Finding ourself in the midst of scenes that would make us content for a sojourn of months, instead of one night, we remained until the next morning. Nor was our pleasure limited to the material comforts which we are so well qualified to enjoy, but it was greatly enlivened by the social and intellectual embellishments, which enliven many a bye-place in the West. Mr. F.'s fields are extensive, and abounding in crops.[32]

"A mile farther up, on the road to St. Paul, we found Mr. J. S. Norris. He was employed in getting in his grains. His location is admirable. It commands a far extended view towards the St. Croix, and a distinct view of every part of his cultivated fields, which lie in a slope considerably below the level of his house. In Mr. Norris' movements about his work we see evidences of the pleasure and satisfaction that may be found in the pursuit of agriculture rather than in the perplexity and care devolving upon a life in town.

Our immediate return being now positively requisite, we reluctantly omitted calls upon several other gentlemen in that neighborhood, and struck over the high prairie towards St.

[32] Joseph W. Furber settled in Cottage Grove in 1844, after lumbering for four years at the falls of the St. Croix. He was a representative in the Wisconsin territorial legislature from St. Croix County in 1846, and in 1849 he was speaker of the House in the Minnesota legislature. Warner and Foote, eds., *St. Croix Valley*, 365; Henry L. Moss, "Biographic Notes of Old Settlers," in *Minnesota Historical Collections*, 9:151.

Paul, by way of the Middletons and McHatties, all thrifty farmers.[33]

"The settlers of Red Rock, and Cottage Grove, are as intelligent, courteous, enterprising and industrious a people as can be found anywhere. Most of them came from the State of Maine. They combine the peculiar qualities of the New England yankee, with that travelled acquaintance with men and things, that prepares them for almost any society where their lines may be cast.

"We have viewed this section of Minnesota with surprise and delight. In respect to its beauty and fertility, it will vie with the best sections of upper Illinois. And taking into account its unqualified healthfulness, we pronounce it emphatically the best section of country in all the West. — Where else can the immigrant find the three essential qualities, fertility, health and beauty combined?

"The area of clear prairies, fringed with timber, must comprise, we think, an extent of some thirty or forty miles by a breadth of from two to ten miles."

On a day in September, 1849, Goodhue explored on horseback the area below the village limits, then known as "Pig's Eye" — the name by which St. Paul was first known, and the present name of an island in the Mississippi and a near-by marshy lake. Included in this exploratory jaunt was what is now Indian Mound Park. His discoveries are recorded in the *Pioneer* of September 19, 1849:

"The connecting link between St. Paul and Red Rock, which we described, in our last, is Pig's Eye. This locality,

[33] James S. Norris was one of the earliest farmers in Minnesota. With Joseph Haskell as a partner, he began farming near Afton in 1840, and the next year he settled on a claim in Cottage Grove. He was a member of the territorial Council in 1849, speaker of the House in 1855, and a member of the constitutional convention in 1857. James Middleton, with his large family of sons and daughters, and John and Alexander McHattie settled on claims in what is now Woodbury Township in 1845. Moss, in *Minnesota Historical Collections*, 9:152; Loehr, ed., *Minnesota Farmers' Diaries*, 11; Warner and Foote, eds., *St. Croix Valley*, 386, 396.

of which much has been said, but which few of our denizens have seen, is bounded on the north, by Weld's Bluff, which is seen from St. Paul; on the south, by Red Rock; on the West, by the timbered bottoms of the Mississippi, and on the east, by a region of uncertainty.

"Turning around Robert's corner at the lower landing, we pass down through a heavy growth of timber, cross Trout Creek, and McLeod's Creek,[34] finding the path good for a horse, most of the way. Ascending upon the first table above the river, we come suddenly, upon the grounds of the

"*Indian Encampment,* which has elicited some speculation for a few days past, it being distinctly in view of St. Paul. We found the frames of a dozen lodges which the proprietors had left the day before, and one lodge covered with skins, and occupied by a family. They were awaiting their friends from Little Crow,[35] before they take the trail of their predecessors for the cranberry meadows. A lodge is ribbed with twelve poles, fifteen feet high, straddling at the base, and tied in a bunch at the top. These poles, when covered with skins, leaving a low aperture in one side, make a lodge. A lodge, is, perhaps, to be regarded as the Indian's home, rather than the wigwam, which is built more like a house. To the stranger, the home of the Indian is a curious scene. As you stop before the entrance of a lodge, you will probably receive a greeting salutation from the inmates, many of whom return your 'good morning,' in plain English. While returning your compliments, they usually retain their squatting or side lounging posture, and if their feet are towards you, they change their position no farther than to look at you over their shoulder. The females usually reciprocate a respectful salutation with a pleasant smile. In this expression they are rather fascinating; they show, generally, a set of ivory which

[34] McLeod's Creek is now Phalen Creek.
[35] This was the Indian village of Kaposia, where the Sioux chief, Little Crow, lived.

a queen might envy. Some saddle-trees lying at the door, some tethered ponies in the nearest grass, and a little howling cur all over the lot, complete the picture. The Sioux are on their yearly migration to the cranberry meadows, lying some ten miles north of this, where it is said they will this season gather an abundant harvest.

"*The Bluff.* We scramble up the bluff, and pass the house of Mr. [William] Evans, one of the most desirable sites for a dwelling about St. Paul. A half a mile beyond, we arrive at the house of Mr. E[ben] Weld. His lands are beautifully situated, as everybody can see, looking from St. Paul. Mr. Weld, we presume, from his elevated position, does not regard himself as coming under the supervision of the authorities of Pig's Eye; therefore, to make all demarcations distinct to our eye, he leaves Patrick, the knight of the frying pan, to get dinner, while in a most familiar sally, he goes out bareheaded to show us Pig's Eye, which at a point a few rods back of the house lies stretched in one street below. But hold! Here are some artificial

"*Mounds,* upon which we must stay and speculate. Some twenty mounds, extending a mile from Mr. Evans' along past Mr. Weld's, are a subject of wonder and admiration. They are about fifteen feet high, and rounded hemispherically, as with a trowel. They are to be associated, historically, with the other innumerable monuments of this class, in the great Mississippi valley, which in their ancient and inscrutable origin, baffle even conjecture. The present races of Indians know as little about them as ourselves. Mr. Weld intends to excavate one of them, and furnish us a report of his discoveries.[36]

"Passing some hundred yards from his house, by the old

---

[36] The first recorded excavation of these mounds, now within Indian Mound Park, was made by the Reverend Edward D. Neill in 1856. Later surveys and excavations were made by a committee of the Minnesota Historical Society in the 1860's and 1870's, and by T. H. Lewis a few years later. The results of these examinations may be found in Neill's *History of Minnesota,* 208, n. (Minneapolis, 1882); N. H. Winchell, *The Aborigines of Minnesota,* 261 (St. Paul, 1911); T. H. Lewis, "Mounds and Stone Cists at St. Paul,

and picketed grave of a Catholic Frenchman, who was forbidden a burial in the church-yard, for a spirit of impenitence shown his last confessor, we recline upon the brow of the bluff and behold upon the bottoms, some one hundred and fifty feet below us,

"The Kingdom of Pig's Eye. Here is a real locality, though to our own apprehension, Pig's Eye has heretofore 'nominis stat umbra,' — been of doubtful existence. We are informed for the first time of the

"Etymology of the Name, Pig's Eye. Once at a time within the memory of several of our citizens, there flourished upon the plain before us, a Frenchman, named Parrant. He was a ruling spirit, and otherwise distinguished, by all who had ever viewed him, as notable for having one eye, unequally matched with its distant yoke mate, and precisely the shape of a pig's eye. He being best known as the man of this peculiar visual organization — his identity became in the process of time, stamped with that name. He subsequently opened a grocery at the lower landing in St. Paul. On one occasion, a gentleman inditing an epistle at Mr. Parrant's desk, dated the letter, for want of a more definite designation, 'Pig's Eye, such a month, 1842.' The letter received in return was directed to Pig's Eye — in good faith. Hence the name. But after the erection of the Catholic church in this place, the name of St. Paul exorcised the name of Pig's Eye, and the latter was driven back, as under the vagrant act, to its present place.[37]

Minnesota," and "Pre-historic Remains at St. Paul, Minnesota," in the *American Antiquarian,* 18:207–210, 314–320 (January, 1896); and A. J. Hill, "Mounds in Dakota, Minnesota and Wisconsin," in *Minnesota Historical Collections,* 6:312–314.

[37] Pierre Parrant, a Canadian voyageur who was in the Minnesota region as early as 1832, made successively, between 1838 and 1843, several claims on the site of St. Paul. From the various hovels which he erected he sold whisky to Indians, voyageurs, traders, and soldiers from Fort Snelling. His last claim was below Dayton's Bluff, at the location described by Goodhue. According to Williams, Edmund Brissett was the man who dated his letter "Pig's Eye." The letter was written to Joseph R. Brown, then at Grey Cloud Island. Williams, *Saint Paul,* 64–66, 74, 84–86.

"Pig's Eye extends in one street, some two miles to Red Rock. It has some forty families, and about the same number of able-bodied men, who are usually in the employ of the Fur Company, as voyageurs. They are Canadian French. Though husbandmen, after having planted their fields, they hold themselves in readiness, as minute men, to attend the call of their employers, up the river; leaving the culture of the crops to the females. Nor is Pig's Eye devoid of

"*Romance.* We descended the bluff, passing a spring which rushes from the hill side, with a stream of the size of a hat, and made our way to a cabin. This cabin is occupied by a French family, and situated between a melon patch, and a most luxuriant corn field. Applying for the purchase of some melons, we were waited upon by a maiden some sixteen years of age, of modest address, who is said to pride herself on nothing but her dexterity in hoeing corn. She has received the attentions of several suitors, but agreeable to the connubial code of the Calmuch Tartar belles, who never yield except to the lover who can overtake them on horseback, so she demands that the winner of her hand shall out-strip her in hoeing corn. That man, after many trials of celerity, has not yet been found. No one comes up to the scratch. Thus far she remains Mademoiselle Francaise, who never acknowledges the corn.

"*The View from Mr. Weld's.* The view from Mr. Weld's extends down the glistening channel of the Mississippi, some twenty miles, where, in the vicinity of the confluence of the Mississippi and St. Croix, a high bluff, mounting to the sky, closes the scene. The intervening space takes in Pig's Eye, Red Rock, Kaposia, (Little Crow) a mission residence under the worthy superintendence of Rev. Dr. Williamson,[38] and the southern parts of Cottage Grove prairie – a magnificent

[38] Dr. Thomas S. Williamson, a physician and a Presbyterian missionary to the Sioux in Minnesota since 1835, was stationed at Kaposia from 1846 until the abandonment of that mission when the Sioux were removed to their reservation following the treaties of 1851. Folwell, *Minnesota*, 189, 210, 211.

scene. — Directly across the river, the Sioux lands lie far and wide to the view. Rich meadows connect the wooded margin of the river with the ascending lands beyond. These meadows, which extend a distance of some two miles by a mile, are mirrored in an oblong lagoon or lake, giving them a bright and charming appearance. At one point on Mr. Weld's farm, the eye compasses, from the smooth hills beyond Ft. Snelling, to the limits of view in the south, an extent of some forty miles.

"Carver's Cave, which is now choked with an avalanche of gravel, remains for notice hereafter.[39]

"Commencing with Pig's Eye, we have now come to the end of our *tale*, having determined to go the whole hog."

It is surprising that Goodhue did not discover the region northeast of St. Paul until he had been in Minnesota for more than three years. That now well-settled suburban area he saw in its primitive charm, with its virgin meadows, its black-oak thickets, its "rolling oak openings," and its many lakes, before their shores were lined, as they are now, with summer cottages and all-year homes. The French names on the mail boxes at Little Canada are all that is left to remind us of the exotic little community of voyageurs as it was when he visited it; and Manitou Island in White Bear Lake, which Goodhue describes as "a vast flower pot," where, "in solitude, the eagle builds her nest," has lost its wild loveliness to a more sophisticated beauty, for it is now covered with handsome houses and fine gardens. In the *Pioneer* of June 24, 1852, he describes this "Region of the Lakes":

"Here we have been lauding other regions of Minnesota, for more than three years, without any knowledge, or the faintest idea, of the delightful region of the lakes, northeast of St. Paul. Last Saturday, we proceeded out through Little

[39] The cave took its name from Jonathan Carver, who, while on an exploring expedition in the area of Wisconsin and Minnesota, held a council with the Sioux at the cave on May 1, 1767. Folwell, *Minnesota*, 1:53–64.

Canada, to inspect that part of our own neighborhood; but it is truth to say, that it surpasses our power of description to do justice to it. The lakes in and around Little Canada, with the small farms that surround them, the sharp-roofed, French looking houses there, built of tamarac logs, and the log barns, thatched with straw, precisely as they were by the peasantry of France in the time of Louis XIV, and as they still are in France and in Canada, (for a Canadian abhors

RED RIVER CART

innovation,) the primitive looking ox yoke, upon the steers that are about one-half head and horns, the tamarac fences, the patches of beans and onions, and the rude Red River cart [40] and pony in the door yard, where half a dozen lean dogs are bristling and twice as many lean swine, all these features are new to hundreds of people living in St. Paul; and are interesting to us; for these people are our neighbors, older residents here than we are, and very contented, worthy

[40] Red River carts were used in the trade between St. Paul and the Red River settlements. The Minnesota Historical Society has in its museum one of these two-wheeled carts, made entirely of wood and a little rawhide. The cart was drawn by an ox or pony, and carried a load of half a ton.

people, whose acquaintance none of us sufficiently cultivate, (except perhaps, a day or two before elections.) Every thing that these people of simple habits, want, they raise or procure.

"But when you hire one of Benson's fine horses and carriage, to go to Little Canada, you will so soon be there, that Benson will not expect you back, before you have time to drive half a dozen miles further on. You will never be out of sight of some beautiful, pebbly lake, large or small, on the right or the left of you— as you pass on through the rolling oak openings —; here you will see the spindling spires of a tamarac swamp — the tamarac, that most poetic of all the evergreens — and there you will see a small meadow of natural grass, smooth, level, rank, growing in what may once have been the bed of a shallow lake — here is a ridge of excellent land, a warm, sandy loam, far richer than it seems, as is proved by its cultivation, covered with a sparse growth of gnarled white oaks — next perhaps is a thicket of black oaks, small, but numerous, like the family of John Rogers —; you find the road, although new, very good, and smooth enough for sober people; although fishermen even if editors, returning with a wagon load of fish which they had bought of more skilful anglers, might easily have some of their fishing poles jolted off, without knowing it.

"Now here you come to two lakes, divided by a peninsula; and on the shore of one of these, White Bear Lake, is the house and field of Mr. Barnum.[41] It is a charming spot, with a view of the lake in the front, extending for miles, the lake surrounded with gently swelling hills, covered with trees, and the whole shore lined with pebbles, white, red, black, and of all colors, including some very beautiful cornelians. In the midst of the lake, like a vast flowerpot, is an island crowded with rock maple trees — so dark beneath the canopy of luxuriant trees, that you can scarcely see to read by daylight — a

[41] Villeroy B. Barnum's claim was between White Bear and Goose Lakes, in what is now Cottage Park.

vast temple of trees, and in the shadowy aisles of which, are
birds that sing most sweetly, of a plumage that shows them to
be strangers to sunlight. Here, in solitude, the eagle builds
her nest of sticks and breeds and educates her fierce children,
feeding them upon the bass and the pickerel, fresh snatched
from the surrounding lake, that is fairly rippling with its
millions of finny inhabitants. The island belongs to Mr. Freeborn of St. Paul, who is also opening a large farm and building
a good house, on the west side of the lake.[42]

"Pass we on, by [Isaiah] De Webber's, over a tract of as
level, rich ground as can be found in Illinois, Iowa, or Wisconsin, towards Bald Eagle Lake, a distance of about two miles. On
the left is the field of Mr. Geo. W. Moore, of the Minnesotian
office,[43] which it is a wonder that the art and mystery of type-
setting, can restrain him a single month from the occupancy of
— oats growing knee high — and west still further, through the
sparse oak openings, covered with a dense intermixture of
grass, pea vine and hazel, is Richard McLagan's new farm, and
beyond it, a dense tamarac swamp, belonging to Mr. Moore;
and still further east, the houses of Mr. [Hugh I.] Vance and
M'Lagan, on the shore of Bald Eagle Lake — another of those
charming sheets of water, 5 or 6 miles long, indented with
woody peninsulas of woodland, and fringed all the way
around, outside of its pebbly margin, with trees of oak or
tamarac, and a beautiful little bouquet of an island in the midst
of it, covered with rock maple trees, where we found in the se-
cluded home their mother gave them, two eaglets. Mr. Pierce,
is also making a farm there. It is about midway between St.
Paul, St. Anthony and Stillwater. But little is known of the
region still further northeast; but so far as we can learn, it is

[42] William Freeborn, for whom a Minnesota county is named, at one time
owned a large amount of property in St. Paul and Ramsey County. He removed to Red Wing in 1853. Williams, *Saint Paul*, 197.

[43] Moore was foreman of the *Pioneer* office in 1850 and 1851, and later
became part owner of the *Minnesotian*. Upham and Dunlap, *Minnesota
Biographies*.

just as lovely and fertile and desirable, as that we have just
described. People in Minnesota, and people out of Minnesota
visiting our Territory! Go and visit this fairy land. No love-
lier scenery ever broke upon the vision, outside of Paradise.
Look for yourselves. Go right straight off to Benson, and
hire a conveyance out through the land of White Bear and
Bald Eagle Lakes, and the unexplored regions of lakes beyond.''

GOODHUE'S FIRST HOUSE, LATER THE PIONEER OFFICE

9. Progress at the River's Bend

NOWHERE IS THE GROWTH OF ST. PAUL FROM A HANDFUL OF hovels to a thriving, bustling village so well described as in the *Pioneer*. In its columns are recorded the grading of streets, the building of houses, churches, hotels, shops, lumberyards, sawmills, the advent of the butcher, the confectioner, the ice man, the milk man, the coming of preachers, doctors, druggists, lawyers, and all the excitement and activity of a fast-growing frontier town.

In the first issue of his paper, Goodhue describes the new Minnesota capital as it was in the spring of 1849, no longer the sleepy little hamlet of preterritorial days, but "rife with the exciting spirit of advancement"; and he points out the advantages that some day will make it "the St. Louis of the North":

"This town, which was but yesterday unknown, for the reason that it had then no existence, is situated on the east bank of the Mississippi river, about five miles south of latitude forty-five degrees north — being about in the same latitude with the northern extremity of New Hampshire and Vermont, and the central portion of the State of Maine. St. Paul is at the head of navigation on the river, being only eight miles by land below the Falls of St. Anthony, of which we shall say more hereafter. In approaching St. Paul by passage up the river, after making a large bend around the Sioux reservation on the western shore — a beautiful tract of well-wooded land — at a distance of about half a mile below St. Paul, the entire village breaks suddenly upon the view, resting upon a bluff nearly one hundred feet above the level of the river, and extending up the river about half a mile. At each end of the town, the bluff is cloven down, so as to afford a moderate grade down to the river; and these two points of access to the river, make the Upper and the Lower Landing. A more beautiful site for a town cannot be imagined. It must be added that bilious fevers and the fever and ague are strangers to St. Paul.

"A description of the village *now* would not answer for a month hence — such is the rapidity of building and the miraculous resurrection of every description of domicils. Piles of lumber and building materials lie scattered everywhere in admirable confusion. The whole town is on the stir — stores, hotels, houses, are projected and built in a few days. California is forgotten, and the whole town is rife with the exciting spirit of advancement.

"Aside from every consideration of the importance attached to St. Paul as being the place designated by law for the organization of the Territorial Government of Minnesota, and independent of its advantages merely as a healthful town on the Mississippi river, (quite an anomaly, at least south of us) it is obvious to the most casual observer that St. Paul, at the head of river communication, must necessarily supply the trade of all the vast regions north of it to the rich plains of the Selkirk Settlement, and west to the Rocky Mountains, and east to the basin of the great lakes, and is destined to be the focus of an immense business, rapidly increasing with the growth and settlement of the new regions lying within the natural circumference of its trade. It will be recollected, also, that all the supplies for Ft. Snelling, Fort Marcy, and the fort to be built on our northern frontier, opposite to the Selkirk Settlement, must pass through St. Paul, as well as the supplies to the Indians of the several tribes at their payments, and the outfit and supply of the extensive fur trade in the north-west.[1] That extensive region of beautiful lands bordering on the St. Peters river, as well as all the other tributaries

[1] Fort Ripley was established as "Fort Marcy" in April, 1849, was renamed "Fort Gaines" a short time later, and in 1850 received its present name. It was not until July, 1870, that a fort opposite the Selkirk Settlement — Fort George H. Thomas — was established. Its name was changed to Fort Pembina

of the Mississippi north of us, will soon be settled, and *must* obtain their supplies through St. Paul. Is it strange, then, that St. Paul is beginning to be regarded as the St. Louis of the North?"

In spite of prodigious building activities, housing conditions in the young village were not unlike those that faced St. Paul a century later. "We advise settlers who are swarming into Saint Paul in such multitudes," wrote Goodhue in the *Pioneer* of April 28, 1849, "to bring along tents and bedding, to provide for their comfort until they can build houses; as *it is utterly impossible* to hire a building in any part of the village; although builders are at work in every direction, completing houses." A month later, in the issue of May 26, he reported "The Progress of St. Paul" in the matter of building:

" 'Scratch up, scrabble up, tumble up, any way to get up,' seems to be illustrated in the sudden growth of the buildings in St. Paul. Logs which were in the boom at the Falls last week, are now inflated into balloon frames at St. Paul, ready for a coat of fresh paint. Lots which were the other day considered quite remote, are now 'right in town.' More than seventy buildings, it is said, have been erected here during the past three weeks; and the town is so changed in its appearance and has so multiplied its inhabitants, that a person absent for three weeks, on returning, almost fancies that he has been taking a Rip Van Winkle slumber. The two landings have already locked their arms in a fraternal embrace."

One of the first public conveniences acquired by the village was a town pump, reported in the *Pioneer* of July 5, 1849:

"Within the present week the citizens of St. Paul have erected in the lower square a pump.[2] Of course nothing could be more desirable, or to the city more appropriate. For what

in September of that year. *Pioneer*, January 2, 1851; Thomas H. S. Hamersly, *Complete Army Register of the United States, 1779 to 1879*, part 2, p. 151 (Washington, 1880); *Minnesota History*, 12:438 (December, 1931).

[2] The "lower square" is now Smith Park, at Fifth, Sixth, Sibley, and Wacouta streets. It was given to the city in 1849 by the proprietors of Whitney and Smith's addition, Cornelius Whitney and Robert Smith, and

is a town without a 'town pump?' It is 'a church without a bishop'! How will a stranger know when he arrives in our steepleless city unless it has the centre marked with a pump! A town pump is useful on numerous accounts. It is the centre exchange, where merchants and financiers do the fiats of commerce. It is the place for placards of advertisement; a reference for details of information upon all doubtful questions—as when we say, 'inquire of the town pump.' It might do for the stand of a temperance lecturer. It might answer as a whipping post for rogues of low degree; and might perhaps subserve a patriotic purpose as a ducking engine with which to quench the head of over zealous office-seekers."

The improvements noted in later issues indicate that St. Paul was emerging rapidly from its primitive state, and taking on something of a metropolitan air. From the *Pioneer* of September 19, 1850, for example, we learn that the "conveniences of a city, are gradually increasing in Saint Paul. The confectioner, the ice cart, the milkman, are among the new conveniences here; and last and not least, a regular market for fresh meat. The butchering establishment of Mr. Mosher, his arrangements for buying beeves and for killing, dressing, preserving, and carrying out meat for sale, are as neat and convenient as if he had served a regular apprenticeship at the business in Brighton. It gives us pleasure to see these things done up in the right way." [3] Evidence that the "scratch up, scrabble up" dwellings of 1849 were gradually giving place to better and more permanent houses is found in the issue of December 19, 1850, which notes that "several delightful residences" have been built "upon the brow of that natural terrace of hills in the rear of St. Paul." "Nature never planned a spot," wrote the editor, "better adapted to build up a showy and delightful display of architecture and gardening."

named for the latter. Lloyd Peabody, "History of the Parks and Public Grounds of St. Paul," in *Minnesota Historical Collections*, 15:612.

  [3] The *Pioneer* of October 3, 1850, reports the failure of Joseph Mosher's business.

While Goodhue pointed out with satisfaction the improvements that were daily taking place, he was always ready to call attention to the town's bad features, which he was impatient to have remedied. The town marshal, who probably had his difficulties in applying the scant public funds to their best use, was often the butt of the editor's impatience and ridicule. "He goes sailing about town," complained Goodhue in the *Pioneer* of August 21, 1851, "like a schooner pitching about in a heavy swell; but nothing is accomplished." He invited the marshal, the next time he was "in ballast," to "sail around and take observation" of sidewalks that needed mending, a bridge that should be repaired, and other matters that called for his attention.[4]

Goodhue was firm in his belief that St. Paul one day would be a great city, and he wanted it to be a beautiful city as well. He criticized the way in which the village was laid out, in "skewdangular" town lots and ill-shaped blocks, and recommended a complete resurvey of the town. He advocated that no buildings be erected on the margin of the bluff toward the river; instead, a sidewalk should be laid and elm trees planted through the length of the town. It was to be more than three-quarters of a century before this dream was to be but partially fulfilled.[5] One subject upon which he harped continually was the importance of widening streets. Typical of his editorials on this subject is a paragraph in the *Pioneer* of November 21, 1850:

"We would earnestly invite the attention of our town authorities, to the importance of widening some of the streets of Saint Paul; especially Fourth Street, ought to be widened at least 20 feet, forthwith, before the expense accrues, as it inevitably soon will, of accomplishing the same thing by removing a whole row of buildings from each side of it. Fourth street ought also to be immediately graded through the

[4] *Pioneer*, August 21, 1851, February 26, 1852.
[5] *Pioneer*, August 15, 1850, March 27, October 2, 1851.

bluff which now separates the upper from the lower plateau; and it ought also to be graded, of a good width and at an easy grade, from where it crosses Roberts street, down through the ravine, under the bridge that Jackson street crosses over upon; so that we may be able to get to the landing without passing down a precipice. Some such matters, pertaining to the permanent, prospective interests of Saint Paul, and es-

BRIDGE AT FOURTH AND JACKSON STREETS
Lot Moffet's "Temperance House" is shown at the left.

pecially the widening of the streets, invite the earnest consideration of the President and Town Council."

Again, in the *Pioneer* of March 20, 1851, he wrote:

"Friday the 14th—Another summer day. Signs of activity and preparations for building, in every part of town. St. Paul is stretching like a young giant after a nap. The [Norman W.] Kittson and the [Stanislaus] Bilanski property, are to be laid off in lots, as additions to the town.[6] Will the proprietors have

[6] The Kittson addition was platted by Charles W. W. Borup in 1852. The Bilanski property was between Trout Brook and Phalen Creek.

the sagacity to make liberal lots and wide streets? One hundred feet is none too wide for a street. Remember, that in a short time, there will be rows of tall brick buildings on both sides of those streets. Why not make room, not only for the business that will throng these streets, but also to let the sunshine and the air down into them? The proprietors of St. Paul, hitherto, seem to have had Constantinople for their model, in laying out the town."

In the issue of August 28, 1851, Goodhue called attention to the need for a sidewalk and lights along Bench Street, which, beginning at the lower landing, climbed the bluff, long since cut back, and joined Third Street at Wabasha:

"It would be a real benefit to Saint Paul and would also be highly creditable to the town, if a good side walk were erected on the south side of Bench street, through the whole length of it. Bench street, on that side, ought, also, to be well lighted, with a row of spirit gas lamps, set upon lamp-posts; the expense will be little and the convenience great; for that street is always literally thronged with travel, and in dark nights, there is always danger of stepping over the bluff."

Evidently the townspeople paid some heed to his suggestion; but they failed to go far enough, for the following spring, in the *Pioneer* of March 25, he dealt with the subject more emphatically in an article headed "Plank Side-Walks":

"Will the people, lot holders and all, take hold and extend the side-walk that is now laid down on Bench st., through to each end of the town? If this is to be done, now is the time to do it. As you desire comfort in walking, for yourselves, your wives and your daughters — as you take pride in St. Paul, *put these side-walks through.* Next to good hotels, nothing so favorably impresses strangers, as clean side-walks. They are a town's certificate of good public character. All

Williams, *Saint Paul*, 48, 121; Henry S. Fairchild, "Sketches of the Early History of Real Estate in St. Paul," in *Minnesota Historical Collections*, 10 (part 1): 431.

HORNS OF THUNDER

those things that mark advanced civilization, all comforts
observable about our town, public or private, are so many
allurements to capital and to men and women of taste, to
settle with us. There is not a man living in St. Paul, who
owns a lot, but would make money by building a side-walk
along it, and a handsome fence around it, and by planting
at least one tree on it. Let us see now, which side of Third
and St. Anthony streets,[7] will first carry out a side-walk,
through town; and which end of town will do it. These walks
have more to do, not only with the prosperity of the whole
town, but with enhancing the value of business lots which they
pass, than many persons are aware of."

The *Pioneer* of September 4, 1851, presented a plan for
"A Public Promenade in St. Paul." The route that Goodhue
had in mind for such an avenue, from Trout Brook past the
Capitol, which was then being built on Exchange Street between Cedar and Wabasha, probably would have cut across
the original town plat from Ninth and Wabasha diagonally
to Fort Street, now Seventh:

"Now is the time — next year, it will be forever too late, to
have a large public avenue laid out, which will in time be
ornamented with shade trees and fountains and statues — the
property forever, of all, the rich as well as the poor, of the
multitude of human beings who will inhabit Saint Paul. We
have no public ground — or nothing that deserves that name
— no streets of sufficient width for pleasure promenades; and
now we propose that an avenue be opened from Trout Brook
near the mill,[8] to extend along by the Capitol, at the foot of
the second bench, 150 feet wide, in a straight line, to a point
opposite Fort Snelling — to be forever a public avenue, over
which our citizens may walk or ride — to be ornamented in
time, with whatever adornments the wealth of our town may
afford.

[7] Third Street west from Wabasha was known as St. Anthony Street.
[8] This was a grist mill. It is shown on a *Map of St. Paul* by George C.
Nichols, published in 1851.

"Proprietors of the lands through which it may pass, may rest assured, that for the erection of elegant public or private buildings, the ground upon each side of such an avenue, would in a few years become of immense value; nay, if they would meet together immediately and donate the ground, and have such an avenue laid out, their grounds would at *once* be enhanced in value, far more than the worth of all the ground required for the avenue. Will the proprietors of those grounds meet and accomplish this work, so important to the beauty, health and welfare of Saint Paul, as well as so advantageous to their own private interests? Who of them, will commence the work, by notifying a meeting of the proprietors, by a call, which we will cheerfully make in our columns? . . ."

"A Plan for Improving the Levee of St. Paul" was the subject of an editorial in the *Pioneer* of January 15, 1852:

"The steamboat business of Saint Paul, is all done at two landings, the Upper and the Lower landing, distant from each other, about half a mile, with a very high bluff, say from sixty to ninety feet high, intervening and forming a wall to the very brink of the river. This separation of the steamboat business, is rather an unfortunate feature of our town. It begets an unpleasant spirit of rivalry and prevents that centralization of business, which is to be desired; and is moreover attended with much needless expense to steamboats; which have to get up steam expressly to run from one landing to the other; and much inconvenience to consignees, who often have their freights discharged by mistake, at the wrong landing.

"To remedy this evil (for it is an evil) in the way it *ought* to be remedied, the Corporation ought now to do what should have been done in making the survey of the old town of St. Paul; that is, vacate ground enough on the east bank of the river, between the two landings, to admit of grading the bank suitably for a levee, all the way down Bench Street. All the ground south of a line drawn from the foot of Third Street intersecting with Sibley Street, and then straight to the

American House,[9] *ought* to have been laid off as public ground, to be graded down to the river. As this was not done and probably cannot now be done, the Corporation ought to vacate all the ground between Third street and the river, for the same purpose. If even this cannot be done, on account of *vested rights,* then the proprietors of lots on the south side of Bench street, ought to be permitted to cut Bench street down, raze it down nearly to a level with the river.

"Bench Street, and the ledge between it and the river, thus cut down to the water edge and widened as it easily might be,

THE AMERICAN HOUSE

by encroaching a little upon the river, would afford a space not less than 200 feet wide — ample room for warehouses along the north side of it, and not less than one hundred feet for a levee, between the ware-houses and the river. These ware-houses would occupy the place of Bench street, (after Bench street was excavated,) and the north end of them would abut against the perpendicular wall. Goods stored in them might be carried either up or down the levee, or they might be raised with windlasses, through the ware-houses, to

[9] The American House, built by Henry M. Rice and opened in June, 1849, was "a long, white wooden building with a portico running the whole length of it," at the corner of Third and Exchange Streets. It burned down in 1863. See Newson, *Pen Pictures,* 112; Williams, *Saint Paul,* 224; and the *Pioneer,* June 14, 1849. Newson wrote: "Here politicians met and discussed questions of great public moment; here balls and dinner parties were given; here strangers and citizens gathered for social intercourse; here bargains in real estate were made."

a level with Third Street; and Third Street ought to be widened so as to occupy all the space between Third and Bench, making it a grand business avenue.

"This looks like a large undertaking; but it may be done, and the future business of St. Paul, will well warrant the accomplishment of it. It looks more probable *now* that it *may* be done, than it did in the spring of 1849, that a noble stone aqueduct and a street regularly graded over it, would ever be built through the ravine, between Roberts and Sibley streets. And we consider it by no means certain that the rock that must be quarried in making the excavation of Bench street and the lots south of it, would not more than pay for the whole cost of excavation, for building purposes. It seems evident that the ledge of the upper plateau, is destined to be the principal building material in St. Paul. It is one vast quarry of rock, of the most suitable quality and thickness; and certainly it is easier to quarry it in the edge of the bluff than any where else."

The columns of the *Pioneer* were full of suggestions and plans for supplying St. Paul with every conceivable improvement, from a water system to a town clock. The editor pointed out the need for a fire company and equipment; for a jail, since "crime stalks at large and criminals go unwhipt of justice, for want of a place of confinement"; for more hotels; for a public market house; for a cemetery; for daguerreotypes "to be taken annually and preserved as historical records of the growth of the town." Time and again he urged the establishment of factories of all kinds — for paper, powder, soap, candles, furniture, leather, and countless other articles. "The only way to real independence," he wrote, "is to build up our manufactures." [10] The demands of the incoming settlers for building materials could not begin to be met in the rapidly growing village, and in the *Pioneer* of June 3, 1852, Goodhue

[10] *Pioneer*, August 15, November 28, 1850; August 7, 28, September 11, October 16, 1851; February 12, June 3, 1852.

points out the need for the manufacture of brick as well as lumber in St. Paul:

"When the Dutch began to build Gotham, they brought bricks over from Holland to make houses of. The other day, we saw a wretched lot of brick taken off a boat, shipped from Dubuque to St. Paul. Here it has been rub and go then stick again, with St. Paul, ever since it began to grow, for want of lumber and for want of brick. Pine lumber always sells

ST. PAUL'S FIRST JAIL

higher here than in St. Louis, because the demand for it is so great. Our three saw-mills,[11] and what lumber we get from St. Anthony, do not begin to supply the demand; and as for brick, there has never been half a supply. Prime logs are plenty here and cheap. We want steam saw-mills, good ones, twenty of them. St. Paul is the best point in the whole west, for every sort of lumber manufacture. We want more capital in the manufacture of lumber and brick, and in almost every

[11] The three sawmills were those of John R. Irvine and Wasson and Barnes at the Upper Landing, and of Dana, Oakes, and Company at the Lower Landing. *Pioneer*, March 6, October 3, 1850, October 9, 1851; *Democrat*, October 28, 1851.

other sort of manufacture. To go into the manufacture of brick here, on the right plan, on a large scale, with sheds, machines and everything complete, will take a capital of $3,000. With that when conducted judiciously, and the business well managed, we know of no surer way to wealth."

St. Paul citizens were soundly berated for certain evils and nuisances which they apparently tolerated. With bitter sarcasm, in the *Pioneer* of July 29, 1852, the editor called attention to a most serious evil, under the heading "A Word to Parents in St. Paul":

"Perhaps you are aware that there is a free school, at the lower landing in St. Paul, where your children can be taught all peccadilloes and vices, from lying and profane swearing, up to the higher calendar of crimes. You have only to turn your children out there, with the rest, – let them go wild along the docks in the water and out of it, a sort of amphibious condition, for a few months, snatching irregular meals or a little slumber at home by night and away to the dock again. They will soon be beautiful graduates, every one of them with a diploma from the Devil. Oh, but this is a great institution, these free American schools, along the shores of the Mississippi!"

Education, to Goodhue, influenced by his background and thoughtful for the future of his own small children, was of the utmost importance; and he frequently decried the lack of adequate schools in St. Paul. On March 27, 1851, he wrote: "Our children are coming, coming, coming, to take our places on the stage of action. Shall we do nothing, or next to nothing for the education of our children, while we squander thousands for churches, balls, and politics?" His mind must have been occupied more than usual with the youth of the village at that time, for in the same issue he printed the following:

"Truth compels us to say, that there is not a building in all St. Paul, fit to be called a District school house. The only building known as such, is hardly fit for a horse stable. – There

was another miserable substitute for a school house, on Bench
street, belonging to the upper District; but that was sold the
other day, to satisfy a mortgage of less than $200.00. All this
in an opulent town, swarming with children, little untaught
brats, swarming about the streets and along the levee in utter
idleness, like wharf rats. All this in a town too, that boasts
of half a dozen steepled churches. . . ."

Time and again Goodhue deprecated speculation in town
lots. "Time, industry, capital—these, and not a spirit of wild
speculation, will build up our town," he wrote in his paper for
May 22, 1851. In the issue of June 27, 1850, he discussed the
subject at some length:

"Owners of town lots in new places, almost always set too
high a value upon them. It is so in the town of Saint Paul.
Speculative prices have ruined many promising towns. No
village commencing its career, can start with a prospect of
distancing others, if it carry much dead weight. The cash
price of town lots in Saint Paul, is *too high*. It is industry,
it is labor, it is actual *production*, not gambling and speculation which produces wealth. We may string town lots all
the way from Point Douglass to Sauk Rapids, without adding
a dollar to the wealth of this Territory—line the river with
town sites, as the Maumee was lined with paper towns, and
who will be benefited by it? One town with the wealth and
capital concentrated in it, which can be concentrated in it,
which can be profitably invested in the commercial business
at the head of boating on the Mississippi, would be worth
more to this Territory, than five times the same amount of
capital *fizzled* away in trying to build up half a dozen rival
towns.

"For years to come, town property will be the poorest
property in Minnesota. We are speaking our sentiments now,
in plain English. We want to see more industry and production and less gambling and speculation. The bounteous treas-
ures of the virgin soil, let those be sought after with the plow

THE CHAPEL OF ST. PAUL

[From a water color by Robert O. Sweeny, in the possession of the
Minnesota Historical Society.]

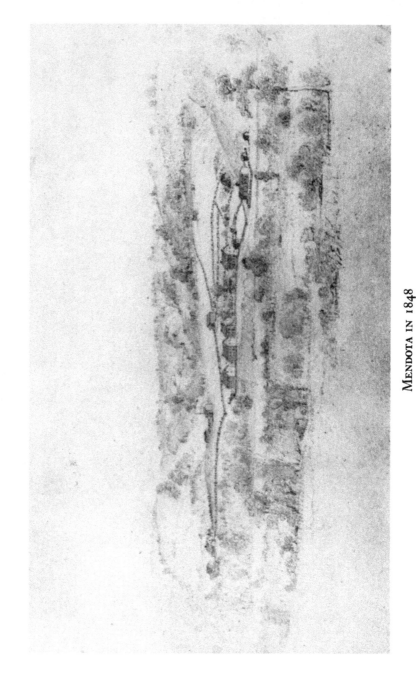

MENDOTA IN 1848

[From a photograph of a pencil sketch by Seth Eastman, in the possession of the Peabody Museum, Harvard University.]

and the hoe. Consider these facts, you shrewd men, who hold on for high prices, lest some purchaser should hereafter realize a profit upon his lot, by the growth of the town; that the island which now constitutes the city and county of New York, was purchased of the Indians in 1626 for twenty-four dollars. This seems cheap; yet if that sum had been invested at compound interest, at 7 per cent, the accumulated capital would now amount to sixty-four millions of dollars, or more than the city or county of New York is now worth, deducting what has been expended on the real estate since it was purchased from the Indians.

"St. Paul is growing rapidly, fast enough, no doubt. It is better to build too little than too much. Look at and compare Galena and Dubuque. While Galena has kept her capital employed in lucrative trade, Dubuque has put *her* capital into piles of brick and mortar. Galena is able to build steamboats and to grasp the trade of the Upper Mississippi, while Dubuque can only look at her fine buildings and say "these are mine if they were paid for and for *rent* if there were business tenants to occupy them." To individuals or to towns, *a diversion of needful capital from its regular, legitimate channel of business*, invariably brings disaster."

For all his scolding, Goodhue was quick to defend St. Paul from any criticism from the outside. Under "The Morals of Saint Paul," in the *Pioneer* of March 20, 1850, he defended his town against charges of ungodliness, which apparently had come to his ear:

"We think there is a disposition in some quarters, to underrate the morality of our town. Letters have been written abroad, representing us as a very graceless, God-forsaken people. A stranger, reading these letters, might naturally expect to find us a community of rowdies, wholly disregarding Sunday, trampling upon the Cross like so many Japanese, armed to the teeth for an affray, with pistols, dirks and bowieknives.

"Let us now look at facts. Less than one year ago, the few inhabitants here were mostly Canadian French; who were and are, as peaceable and quiet people as there are in the whole world — people who never violate the law if they know it, devoted worshippers, who are scrupulously punctual in the discharge of their religious duties. With the opening of navigation last spring, immigrants poured in from various quarters. Shelters, not houses, but even shelters had to be struggled for. We were strangers to each other — every man had to take care of himself. Except the Catholics, society existed only in its separate elements; there was neither religious, social, or political organization. It is true, as might be expected, that we had a large influx of idlers, office-seekers and black-legs; for which our townsmen generally are not responsible. Many persons came here with groceries, because this was an attractive point for capital and population. There is again, an enterprising, speculative class of persons in the world, who hover over the army of emigration, wherever it marches. Will not the eagle obey the instincts of his nature? Where money is found, there will be gambling. It always was and will be so. Were a *gulch* of gold found under the very walls of the New Jerusalem, the faro-dealer with his honest box, would be one of the earliest on the spot, dealing from the head of a whiskey barrel.

"Of all the non-producing classes, the most are transient. Such we have amongst us, drawn in during the winter, from neighboring villages, because Saint Paul is *the* place, the point of attraction, above others — the most animated place to spend the winter in. Where they may sojourn hereafter, we know not. It is but justice however to say of all such persons, that however bad their occupation in life and their example may be, they have here almost invariably conducted themselves like gentlemen in their general intercourse in life; they are many of them, very intelligent men; some of them have resorted to this idle sort of life temporarily, for want of better employment, and we hope may reform; but we have had no robberies, no stabbing nor shooting (except the melancholy shooting of Heman Snow by another boy) [12] — no ruffianism — nothing in the way of criminal prosecutions. — The truth is, *there is a moral influence in Saint Paul, as mighty as ever controlled a Puritan village* — more powerful than the law itself.

THE FIRST PRESBYTERIAN CHURCH

"Why, what do we behold? In Saint Paul, unknown on a map two years old, a mere hamlet within one year past, and now with a population of less than 1000, we have three settled Protestant preachers, beside the services of Mr. Ravoux alternate Sundays, of the Catholic church & of Mr. Gear in the Episcopal church. Of these five clergymen, all devoted laborers, some are men of fine taste and true eloquence. We are

[12] This is reported in the *Pioneer* of September 12, 1849.

decidedly a church-going and moral people. Three houses of public worship are built and two or three more in progress of erection.[18] Schools and Sunday schools are not neglected; yet we are not doing enough, we cannot do *too* much, for our moral and intellectual culture.

"To say that Saint Paul is justly characterized as a wicked place, is utterly false."

Shooting in the village streets was more than once the subject of a caustic paragraph, such as that in the *Pioneer* of June 26, 1851:

"Shooting guns in town, is a reckless, vulgar practise, unworthy of any man who does not think more of killing a pigeon, than the risk of killing a human being. It is impossible to permit random shots to be made about St. Paul, no matter in what direction the gun may be pointed, without hazarding lives. Whatever the force or direction of projectiles, the shot or bullet must land somewhere. A random shot, struck a person in the face last Sunday morning on Jackson street. There is a Town Ordinance against shooting within the Corporation; but there is a set of reckless fools, who still keep popping away with guns. We give these gentry notice, that we will complain of the first one we know of violating the Ordinance,

[18]The three Protestant preachers were Edward D. Neill, Chauncey Hobart, and J. P. Parsons, ministers in the Presbyterian, Methodist Episcopal, and Baptist churches, respectively. Neill was superintendent of public instruction in the state and chancellor of the University of Minnesota from 1858 to 1861; chaplain of the First Minnesota Regiment in the Civil War; United States consul to Dublin in 1869–70; president of Macalester College in 1873, and from 1884 until his death in 1893 its professor of history, literature, and political economy; and the author of a *History of Minnesota*, published in 1858. The Reverend Ezekiel Gear was chaplain at Fort Snelling, and Father Augustin Ravoux had under his charge the Catholics of St. Paul, Mendota, Lake Pepin, and St. Croix. See Upham, *Minnesota Biographies;* and Williams, *Saint Paul*, 113–115, 212, 245, 278, 318. On October 10, 1850, Goodhue wrote in the *Pioneer:* "The Episcopal Church was raised on Tuesday morning last. There are now in the course of construction three churches in the town of St. Paul, viz: The Presbyterian church (brick) nearly enclosed; the Baptist church (frame) also nearly enclosed, and the Episcopal — these, with the Methodist (brick) built last summer, and the Catholic, will make five churches in St. Paul.

and try to ascertain whether our town must be made a shooting gallery of, for half a dozen fools, who would confer a
particular benefit upon the town, by standing at the other
end of their guns when they shoot them, or by making targets
of each other. As for shooting guns on Sunday, it is so un-
christian, uncivilized, barbarous, *beastly*, that even the Sioux
across the river, are too respectful to do that; and any person
who will discredit and disgrace St. Paul, by firing a gun within hearing of our church-going town, is utterly reckless, and
ought to be looked upon as an abandoned ruffian."

Another nuisance that tried the editor's patience sorely was
the matter of hogs running at large in the town. In the *Pioneer*
of June 28, 1849, he expressed his annoyance with the hogs
that rooted under the loose floor of his office, jostling his
chair with their backs; and on September 26, 1850, he printed
this paragraph:

"Our town Corporation, has not succeeded in suppressing
hogs; they still run at large. They are an intolerable nuisance,
filling the town with fleas, unrooting every soap barrel, box,
or whatever else they can find — four legged thieves, which
their owners expect to have fattened by what they can steal
from their neighbors; and the proprietors of them, who salt
them down are virtually concealing stolen property. He who
steals from his neighbor's garden, is a more decent thief than
he who keeps hogs and hens to commit petty larcenies for
him."

While Goodhue was generous in his praise of other communities in the territory, he would not tolerate an insinuation
that any of them had commercial superiority over St. Paul. The
Pioneer and the *St. Anthony Express* waged continual warfare
over the advantages of their respective towns. St. Anthony,
Goodhue conceded, was beautifully situated, and the water
power at the falls would undoubtedly make it a town of importance; but steamboats, he was convinced, could not navigate to
St. Anthony, except during high water, and St. Paul had the

more advantageous location at the head of navigation on the Mississippi. The editor of the *Express* was well able to take care of St. Anthony's interests. On one occasion he thanked the *Pioneer* "for its periodical slashing against St. Anthony; creating no little sport in the 'sister city.'" "Why, neighbor," he continued, ". . . it would do your soul good to see the urchins up here, performing those mysterious gyrations of the fingers, as applied to the nasal organ, when they read of *your boulders.* By the bye, what a rumpus little Tray made as the moon rose, and yet the moon made *regular trips* – just as the boats will to St. Anthony, the coming season." [14]

In 1850 Henry W. Hamilton of Ohio published a series of letters, written during his travels in Minnesota and Wisconsin, under the title *Rural Sketches of Minnesota, the El Dorado of the Northwest,* in which he wrote: "St. Paul, being the seat of Government, and considered abroad as the head of navigation on the Mississippi, is at present the . . . town of most importance in the Territory. This will not always be the case. A glorious little town 9 miles up the river . . . is bidding for the laurel and the wreath." This brought forth from St. Paul's stanch champion the following editorial, published in the *Pioneer* of December 26, 1850, under the title "Saint Paul and Saint Anthony":

"We have seen a frivolous little pamphlet, lately published by a Mr. Hamilton of Ohio, all about Minnesota. The writer appears to have been particularly enamored of the young lady 'who taught the first school ever opened in Minnesota' [15] – also of 'a glorious little town about 9 miles above Saint Paul.' *Our* village is a place of *some* importance just now, being the capital and being considered *abroad,* the head of permanent steamboat navigation. Mr. Hamilton strongly intimates that the *real* head of steamboat navigation, is at St. Anthony. That

[14] *St. Anthony Express,* April 16, 1852.
[15] The schoolteacher referred to (page 15) was Harriet E. Bishop, who established a school in St. Paul in 1847.

boats of sufficient power, can run to the Falls in high water, is well known; that they *cannot in low water*, is equally certain. In a dry time, boats reach the *bottom*, before the *head*. There is the *rub*, Mr. Hamilton. Without 'Locke on the human understanding,' the minds of mankind can be elevated to the comprehension of a simple law of hydrostatics; but without locks on the river, boats cannot be got over the rapids and scattered boulders and fragments of rock broken off and carried by the cataract, for miles, below Saint Anthony, into the swift shallow current of the river. *That* is the way to tell the truth.

"We do not, in the slightest degree, underrate the natural advantages of Saint Anthony. We admit, to the fullest extent, all that has been said of the beauty of scenery there — and the value of the hydraulic power and of the industry and intelligence of the men, and the beauty of the women. But after all, nothing is equal to truth. The people of Saint Anthony who are candid, will not thank Mr. Hamilton or any body else, for representing abroad, that steamboats could, if they would, run above Fort Snelling, through the whole season of boating. We do not say that Saint Paul will always be the most important town in Minnesota. We do not say that Saint Anthony will *not* be. Men will honestly differ in opinion about such matters; but they need not *quarrel* about it. Capt. George says, that man made Saint Paul, but God made Saint Anthony. This is in part true. God made the thundering cataract there, and Franklin Steele put a yoke upon its neck and it is now obedient to do the work of millions of men; but the same God also made eighteen miles of very crooked river below the Falls, and very swift, and scattered flocks of boulders, and ridges of ledge in the channel. The same God also left a very pretty spot for a steamboat depot, where Saint Paul is; and made a beautiful extent of undulating plains, easy to grade for a plank road or a railroad, all the way from Saint Paul to Saint Anthony, a distance of about 9 miles. The same God designed that these towns should be mutually beneficial to each other. That each of them must inevitably add importance to the other — that they are in no sense rivals, but that they are partners, is as true as the simplest axiom of political economy.

"Really there *can* be no rivalry between them, no more than there can be between a steamboat and a cotton factory, or a coal barge and a trip hammer. A railroad is as indispensable between them to advance the interests of each town, but especially of Saint Anthony, as a cart or a wagon is, to a farmer. — What a manufacturing town wants, is easy access, cheap communication, to facilitate its business. Arrivals by locomotive trains would be as valuable to Saint Anthony, as arrivals would be by steamboat. It is wholly a question of economy. If a railroad were built from here to the Falls, nine miles, the river would still be open for boats; and if boats could run at all to Saint Anthony, and could run eighteen miles, and carry against the competition of the railroad, they would do the carrying and Saint Anthony would enjoy the benefit of reduced rates and fares. Even if there were no obstruction whatever to the navigation of the river, to the foot of the Falls, a connection of the *upper end* of Saint Anthony, by railroad, with Saint Paul, would enlist the favor, interest and patronage of the upper end, in favor of the railroad which would bring business to their very doors; and against the steamboat landing at the lower end of Saint Anthony, which should endeavor to keep at that end of the town, a monopoly of stores and ware houses, as it already has, of manufacturing and hydraulic power."

A picture of conditions in St. Paul in the summer of 1852, when Minnesotans were impatiently awaiting the ratification of the Indian treaties negotiated the year before to permit settlement west of the Mississippi, is given in the *Pioneer* of June 17, 1852, under the title "Business in Saint Paul":

"The delay in ratifying the treaties has very seriously affected the business of our town and of the Territory. Men are waiting and waiting, and doing nothing, until the treaties are ratified, who would otherwise invest and be actively engaged in their various avocations. The suspense has its effect upon the price of real estate — not that prices recede or are likely to recede; but then the demand is not active and lively,

MARSHALL'S SLIGO IRON STORE

as it otherwise would be. As for building, it progresses as rapidly as ever, and quite as fast as the supply of materials can be had.

"By the way, we see that Mr. Marshall has opened an extensive lumber yard, extending from Bench to Fourth street. So now we have a lumber-yard at each end and one in the middle of town,[16] besides orders filled at the three mills in St. Paul and at St. Anthony; and yet lumber sells much higher here than in St. Louis, and immense rafts of logs are going down by our town — a fact that demonstrates the utter inadequacy of the lumber manufacture in our town; and again we repeat, forty more saw mills are immediately wanted in St. Paul. There is one little mill now running here, which we are

[16] According to his advertisements in the same issue of the *Pioneer*, William R. Marshall's new lumber yard was in the rear of his "Sligo Iron Store," where he also sold groceries at wholesale. Marshall became very prominent in Minnesota affairs. He founded the *St. Paul Press* in 1861, and he took part in the Civil and Indian wars as a colonel and brevet brigadier general. From 1866 to 1870 he was governor of the state. The St. Anthony Mill Company had a lumber yard in St. Paul at Jackson and Seventh Streets, according to an advertisement in the issues of the *Pioneer* for 1852.

informed is clearing over thirty dollars a day. Pine logs delivered in St. Paul, cost less than *stumpage*, or the privilege
of cutting the trees alone, costs in Maine. So we are informed.
Such facts ought to command the immediate attention of adequate mill capital, from abroad. There is a very considerable
demand for lumber, in all the region of country around us,
besides quantities shipped up the Minnesota river, where we
are told there are already two young towns, larger than St.
Paul was at the date of the Organic Act in 1849.[17]

"Trade is rather dull; although it is rather more brisk
within the last week. In the aggregate, there is a very large
amount of merchandise sold every day in St. Paul. Some
branches of trade, are no doubt, overdone; but we have never
yet seen a town, where prudence, sagacity, and a proper attention to business, of any sort, was generally better rewarded
than here. The work of grading the streets down to the river,
and providing properly for our increasing steamboat commerce, has been taken hold of here, and pushed forward with
the energy that is the characteristic of our town. There is no
other town, big or little, that has more courage than this, to
put its shoulder to the wheel of a great enterprise, and *move* it.

"Farms, a great many, are being opened in all directions,
and on both sides of the river. That is right. No danger but
what the town will grow fast enough — towns often grow
too fast. Many of our people are exclaiming brick! brick! the
town is perishing for want of brick! (Like the circuit-rider
at a camp-meeting, when the pen was suddenly filled with
inquirers, who exclaimed 'straw! straw! souls are perishing for

[17] Goodhue probably refers to Le Sueur and Traverse des Sioux, which
were platted in 1852. Le Duc, in his *Minnesota Year Book for 1853*, 29, describes
Le Sueur as "regularly and handsomely laid out," with a hotel, a warehouse,
a blacksmith shop, ten two-story frame buildings, and a wagon shop and other
places of business under construction. Of Traverse des Sioux he writes:
"During the past summer [*1852*] several claimants have taken possession of
the site, and a part of it has been laid out into town lots which are rapidly
being improved. Traverse des Sioux at 6 months of age, could boast of 4 stores,
1 warehouse, and a chapel, besides dwelling houses."

want of straw!') But it is not so. Brick may do a town more hurt than good. We do not want to see our town full of three story bricks under mortgage, like towns we know of, at which, steamboats running between St. Louis and St. Paul, sometimes stop to leave a passenger or take on a hen-coop, without any adequate business to sustain it. There is no more salvation for towns, in brick, than there is for souls in straw.

"Frank Steele, Esq., is building a wharf boat, one hundred and fifty feet long, to be kept by Mr. Montfort [*A. C. Monfort*], the former popular clerk of the steamboat Dr. Franklin, No. 2, just above [William H.] Randall's levee, an excavation for a levee being now in progress, to afford convenient access to the wharf-boat.[18] [Isaac] Markley & Co., are pushing forward the grade of Third street, to intersect Sibley street, which leads to the lower landing, with the utmost vigor. Mr. [John M.] Castner is effecting a grade of Jackson street, by which the present avenue to the lower landing will be made easy. Mr. [W. C.] Morrison is reducing the grade of Third street, where it rises from the lower to the upper plateau.

"One or two things we wish to invite attention to. One is, to the importance of making but a single grade of Jackson street, from Fifth, or perhaps Sixth street, to the river. The importance of doing this, and doing it now, or at least of determining now, that such shall be the grade, is very obvious. Let this be done, and let Sibley street, which is parallel to it, be carried up at the same grade. In that way, and in no other, the old town may be easily connected with Smith & Whitney's addition, and Kittson's addition. Do the best we can, it is difficult to match together and connect in anything like a harmonious whole, the awkward fractions and additions constituting the town.

"Another thing to which we invite attention, is the narrow,

[18] William H. Randall, one of the original proprietors of St. Paul, graded the lower levee and improved some of the streets in the town at his own expense. He had a stone warehouse on the levee. See below, pp. 246, 252, and Williams, *Saint Paul*, 156.

short-sighted, little policy, of building ware-houses on the very bank of the river, instead of leaving a wide levee, at least two hundred feet wide, in front of them. Levee room is of the very utmost importance. You can enlarge ware-houses, but not so easily levees, at least without disturbing currents

THE UPPER LANDING
The bridge, a causeway of logs, is in the right background.

and creating sand-bars, by artificial obstructions thrown forward into the river. Every building at the lower landing ought to be immediately moved back to a distance of two hundred feet from the river. Neglect it now, and it will result soon, in driving the business above or below, to *where more levee room can be found*. The bridge to the upper landing, is nearly completed. What the plan of improvement there is, or how anything like an adequate provision for a levee business, is to be made, we are not sufficiently informed; but certainly, the expensive work already done there, goes to prove what we have already said, that there is no enterprise too difficult for St. Paul to undertake. For our part, we shall never be satisfied until our original plan can be consummated, of cutting down Bench street, and making one grand levee, the whole length of town."

The following doggerel, published on January 2, 1850, as a New Year's address from "The Minnesota Pioneer to Its Patrons," expresses Goodhue's faith in the future of St. Paul:[19]

When the Old Year thawed out last spring,
Quoth he "I must be travelling."
So, on the Highland Mary came,
And for "up river" booked his name.
Quoth he, this, Captain Atchison,
Is quite a stream we are upon?
As large, says Cap., familiarly,
As rivers often get to be.
Quoth the Old Year, 'ere I go down,
I mean to locate me a town —
A town that in the shade will throw
My *other* town, San Francisco.
In France, they've got things now at rest,
They're poor republicans at best;
They had a flare up, too, at Rome,
That made me wish myself at home.
Give Italy enough of rope —
She'll hang herself or hang the Pope;
And as for Hungary, 'tis quite
A useless thing for her to fight.
Where, flourishing has ever grown,
A Republic grafted on a throne?
I'm glad, from Europe to get back,
Altho' your President's Old Zach;
And now I want to get away
Up north to escape the cholera.
For vigorous health no climate dare
With Minnesota to compare.
The cities on the river must be three,
Two that *are* built and one that is to be.
One, is the mart of all the tropics yield;
The cane, the orange and the cotton field;
And sends her ships abroad and boasts,
Her trade extended to a thousand coasts;
The *other*, central for the temperate zone,
Garners the stores that on the plains are grown;

[19] This was reprinted in part in Williams, *Saint Paul*, 247.

A place where steamboats from all quarters, range,
To meet and speculate, as 'twere on 'change.
The *third will be*, where rivers confluent flow
From the wide spreading north thro' plains of snow;
The mart of all that boundless forests give
To make mankind more comfortably live,
The land of manufacturing industry,
The workshop of the nation it shall be.
Propelled by this wide stream, you'll see
A thousand factories at Saint Anthony:
And the St. Croix a hundred mills shall drive,
And all its milling villages shall thrive;
But then *my* town — remember that high bench
With cabins scattered over it, of French?
A man named Henry Jackson's living there
Also a man — why every one knows L. Robar:
Below Ft. Snelling, seven miles or so,
And three above the village of Old Crow.
Pig's Eye? Yes; Pig's Eye! That's the spot!
A very funny name; is't not?
Pig's Eye's the spot, to plant my city on,
To be remembered by, when I am gone.
Pig's Eye, converted thou shalt be, like Saul:
Thy name, henceforth shall be Saint Paul
When the Wisconsin's wedded to the Fox,
By a canal and solid steamboat locks;
When freighted steamboats leave St. Paul one day
And reach, the next but one, Green Bay,
When locomotives regularly draw
Their freighted trains from distant Pembina
And o'er the bridge, rush, thundering, at St. Paul,
And at Dubuque, to breathe, scarce make a call
But hurry onward to the hot Balize,
By flying farms, plantations, houses, trees —
A levee lined with steamboats to each end;
When one great city covers all
The ground from Pig's Eye to the Falls,
I then will claim St. Paul for mine,
The child of 1849.
Pig's Eye, converted, thou shalt be like Saul,
Arise; and be, henceforth — Saint Paul!

10. Cotillions and Culture

SOCIAL LIFE IN EARLY MINNESOTA, ALTHOUGH IT HAD ITS CRUDER aspects, was in many ways superior to that of the average western community. The settlements were small, and social gatherings were necessarily democratic; but they included a good representation of men and women of culture and education. A St. Paul woman who settled in Minnesota as a girl in 1849 wrote many years later: "I cannot imagine a finer society than existed in the villages of Mendota, St. Paul, and St. Anthony, and at Fort Snelling." Nevertheless, she was forced to admit that "those early days bore ample testimony" to the fact that "the restraints of an older and long settled community are thrown off . . . to a large extent in newly settled districts." [1]

Dancing parties, sleigh rides, and visiting helped Minnesotans through the long winters, when the freezing of the river cut them off from communication with the outside world. The holiday seasons were especially gay. There was a great deal of social intercourse between the communities of the territory, and functions held at any of them were usually well attended by people from the other places. In St. Paul, most of the balls and other large parties were held at the Central House on Bench Street, the American House on Third, or in Mazourka Hall, an upper floor in a wooden structure at Third and Exchange streets, built by the Elfelt brothers, Abram, Edwin, and Charles, to house their drygoods and grocery business, which occupied the remainder of the building. The hall, according to Goodhue, was "adorned with classic paintings, from the prolific brush of Mons. Schinotti, representing the Nine Muses, and several respectable celestial ladies of the Pantheon; especially Diana." [2] In St. An-

[1] Cathcart, in *Minnesota Historical Collections*, 15:522, 525, 545.
[2] *Pioneer*, December 25, 1851.

thony, the St. Charles Hotel was the fashionable spot; and Stillwater parties were held at the Stillwater House or the Minnesota House. In great demand at dancing parties in all the Minnesota communities was the Sixth Regiment Band from Fort Snelling, composed of some fifteen musicians led by Sergeant R. T. Jackson, and famous up and down the Mississippi. Another popular band was that of a group of colored men from St. Paul, led by William Taylor, a barber,

MAZOURKA HALL AND THE JAM SALOON

who "called figures" for the dances in a musical voice, strong and clear.[3]

Occasionally there were lectures in the larger villages. In the winter of 1849–50 the St. Anthony Library Association sponsored a series of lectures, the first of which was given by the Reverend Edward D. Neill of the Presbyterian Church in St. Paul. Neill also gave addresses before St. Paul audiences on historical subjects. Another popular speaker was Captain John A. Wakefield, who gave a number of temperance lectures. The *Pioneer* of February 13, 1850, announced that Wakefield would deliver "a philosophical and scientific temperance lecture . . . illustrating his subject with anatomical diagrams of the human stomach. It will be useful to all; but

[3] Williams, *Saint Paul*, 249; Cathcart, in *Minnesota Historical Collections*, 525.

especially interesting to the more highly cultivated class of minds." Sarah Coates, a homeopathic physician, gave a series of lectures an anatomy and physiology for St. Paul women in the summer of 1851.[4]

In the early 1850's a literary club and two lyceums held weekly meetings in St. Paul. For those of less cultivated interests there was Charles Cave's "Splendid Bowling Saloon, with appropriate accompaniments," and a "Liquorary Association," which, according to an advertisement in the *Pioneer* of January 23, 1850, held nightly meetings "for the discussion of Oysters, Sardines, Pigs feet, etc." St. Paul ladies had a sewing society, and a Masonic lodge was organized in the village in 1849. In that year also a "Mr. Gayetty" organized an intrumental band, and in 1852 a "Mr. Stone" held a writing school. "In the early part of the evening," wrote Goodhue, "Mr. Stone teaches a writing school; and in the latter part, the school is resolved into a cotillion party. . . . Thus two birds are killed with one Stone."[5]

With the opening of the river in the spring there were steamboat excursions and picnics. Now and then a group of family singers, such as the Bakers and the Raymonds, or a company of actors found their way to that northwestern outpost of civilization and gave concerts and plays. In the summer of 1850 a "Mammoth Circus," which advertised itself as an "unequalled, unique, and splendid company of equestrians, gymnasts, acrobats, pantomimists, comedians, olympiads, and Herculeans," visited St. Paul and Stillwater, where its members gave exhibitions of their "inimitable daring, hippodramic, scenic, descriptive, pantomimic, fancy and

[4] Neill, *Minnesota*, 521; *Pioneer*, August 14, 21, 28, 1851. It was on her trip to St. Paul in 1851 that Miss Coates met the well-known steamboat captain, Daniel Smith Harris, whom she married that year. Truman Coates, *A Genealogy of Moses and Susanna Coates . . . and Their Descendants*, 59 (n.p., 1906).

[5] *Pioneer*, October 4, 11, 1849, January 30, February 6, 1851, March 4, 1852; Williams, *Saint Paul*, 235; Stella Selby to Elizabeth Fuller, December 12, 1852, in the Fuller Papers.

comic Equestrianism, corpuscular devices, acrobatic poises, gymnastic acts, Herculean feats, and other novelties of a classic, dignified and interesting order." The Fourth of July was usually observed by elaborate exercises, with fireworks, parades, orations, and balls.[6]

Goodhue's accounts of social affairs in the columns of his paper reveal "society" as it existed on the outer verge of the 1850 frontier, with the mixed elements of Minnesota's communities striving to adapt the manners and customs of the East to raw frontier conditions. Seldom was a private party noted in the *Pioneer*, doubtless because pioneer houses were ill adapted to entertainment on anything but the smallest scale. The functions described were mostly democratic community gatherings, which anyone with the price of admission might attend. In the *Pioneer* of January 2, 1850, the first New Year's celebration in Minnesota is described:

"It is proverbial that Saint Petersburgh, and the capitals of the other cold countries, are the gayest places in the world, during the reign of winter. The festivities and hilarity of our town on New Year's confirm the truth, that cold weather can never freeze warm hearts. Saint Paul was, yesterday, swarming with animated fashion. The side boards of many of our citizens were provided with free entertainments, which would do credit to the wealthy burghers of Gotham. At 11 o'clock A. M. our people assembled at the Methodist church, to attend the exercises of the Minnesota Historical Society; where an introductory lecture was delivered by the Rev. Mr. Neill, which was not merely instructive, but thrillingly eloquent; his subject, the early voyageurs of the North West, being enlivened with that sort of vitality — in short — one could seem to see actually stirring before him, all the events described. Every listener was delighted, and the exercises were enlivened by the instrumental band from Fort Snelling.[7]

[6] *Pioneer*, July 11, 1850, August 14, 1851.
[7] This was the first annual meeting of the Minnesota Historical Society, which was incorporated in October, 1849. Neill's address was published in

"In the evening there was a throng—a perfect rush, of every body from every where, to the ball at the Central House. It was the largest collection of beauty and of fashion, we have ever seen in the West; there being nearly or quite one hundred gentlemen with their ladies present. The only hindrance to perfect enjoyment was the excessive numbers at the party, there being room for only five sets of cotillions...."

The holiday season of the next year was especially festive, according to the *Pioneer* of January 2, 1851. The season included Thanksgiving Day as well as Christmas and New Year's, for in early Minnesota the governor usually proclaimed a day late in December as Thanksgiving:

"As we anticipated, this winter is a season of much gaiety in Minnesota. The holidays have been particularly rich in social entertainments and interesting religious exercises. On the evening of the 24th, there was a ball at Mr. Moffat's, where, we are bound to say, the entertainment was admirable.[8] The next day, Christmas, there were religious exercises at the Catholic and the Episcopal churches, and in the evening, the latter church was brilliantly illuminated. The same evening, there was a ball of unusual splendor at Mr. Brewster's new hotel, in Stillwater, attended by more than one hundred gentlemen and ladies, eight cotillions occupying the floor at once.[9] The next day, thanksgiving, the bells pealed merrily at sunrise and at sunset, and religious exercises were observed in the churches, of a most interesting character. Mr. Neill delivered a historical address, illustrated with stirring incidents of early times, and contrasting the infancy of our favored Territory with that of the Puritan colonies, which thrilled every heart, and pronounced a beautiful eulogium

the society's *Annals* for 1850, and republished under the title "The French Voyageurs to Minnesota during the Seventeenth Century," in *Minnesota Historical Collections*, 1:1–18.

[8] Lot Moffet was the proprietor of the St. Paul Temperance House, commonly known as "Moffet's Castle," on Jackson Street.

[9] John W. Brewster was the proprietor of the Lake House, built in 1849. Folsom, *Fifty Years in the Northwest*, 400.

upon honest toil. We hope all will read it. The highest credit is due to Mr. Fort, by whose exertions a choir of sacred music has been formed, which would do credit to any church in Christendom.

"In the evening, there was a magnificent ball at Mazourka Hall, which Mr. Elfelt has fitted up with transparencies, paintings, pictures and chandeliers, in a style of superb elegance. Sleigh-riding, visiting, open doors and rich entertainments on New-Year's Day, and a magnificent ball on New Year's eve, coupled with suitable religious exercises, have rendered memorable our holidays."

In the same issue the editor commented that "Many of the people of St. Paul, observe the good old Dutch New York fashion, of keeping open house on New-Year's and brightening the rusty chain of social intercourse, by making friendly calls upon the ladies and partaking of good cheer." And he added: "We welcome those who may call at our house." A contemporary wrote that on New Year's afternoon "the better class of our gentlemen" made calls, while others idled about in the "grog shops."

Readers of the *Pioneer* beyond the bounds of Minnesota may have got the impression that society as it existed on the upper Mississippi was highly sophisticated, when they read of St. Paul "swarming with animated fashion" on New Year's Day, of "magnificent balls," and of the "superb elegance" of Mazourka Hall. If so, that impression must have been dispelled by the account in the issue of January 23, 1850, of "The Ball at the Central House," in which the editor found it necessary to point out "some improprieties to be avoided at balls":

"The Ball at the Central House, Thursday evening, was attended by about 30 gentlemen and 30 ladies; and was far the most pleasant party of the season. It is more agreeable to attend a small party, to have plenty of room and an opportunity for becoming acquainted with all who are present, than to be one in a vast crowd of persons who all have as much as they can do to keep from being engulfed by the living masses. Then how much more rational, to take a light repast of hot coffee and tea, with such palatable eatables as can be taken in the way of a collation, leisurely, than to scramble for an uncomfortable seat at a table loaded down with the substantial fare required to appease the hunger of a party of English fox-hunters, with a chance of having a good dress ruined with grease and gravies and sauces? Dancing is designed as a sort of mental as well as bodily recreation. It requires, to be enjoyed, a lively, poetic temper of mind, to which indulgence in grosser temptations of the table, is not conducive. Dancing, properly conducted, with chaste, correct music, has a tendency, not only to improve the manners, but to elevate, to etherialize the mind.

"The ball-room should be the home of decorum and propriety. The bar-room should never be carried into the ballroom. The ball-room is a place where every gentleman will avoid any degree of coarseness. It is no place for *cant words* and *Westernisms*. It is no place for gentlemen or ladies, to indulge in grotesque costume or eccentricities of action or smartness of expression. Any person who tries to be conspicuous in a ball-room, by anything fantastic in dress, odd in carriage or remarkable in expression, may depend upon being regarded as a vain or vulgar person, by the well-bred.

"There are some improprieties to be avoided at balls, which it may be well enough to mention.

"1st. Avoid the meanness of neglecting to pay your bill. No man of the least self-respect, would think of sponging his evening's entertainment. As for those who enter into a sort of half communion with the ball — who plant themselves in the way of the company while dancing, who eat supper, who do every thing but dance and pay their bills, it is the duty of managers to turn them straight out of doors. They are an intolerable nuisance — like men who climb up and ride on the boot of the stage, rather than pay their fare and take an inside seat.

"2d. Gentlemen should not wear pumps nor thick boots in a ball-room; nor worse yet, moccasins, unless they wish to join in a scalp-dance; but fine boots. No person should presume to dance without gloves. Clattering, thumping time, pigeon-winging and all fantastic splurges with the feet, are extremely vulgar. It is improper to shake hands in a ball-room.

"It is ill-bred, for one or two couples to attempt to show their skill in waltzing, while cotillion sets have nothing to do but stand upon the floor and witness a human whirligig until it runs down. It is ill-bred, yes! and ill gotten bread, for a lady to sweep a quantity of cakes and nuts into her handkerchief, at the table, to carry home. She might as well pocket the sugar bowl and the tea-spoons.

"Of course no lessons in these elementary principles of etiquette, are needed in the refined society of Minnesota; but we have readers in the Sandwich islands." [10]

Two years later, when he reported the "Odd Fellows' Ball, on Monday Night" in the *Pioneer* of February 26, 1852, the editor was pleased to note "quite an improvement" in the balls held in Minnesota, although he was not altogether pleased with the way the women dressed:

"The Hall was crowded; and the company, when not dancing, was engaged in a general buzz of conversation. It was the most *talking* ball we ever saw. Another characteristic, was, that the ladies, with few exceptions, were very plainly dressed; some were rather too cheaply dressed. An affectation of extreme simplicity of dress, is about as ridiculous as extravagance, and an indulgence in fantastic dress and tinsel splendor. As to the gentlemen, they were mostly Odd Fellows; and of

---

[10] In his paper for January 16, 1850, Goodhue proudly acknowledged "the receipt of one year's subscription to the Pioneer, from the under Secretary of the Sandwich Islands."

course they appeared in the magnificent regalia of their order. Never was a cavalcade of spotted circus horses, more gaudily caparisoned with sparkling breast-plates, ornamented surcingles and starry martingales, with here and there a plumed tinsel cap. . . .

"There is quite an improvement observable in our balls. We no longer hear stamping and shuffling and thumping the time out with the feet; but the dance moves along, lightly, gracefully, swimmingly. Waltzes and Spanish quadrilles were in the programme; but they won't do. The cotillion, like the English language for the *tongue*, is the common language for the *feet*; and the mass of Americans, never will take the trouble to learn but *one* language, for the head or the feet. . . . One thing we have to remark, is, not only the improving taste and elegance of those who attend our balls, but the constant addition to the number of beautiful women and girls, in our town; which is for nothing more truly remarkable than for the very large share of female beauty here resident."

Goodhue found nothing whatever to criticize in the "Ladies' Fair," which he described in the *Pioneer* of December 25, 1851. He was completely charmed with every aspect of the fair, from the "elegant" supper to the "easy elegance" of manners and the "pleasant tone of refined conversation" of those who attended it:

"Charles H. Oakes is a first rate, noble, big-hearted man; as generous a man as the liberal town of St. Paul contains, if he *is* one of the 'Fur Company.' Mr. Oakes gave to the fair, the entire use of his large, new elegant mansion house, well warmed and illuminated from the basement up to the observatory, beside contributing other wise very largely to the entertainment.[11] The weather being pleasant, there was a very

[11] Oakes, a trader with the American Fur Company since 1827, with headquarters most of the time at La Pointe, Wisconsin, settled in St. Paul in 1850. Three years later he became a member of the firm of Borup and Oakes, the first bankers in St. Paul. His "new elegant mansion house" was

large assemblage of persons, by eight o'clock in the evening;
carriages being employed to bring in company from the
distant parts of our widespread town.

"We found there an assemblage of our citizens, of various
ages and of both sexes and of all religious denominations,
many who were there met for the first time, surpassing in
intelligence and real respectability, any assemblage we have
ever before seen in St. Paul; more beautiful, well dressed

OAKES'S HOUSE
[From an engraving on a *Map of Saint Paul*, 1857]

women and girls, and more genteel and accomplished men,
than we supposed could be mustered in our thriving village.
There was an easy elegance of manners and a pleasant tone
of refined conversation, that was truly delightful. Sales proceeded briskly, of the few articles offered; but the most lively
scene of operations, was the Post Office, in one apartment of
the fair, where pertinent, ludicrous and appropriate letters
could be obtained, by any one who desired, at the old rates
of postage, ten cents on delivery.

"*The Supper.* — Of course the supper was an elegant affair; for the Ladies of St. Paul had taken it in hand them-

at Eighth and Jackson Streets. Folsom, *Fifty Years in the Northwest,* 572;
Newson, *Pen Pictures,* 77.

selves; and our ladies too, of the very highest consideration in town. They not only provided and arranged the tables for one hundred persons, in a style of sumptuous elegance, with turkeys, chickens, frosted hams, oyster soups, lobster soups, sardines, and all the substantials of a good supper, but also with pastries and sauces and jellies and piquants of every description; and added their own personal services during the feast, in pouring tea and coffee and supplying the wants of the company.

"There was the utmost practical Democracy and equality, from his Excellency, the Governor, all around to the utmost verge of the company. We left, with a better opinion of the elements of society in St. Paul and higher hopes of the early predominance here, of a christian spirit of enlightened morality and high-toned civilization. What the proceeds of the Fair may amount to, is wholly unimportant compared with the social and moral effect of such a meeting in our town, in making our people acquainted with each other, exchanging opinions, improving manners and elevating the standard of morality, sobriety and civilization."

In 1852 St. Paul celebrated the Fourth of July in two places. The celebration at "the Cave" — which may have been either Carver's Cave or Fountain Cave — was wet, and that held in town under the auspices of the Sons of Temperance, was, of course, dry. Patriotic orations were made at both. In town there were fireworks, bonfires, a torchlight procession, and a ball at the hall of the Sons of Temperance — "the S. O. T.," Goodhue loved to call it. These events, which Goodhue was too busy to attend, he mentioned in a brief paragraph in the *Pioneer* of July 8. Of more interest is his leading editorial in the same issue, apparently written on July 5, and entitled "Fourth of July in the Morning":

"Our people are very generally observing this anniversary on Monday the 5th of July; because the 4th occurs on Sunday. The only impropriety we noticed on Sunday was the annoying noise of fire crackers about the streets, by a parcel of reckless boys, in defiance of the general sense of sobriety that pervaded our town. On Sunday, Mr. Neill gave us an analysis of the character of George Washington; and the choir sung patriotic hymns; and probably there were religious services, equally as appropriate, at the several other churches. On Monday, before sunrise, the bells struck up an anthem of merry peals, as soon as the East was streaked with crimson, while yet the pale moon was dimly shining, far away South West, over the land of the Sioux — the S. B. Ben Campbell, lying all night at the lower landing, opened her eyes, and St. Paul yawned and jumped out of bed and hauled on his pants, whistling Yankee Doodle; and the little boys and girls were up in the twinkling of a bed post — and the bashful maidens that had been sleeping through the sultry night with open windows, leaped up in their snowy night dresses, to close their curtains, as the town was beginning to stir out; and at sunrise the national salute was fired, the report of the cannon echoing and reverberating from hill to bluff and bluff to hill again; and in fact, the 4th of July, came in just as easy and natural and familiar, away up here on the northern frontiers of the Mississippi, as it has anywhere in the whole line of States from Maine hither, that for the hour preceding, had been greeting the king of Day with similar salutations, as they were rolled over into his presence, State after State, in the diurnal progress of our globe from West to East.

"We are to have two celebrations; a water and a liquor celebration; but having much to do this day, 'it is mixed' if we go to either. There is but little pleasure, in marching with a long procession, making a part of a pageant, to parade, through dusty streets, and after listening in a crowded seat, to an oration, which is crowded full of flowers of rhetoric, pressed and cramped and squeezed into a half hour oration, to get a crowded seat at a crowded public table, there to help all the women and girls within reach, to cold pig and stuffing only half baked, and to snatch an unsavory mouthful of it at last, yourself, through sheer hunger—then to listen to fifty intolerable, stupid old stereotyped patriotic toasts for an hour, beside a dozen or more to 'the *la*-dies, God bless 'em!' — to be bored with half a dozen dinner speeches, as long as the ears of the human donkeys that get up and bray them into the ears of the great, undiscriminating multitudes — or perchance to be called up yourself by 'a sentiment, to respond in a speech of wordy nothing,' with gesticulation and voice more violent and emphatic, in proportion as your mind is more empty and your sentences more pointless and senseless — and then to go to bed at night, with a splitting headache—the Lord in mercy deliver us from such celebrations of the Fourth of July."

The Sixth Regiment Band, which provided the music for so many of the dancing parties and steamboat excursions, now and then gave concerts in the various Minnesota communities. One of these, given in the Methodist Church in St. Paul, Goodhue described in the *Pioneer* of February 13, 1850, under the heading "The Concert Last Wednesday Night":[12]

"Unquestionably there is much music in the 6th Regiment Band. What triumph of Art, seems more wonderful than this? — that fifteen men with instruments of music as different as their own faces, can produce such perfect harmony of sweet sounds, that each seems part of all? threading as it were, by separate avenues the wide wilderness of sounds, over undulations, chasms, glassy lakes and wild recesses, suddenly, all the instruments seem to emerge together in the next staff, ready for another of these wonderful evolutions — filling the listener with amazement.

"Hearing this band's performance of several of the standard operas, and the highly artificial compositions of Bellini, Rossini and others, and contrasting it with the three simple

[12] The proceeds of this concert were given to the Washington Monument Association. *Pioneer*, February 6, 1850.

notes of the Dacota, blowing upon his reed, we were never more powerfully impressed with the moral sublimity of Art. What does Nature afford, half as grand as these achievements of human skill? We can find enough to praise and to admire in this band, without inquiring whether it is equal to Gungl's.[13] Some of the performers are equal to the best living. It is needless to mention Jackson the leader, so well known throughout the length of the Mississippi river. His performance upon the bugle, was fully equal to himself, and that is all that *can* be said for him. We consider this band as well as the whole garrison, with its high intelligence — but especially the band, of infinite value to St. Paul — in fact, it is the most powerful element of influence amongst us, for our good, next to the pulpit and the press."

In April, 1851, the Bakers, a family of five singers from Salisbury, New Hampshire, arrived in Minnesota to give a series of concerts at St. Paul, St. Anthony, and Stillwater.[14] Their two St. Paul performances are reported in the *Pioneer* of May 1, 1851:

"No place is too remote for the live Yankee to visit, either from curiosity, or for pleasure or for gain. One benefit results to us, at least from the ascendancy of that bright particular star, Jenny Lind, in the musical firmament; and that is, that all the lesser orbs, paling in her brightness, wander away to enlighten the outer barbarians where they may shine, undimmed by contrast with her lustre.[15] In the monetary world, bad currency expels the good; but in the musical world, notes of highest value, expel notes of inferior value. We thank Jenny Lind therefore, for sending us the Baker family, whose concerts whilom were listened to by thronged houses in the eastern villages and cities.

[13] Josef Gung'l, the Hungarian composer and band master, toured America with his orchestra in the 1840's.

[14] *Pioneer*, April 24, 1851.

[15] Jenny Lind was in America from 1850 to 1852, giving numerous concerts, under the auspices of P. T. Barnum.

"The Bakers came up by the Steamer Excelsior on Wednesday of last week. Their arrival here was preceded by the advent of their agent, Mr. Chandler, who is certainly one of the pleasantest and most popular gentlemen we have seen any where. Their concerts continued two evenings at Mazourka Hall, which was crowded both evenings with a delightful audience. On Saturday evening they performed at St. Anthony and on Monday at Stillwater. Such precision of time, such admirable concord, the minuendo, the crescendo, and all the music that gives artistic effect, was done in a style that could not be improved; and one of the voices, a bass, possesses more compass and depth and richness than any bass we ever before heard — down, down, down a hundred fathoms below the gamut; and we overheard a listener declaring that the singer must be as hollow as a sycamore tree, to produce such sounds. Of the selections of music, we cannot say that we were pleased with all of them."

At Mazourka Hall on August 12, 1851, according to the *Pioneer* issued two days later, occurred "the first dramatic exhibition ever presented in Minnesota." Among the actors in the company was George Holland, the popular ventriloquist and comedian of that as well as a much later day, "whose versatility," wrote Goodhue, "is such that he alone amounts to a dramatic company." That the company was favorably received in the territory is apparent from a paragraph in the *Pioneer* of August 21, 1851:

"The Dramatic Company still continues to entertain as crowded houses every night, at Mazourka Hall, as on the first evening of their exhibition. We hear 'The Serious Family' highly spoken of, in the bill of last Monday night, and that it will be repeated. With a large resident population like ours, and with such accession of visitors as we shall have soon in multitudes, to pass the summers in our town, it is scarcely to be doubted that in a year or two, we shall require, and can well support a regular Theatre in Saint Paul."

11. Steamboats in the Wilderness

THAT THE VAST AREA INCLUDED IN MINNESOTA TERRITORY
west of the Mississippi River would remain Indian country
for long could hardly have been expected. Not Congress,
nor any power on earth, could have kept the throngs of
American pioneers, ever moving westward, from swarming
across the Mississippi, once they had reached the eastern
bank. Almost as soon as the territory was organized Minnesotans were demanding the acquisition of the Indian lands —
the "Suland" they called it — and an unsuccessful attempt
to treat with the Sioux was made in 1849. Following this
abortive treaty, the wheels were again set in motion for the
negotiation of a treaty in the near future.[1]

The leading men of Minnesota realized that Congress would
need not a little pressure to interest itself in spending public
money for a broad tract of land, unknown and uninhabited,
beyond the outer fringes of the frontier. To arouse public
interest abroad in the Sioux country, and thereby pave the
way for Congressional action, they raised funds to finance
four steamboat excursions up the Minnesota River in the summer of 1850. One of the most active of the promoters of this
project was Goodhue, who regarded the excursions "as a
necessary, almost, an indispensable preliminary to obtaining an
appropriation from Congress, for the negotiation of the Sioux
treaties."[2] In the *Pioneer* of August 1, 1850, he set forth the
objects of the explorations:

"The people of Saint Paul, mostly congregated here within
the year and a half last past, from every quarter, drawn to
this town by a conviction now ripening into absolute certainty, that here is destined shortly to be the emporium of the

---

[1] On the treaty of 1849, see Folwell, *Minnesota*, 1:266–275.
[2] See below, p. 258.

trade of all that portion of the temperate zone lying north of it, and extending from the shores of the great lakes to the banks of the Upper Mississippi; embracing a larger area of trade without a rival, and that, too, in the very heart of a continent, than any other town perhaps in the world; situated in the centre of the temperate zone and at the extreme northern point of steady steam navigation by the class of boats profitably employed in the trade above Saint Louis, have deemed no sacrifice of time or of money too great, to explore the interior of Minnesota. While the enterprise of Saint Anthony, has opened navigation by steam the present season to Sauk Rapids, on the Upper Mississippi, and demonstrated the practicability of running small steamboats up that river to the falls of Pokagomon, a distance of 600 miles above us, Saint Paul has explored the other branch of the river above us, the Minnesota, (heretofore more often called the Saint Peter, a name which it will probably now cease to be known by,)[3] for a distance of 300 miles; for the first time startling with the noise of the steam pipe, the most glorious wilderness that ever smiled under the hand of the Creator.

"We have deemed the exploration of the Minnesota river, an object of primary importance on several accounts. As citizens of Saint Paul, lying but 5 or 6 miles below the junction of the Minnesota and Mississippi rivers, the natural and inevitable point of transhipment from the larger steamboats running below, to the smaller boats of different construction, adapted to the navigation of the rivers above us, we wished to know and that the world should know, that the navigable waters above us, tributary to our trade, irrigate an extent of land as great and at least as fertile as the whole length of the

[3] On March 6, 1852, the territorial legislature memorialized Congress to change the name of the St. Peter's River to the Minnesota River. Congress complied with an act, approved on June 19, 1852, providing that the river "shall be known and designated on the public records as the Minnesota River." Minnesota Territory, *Laws*, 1852, p. 70; United States, *Statutes at Large*, 1852, p. 147.

Mississippi from St. Louis to St. Paul. All this has been demonstrated.

"Again, it will be remembered that the whole of the west bank of the Mississippi river from the Iowa line to the northern boundary of Minnesota, is Indian territory; and that the whole country watered by the Minnesota, belongs to the Sioux Indians — that it is a portion of the continent hitherto almost unexplored and unknown — and that Government has now appointed commissioners to treat for its purchase. A better knowledge of its situation, resources, and true value, seemed indispensable to enable the Commissioners and the Senate of the United States to estimate properly what might be a fair and just equivalent for the lands to be treated for."

The first and third excursions were made by the "Anthony Wayne," the second by the "Nominee," and the last by the "Yankee." Each boat left a board nailed to a tree on the river bank recording the extent of its exploration. On the first trip of the "Anthony Wayne" Goodhue was one of the three hundred passengers, which included a St. Louis pleasure party of seventy men and women. He also accompanied the "Yankee" excursion. The *Pioneer* carried no account of the "Nominee" trip, nor of the second voyage of the "Wayne." [4]

Goodhue's exuberant accounts of the first and last of these excursions, with his detailed descriptions of "the fairest, loveliest land . . . that ever the light of the sun shone upon," could have done hardly less than whet the impatience of expectant immigrants for the opening of the lands. And the Indian, the silence of his wilderness broken by the whistle of

---

[4] Of the second voyage of the "Wayne," John P. Owens wrote many years later: "There was no St. Louis pleasure party about this trip — only St. Paul people, some from Mendota, and perhaps one or two from St. Anthony. . . . Col. J. M. Goodhue was not aboard this trip. . . . David Olmsted and Henry L. Tilden were the chief managers of the expedition, and they were two men, that for political reasons just at that time, Goodhue hated worse than he did the 'Old Harry' . . . and he refused to have anything to do with the arrangements." Letter dated Taylors Falls, January 16, 1878, and signed "J. P. O.", in the *St. Paul Pioneer Press*, January 19, 1878.

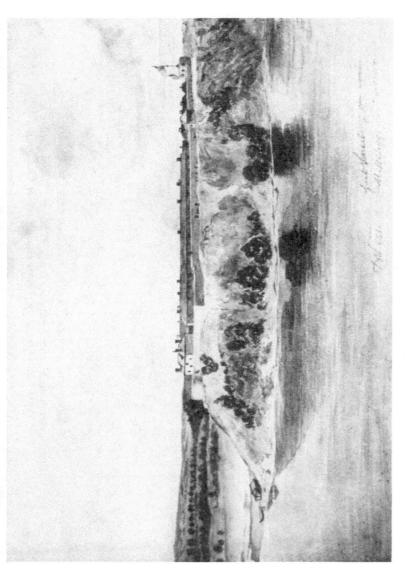

FORT SNELLING IN 1851

[From a photograph, owned by the State Historical Society of Wisconsin, of a water color by Jean Baptist Wengler. The original is in Linz, Austria.]

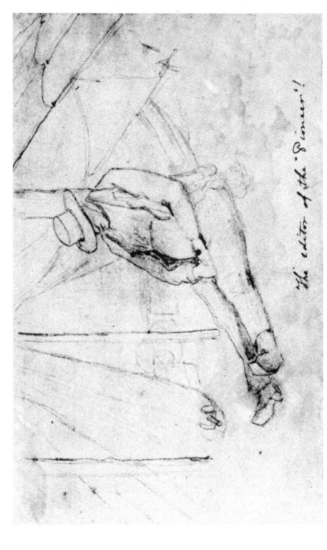

GOODHUE AT THE TREATY OF TRAVERSE DES SIOUX

[From a sketch made at the treaty by Frank B. Mayer. The original is in the Ayer Collection of the Newberry Library at Chicago.]

the steamboat and the voices of the gay excursionists, must have sensed that this was advance notice to gather his possessions and continue his march toward the setting sun.

The account of the first excursion, which lasted but a day and reached the head of the Little Rapids about sixty miles up the river, was published in the *Pioneer* of July 4, 1850, under the heading "A New Chapter in the History of Minnesota — Navigation of the St. Peter River — The Anthony Wayne, the Pioneer Boat":

"On Friday last, the 28th day of June, 1850, that enterprising Steamboat, the Anthony Wayne, enrolled her name in the annals of our Territory; and proved herself worthy of the name of gallant Mad Anthony. The first boat to throw a bow-line ashore under the foaming falls of Saint Anthony, amid the very roar and spray of the cataract — a feat which she repeated again on Thursday last [5] — the boat, on Friday, reaped fresher laurels, by demonstrating that the Saint Peter river, meandering a boundless extent of plains as fertile as the shores of the Nile, is actually navigable for steamboats of light draught, in any stage of water, for more than one hundred and fifty miles; more than this, she afforded hundreds of our citizens and many strangers actual, visual proof, that through the very heart of Minnesota, east and west, extends a country, not surpassed in fertility by the lands of the Wabash valley — well wooded, beautiful as Paradise to the eye, the fairest, loveliest land, by the united testimony of all, that ever the light of the sun shone upon.

"Suddenly, with but two hours notice, the citizens of Saint Paul, who for energy, promptitude and public spirit, are not surpassed by any people in the world, made up a purse of $225, to defray the expense of an experimental trip of the Wayne, one day, up the St. Peter, no boat ever having gone

[5] The first trip of the "Anthony Wayne" to the Falls of St. Anthony was made on May 7, 1850. Both trips were made possible by the unusual floods of that year. *Pioneer*, April 17, May 9, 1850; Williams, *Saint Paul*, 258.

further up that stream than Sixes village[6]—a feat performed, we think, in 1842.—About nine o'clock in the morning, the Anthony Wayne, swung into the channel, at Saint Paul.[7] . . .

"*The Company.* It would astonish all people of ceremony and form, to see how readily 300 well-dressed persons, embracing people of all nations and kindreds under the sun, meeting on this boat, for the most part strangers to each other, formed an acquaintance and mingled together in conversation. Forms of introduction and set ceremonies, seemed to be dispensed with by common consent. All were inspired with a disposition to please and be pleased. The weather was delightful—a clear summer day, warm enough to invite a shade, but not hot enough to render exercise uncomfortable in the pleasant breeze. The music, a small, select band from Quincy, was animated and agreeable; and before we had reached the mouth of the St. Peter at Fort Snelling, a lively cotillion of several sets was in motion, in the spacious cabin —an amusement which the more enlarged Christianity of the West is too liberal to frown upon as a crime, and in which many persons of the purest religious character have the moral courage to indulge.

"*Fort Snelling.* Five or six miles brought the Wayne to the landing under Fort Snelling, which sits there upon the point of the bluff, the faithful sentinel of the Northwest. All honor to the glorious flag there waving; every thread of it is the people's, and the noble soldiers who there defend it, are of us, part and parcel, with sentiments the same as ours, with the same interests, and with feelings throbbing in unison with every pulsation of the popular heart. Of course they wished to be with us, but as the garrison contained but few more than fifty men, officers and soldiers, it was impossible for many to leave the Fort; besides that, Captain [James] Monroe, commanding officer, was hourly expecting a requisition for

---

[6] This was the village of the Sioux chief, Shakopee or "Little Six," on the site of the present town of that name.

[7] Here Goodhue gives a list of the Minnesota passengers.

troops at Sauk Rapids – a reasonable expectation – for the
next day all the troops, down to a corporal's guard, marched
for Sauk Rapids, to quiet the alarming troubles with the Winnebago Indians.[8] Captain [Ralph W.] Kirkham, however,
came on board, with several others, and Mr. Jackson's re-
nowned 6th Regiment band volunteered to delight us on our
way with their admirable music.

"A dozen Indians were at the landing, with their ponies,
covered with bells and trappings. These animals were mounted
by several of our company, who seemed anxious to display
their horsemanship, and galloped about the plain, to the amusement of those on board. We saw nothing very remarkable in
the equestrian line, until a Mr. [James W.] Vincent, from
St. Paul, leaped ashore from the boat, on the back of a beautiful
pony which he had taken along in the boat, and which no bars
can stop; in this way, Vincent, who seemed to grow out of the
animal's withers, did some wild Indian riding, that made the
natives stare. At last the Indians mounted their ponies and galloped away at full speed.

"By this time, we

'Began to feel, as well we might,
'The keen demands of appetite.'

Dinner was soon over, on the principle that 'a short horse
is soon curried.' In fact there was not enough of it to require
much comment; and for the same reason, the Captain,[9] we
know, will excuse us from *any notice whatever, of the supper;* plenty of solids and too much of liquids were paid for
that day, on the Anthony Wayne; but the eatables turned out
like a Sheriff's return of *nulla bona,* endorsed legibly in empty
dishes along the whole length of the Anthony Wayne's table;

[8] The *Pioneer* of June 27, 1850, reported that on June 23 "about 40 Winnebagoes assembled at the steamboat landing [*at Sauk Rapids*] and came to
Mr. [Calvin] Potter's trading house and demanded whiskey, which he refused
them." A fight followed, in which "2 whites were wounded and 4 or 5 Indians
were killed and wounded."
[9] The captain was Daniel Able.

yet, we doubt not, she was perfectly conscientious in exacting *allopathic* pay for *homeopathic* fare; as it was our business, before hand, to learn what was the Wayne's *practice;* so we have no complaint to make — all right — all *perfectly* right!

"*The Saint Peter.* Never was a lighter hearted band of adventurers propelled by steam than the gay multitude thronging the cabin and decks of the Anthony Wayne, as she turned her bow into the mouth of the Saint Peter, to explore that rich valley in the Southwest, along which the covetous eye of the white man has long gazed with prying curiosity, far away toward the distant waters of the Blue Earth river. Fasting is favorable to poetic sentiment.

"The delightful weather, the stirring music of the band, the majestic scenery, every thing, conspired to exhilarate — to say nothing of the iced brandy. The current of the river seemed sluggish, winding along through a vast alluvial intervale, like a silver eel. Uniformly about 150 feet wide, without a snag, a sawyer, a rock, a riffle, or an indenture in either bank, the river really seemed more like a work of art, a ship canal, constructed by the labor and wealth of a great state, than like a natural stream of water, draining an immense area of fertile lands, to the very rim of the Missouri and McKenzie's river basins. — Each shore was a fresh, perpendicular, crumbling bank of alluvion, being more elevated than the grounds more remote from the river, which, as along the Illinois and the lower Mississippi were so much depressed as to form lagoons, filled with water and tall grass, the home of numberless water-fowl; while still more remote from the river, the land rose by a gradual ascent and spread away in the rich luxuriance of a waving inclined plain, its sides crowned with small clustering groves, and a few trees scattered over the whole expanse, upon the east side of the river; while upon the west side, the same description of intervale was walled in at a distance from the river of about one mile, or often less, by

a high, steep, grass-covered bluff. So crooked was the river, that
we seemed all the time to be just at the end of it; but the pilot,
who was certainly very skilful, contrived to wind the boat
along in a labyrinth of interminable twistings, apparently confident that wherever he could direct the bow of the boat, he

BLACK DOG'S VILLAGE
[From an engraving in *Harper's New Monthly Magazine*, July, 1853]

could sweep her stern gracefully around and bring up the rear
without conflicting with the bank of the river.

"*Indian Villages*. At a distance of three miles from Fort
Snelling, by land, but much more by river, we came to Black
Dog's village, on the right bank — a row of huts and tepees
extending along upon the brow of the bluff, say 100 feet high,
and distant from the river a few hundred yards. Along the interval between the bluff and the river, upon the warm sandy

186 HORNS OF THUNDER

loam, they had many little patches of corn and beans planted, which some of the squaws were hoeing; and near by, on the right shore of the river, upon the very bank of it, was Man-cloud's village — a nest of half a dozen huts and lodges, with small patches of ground, planted with corn and beans, cultivated exclusively with hoes. The next village we reached was Good-Road's, distant 9 miles by land from Fort Snelling, on the east side of the river. As the boat approached each village, the Indians and squaws, old and young, with blankets or without, came running to the bank of the river, and standing in astonishment until the boat blew her shrill steam whistle, when all but the old warriors would wheel and run away, half scared to death. As we advanced up the river, the country became still more inviting, spreading away in beautiful slopes from either shore, as far as the sight could extend, with an abundance of forest, entirely free from lagoons and above freshets; and evidently, from the rank growth of vegetation, land of the very highest productive powers. At a distance of about twenty miles, by land, above the mouth, we came to Sixes' village, on the east bank, a very beautiful spot, and a larger village than most others. Here is Mr. Samuel Pond's mission station. It gave us some satisfaction to distribute copies of the last No. of the Pioneer at this place.[10]

"At this place, the boat remained for about two hours, affording a fine opportunity to all who wished, to gain an insight into the wigwams and the domestic condition of the savages. Some of the young squaws brought strawberries to the boat for sale; and several purchases of Indian bows, arrows, pipes and trinkets, were made. Again we are moving onward. The character of the river continues still precisely

[10] Black Dog, Man Cloud (or Sky Man), Good Road, and Little Six (or Shakopee) were chiefs of the Mdewakanton band of Sioux Indians. See Edward D. Neill, "Dakota Land and Dakota Life," in *Minnesota Historical Collections*, 1:263. Samuel W. Pond and his brother Gideon came to Minnesota in 1834 as missionaries to the Sioux. Their story is told by Samuel W. Pond, Jr.. in *Two Volunteer Missionaries among the Dakotas* (Boston, c. 1893).

the same, regular as a canal, and the shores are even more beautiful, being here often bordered with a fine belt of forest trees. At a distance of 35 or 40 miles by land, and at least 60 by water, we reached the village of the Wahpaytons, on the east shore;[11] where the boat again astonished the natives upon the shore, with her shrill steam whistle. Mr. L. Roberts [*Louis Robert*] has a trading house at this place, to which the Wayne brought supplies. Here Pelon and Odell, who were acquainted with the river, informed us that we were at the foot of the Rapids.[12]

"The boat landed at the Indian village; and we had gone quite as far as the most sanguine believed was possible, and were nearly out of wood and of course out of provisions; but to this we were becoming accustomed. There was no appearance of rapids before us. The Captain was enterprising however, and determined to go up to the head of the rapids, above which there is no obstruction for 60 or 80 miles; and accordingly he put the Wayne's nose against the current. She ran along carefully, by soundings, and so far from touching bottom on the rapids, the shoalest water proved to be 8½ feet deep. At the head of the rapids, we overtook a Mackinaw boat, drawn by cordelling. The boatmen upon 'the Rocky Mountains,' (that was her name,) looked astonished and scared, and swung their hats, no more expecting to see a steamboat there than a team of walruses in harness.

[11] This was the village of the lower band of Wahpeton Sioux. The upper Wahpeton lived about Lac qui Parle. Folwell, *Minnesota*, 1:183.
[12] Louis Pelon and Thomas Odell acted as pilots on the trip. Odell came to Fort Snelling in 1841 as a soldier, and was mustered out of service in 1845. The next year he settled in St. Paul. Pelon settled in St. Paul in 1842. See Williams, *Saint Paul*, 199. Goodhue tells the following anecdote about Pelon in the *Pioneer* of July 15, 1851: "Pelon, an old voyageur . . . used to tend Henry Jackson's bar . . . while Saint Paul was only the western suburb of Pig's Eye. At that time all sorts of liquors were sold out of the same decanter; and a stranger coming in, asked Pelon if he had any confectionary. Pelon, not knowing the meaning of the word *confectionary*, supposed, of course, it was some kind of liquor, passed out the decanter of whiskey to his customer, saying, 'Oui, Monsieur, here is a confecshawn, ver good, superb, magnifique, pretty fair.'

"*Returning.* If we had been supplied with wood, the general disposition was to run up stream as long as we could find water; and the officers of the Wayne were the boys to do it; but as we had neither wood, liquors nor provision, and as the Sun was preparing to dip his burning axle in the blue Pacific, the Wayne reluctantly turned her bow down stream, retracing the winding channel of the river at a flying pace, and *balancing* now to the shore on the right, then *swinging* the opposite corner, then *docedo* to a swarthy forest, now it is *chazzez* right, and now left and now *alamande* right and left, and turn the corners, through the flying mazy landscape, to the music of the 6th Regiment Band, while the inmates of the cabin were combining these complex figures of the cotillion which succeeded each other like the beautiful combinations seen in turning the Kaleidoscope. Out of wood! Well; that is one of the outs. How fatal, to be out of wood, out of breath, out of money! An out — a small out, may untune the harmony of a universe. From outs, Good Lord, deliver us! But here, opportunely, we reach the log ruins of an old Indian trading post and an Indian burying place, surrounded with pickets; tie up. The log frame was soon torn down and carried on board the Wayne for fuel; and, would you believe it? The pickets around the grave yard, hundreds of them, were sacrilegiously torn down and consigned to the same use. Here was a most luxuriant growth of strawberry vines, many clusters of strawberries being found upon stems 12 or 15 inches long. The Wayne plays the part of the hyena very well, which was not strange considering how *hungry* she was.

"And now the Wayne moves again down stream — the moon is out, spreading an ocean of softened light around — now a frowning forest — now a vast jungle of grass, and now an undulating prairie, sweep along like a panorama, while countless millions of fire flies are spread every where, flooding a perpetual blaze of light over the dewy plains, as if the moon and stars and all the magazines of lightning on high, had been ground up and scattered broadcast over the earth. Meantime in the cabin, the dance is growing more animated as the night advances. Again we reach the mouth of the river and part with our friends from Fort Snelling, touch a moment, and leave a few more at the upper landing, and presently, at midnight our last cotillion is interrupted by reaching shore at the lower landing in St. Paul. And a day is thus delightfully ended, which hundreds will remember as one of the sweetest of their lives. The next morning at sunrise, the Anthony Wayne was on her way back to St. Louis. Captain Abell, your memory is embalmed in the history of the river St. Peter."

In the *Pioneer* of August 1, 1850, appeared Goodhue's account of the five-day excursion of the "Yankee," which left St. Paul for the journey up the river on July 22. He begins his detailed description of the river at the point reached on the first excursion of the "Anthony Wayne," the head of the Little Rapids:

"All Aboard! The steamboat Yankee, of Galena, was ready on Monday morning, the 22d instant, for the Saint Paul exploring party. The names of her officers are as follows: Capt. M[artin] K. Harris; Clerk, G. W. Girdon; Pilot, J. S. Armstrong; First Engineer, G. W. Scott; Second Engineer, G. L. Sargent. The Yankee is a stern wheel boat, of light draught and powerful engines, about 145 feet long, and 200 tons burthen. She was provided with 200 bushels of Rock Island coal and had her hold full of dry wood; and was supplied with a great abundance and variety of provisions and one ton of ice. It was not until nearly the middle of the afternoon that all the men, and women, and children, with trunks, travelling bags, and band-boxes, were on board and the lines cast off.

"The Yankee floated across the bridge leading to the Upper Landing, and passed out into the river above, by a new route through the upper end of the slough — Touching Mendota, we took on board Joseph Laframboise and family, bound up

the Minnesota river to his trading post at Little Rock.[13] At
Fort Snelling we were joined by a part of the 6th Regiment
band; after which, the Yankee turned her prow into the quiet
current of the Minnesota, and ran on until midnight, tying up
not far below the Rapids. At length the music and the dancing ceased and all was hushed in slumber. At the earliest dawn
of day, the Yankee was again in motion, passing Sixes village
and all the delightful lands which we described on the 1st
trip of the Anthony Wayne. Above the Rapids, we soon came
into a region we had not before seen, and more beautiful,
if possible, than that through which we had passed, being a
varied landscape of prairie and woodland, evidently of the
best quality.

"*Traverse de*[*s*] *Sioux.* The company all seemed delighted
with each other and with all that they witnessed. The river
continued apparently of the same width, without sand banks,
without islands, without tributaries, but with a current increasing in velocity as we ascended, and the channel crooked
beyond parallel, and with many snags and logs in the short
bends. At length we came in sight of the missionary station
at Traverse de Sioux (the Sioux crossing) on the north side
of the river, situated upon a wide slope of prairie, which rose
gradually from the banks of the river and extended far, far
back, covered with luxuriant grass. — Three neat white buildings belonging to the mission, and several Indian huts and
lodges were distant a few rods from the bank, amidst fields
of well cultivated corn, beans, and potatoes, as promising
crops as we ever saw. There was also a small patch of wheat,
just reaped, which looked very plump and heavy.[14]

[13] Laframboise had traded with the Indians in southern Minnesota since
1822. About 1837 he was placed in charge of the American Fur Company's
post at the Little Rock River, southeast of Fort Ridgely on the Minnesota.
Willoughby M. Babcock, ed., "Dakota Portraits," in *Minnesota History Bulletin,* 2:490, n.
[14] The mission station was in charge of Robert Hopkins, who had been a
Presbyterian missionary to the Sioux in Minnesota since 1843. He was

"On we sped. Upon the south side of the river, were Indian corn fields, unfenced, upon the river bottom, the corn planted very thick and like a perfect jungle — almost a solid mass of dark green vegetation crowned with countless spindles. Spreading away a mile or so, this bottom, which is doubtless sometimes covered by the flood, (perhaps annually,) is enclosed by a circling amphitheatre of hills, covered with forest trees; while on the north side of the river is Traverse de Sioux, at the neck of a large peninsula, made by a bend in the river, which after a progress of 3 or 4 miles further, brought us back again within half a mile of the mission. A little above this point we stopped to wood; passengers, crew, and all, assisting. Two or three painted Sioux horsemen came galloping up from the Traverse and seemed to claim tribute. We made them a present of some corn. At a short distance above this place, we found on the north shore a quantity of old rails; which, as they seemed useless to the owner, as they offered no protection to his cornfield, we took, the Captain paying a fair price for them to a gentleman on board, to give to the owner.

"*Cotillion Prairie.* A sunset as glorious as ever shone upon Italy, found the Yankee on the 2d evening, making fast on the south bank of the river, at the upper end of an elevated prairie. Here we all went on shore, and crossing a narrow strip of bottom land, making a speedy trail through the long grass, gentlemen and ladies, old and young, streamed up the side of the bluff, and from its top surveyed a lovely expanse of prairie and woodland far in the south. The full moon was up and the music being on the spot, several cotillion sets were formed upon the grass and there we 'danced by the light of the moon.' — But there was other music also, for which we had not bargained, the band of musquitoes, and as those who dance must pay the fiddler, we thought it best to adjourn before they had presented all their bills. We went back to the

drowned during the treaty negotiation at Traverse des Sioux in 1851. Upham and Dunlap, *Minnesota Biographies.*

boat. Indeed, indeed, that was a terrible night for those, not a few, who were not provided with musquito bars. But within the cabin of the Yankee, the poetry of motion ceased not until after mid-night; and hearts there are that received impressions as indelible as time, that night at Cotillion Prairie, where *all* 'danced by the light of the moon.'

"*Turtle Bend.* By sunrise on the third morning, the Yankee was again in motion. Breakfast; and most excellent fare, having beefsteaks, veal cutlets, salmon, new potatoes, cucumbers, excellent coffee, and in fact the very choicest fare, admirably cooked, from the beginning to the end of the excursion. Here we turn short to the right then to the left — the boat under excellent management. Now we come to the shingle which the Wayne first put up, but of which she afterwards repented, having the fear of the Yankee before her eyes —; on a few miles further — and there, on the south bank, is the shingle of the Wayne, at the foot of a snaggy bend, from which the Wayne turned back, defying any boat to go higher. Here was a sharp bend in the river, and in it four or five snags and imbedded trees. We reconnoitered. The Yankee laughed right out, and just screamed and bellowed at the idea of stopping there. We went ashore on the north bank, it being a deposit of coarse, clean, sharp sand, the best ever seen for mortar, and in the sand found turtles' eggs. Judge Goodrich proposed that the bend be called Turtle Bend; and so Turtle Bend it is from henceforth. By way of extreme but needless precaution, the passengers and crew took a line ashore upon this sandy beach, and held the Yankee's head up to the north shore, the snags being in the centre bend of the stream, while she rounded up, hugging the shore and keeping entirely aloof from all snags; after which we went on our way rejoicing; but by this time the heat was becoming intolerable.

"*Blue Earth River.* What unrivalled beauty of landscape, now we pass through dense forests; now through prairie, and anon stretches away a vast savanna of tall prairie grass, thousands of acres in extent, with a vista of high prairie opening in the distance between forests, as far as the sight can extend. Approaching the mouth of the Blue Earth river, never visited by any exploring party before, since the days of LaCoeur [*Le Sueur*] in 1698, we saw a high mount, almost a mountain, looming up in the distance, which we soon found was near the angle of the confluence of the Blue Earth and the Minnesota.[15] Here our company was startled by a cry of buffalo; which, however, proved to be nothing but a drove of moss covered boulders, far away upon the sloping prairie. A log house became visible upon Blue Earth mound, and a person (some French trader) was looking down the river in mute astonishment no doubt, to see the approach of a steamboat.

"Now we have reached the mouth of Blue Earth, the first tributary of the Minnesota from its mouth up. It is a stream apparently about half as large as the Minnesota, and not navigable for more than a mile or two, certainly, being small and rapid; but in looking up its charming valley, there seemed to be resting there a kind of poetic beauty unlike the rivers of earth. We stopped not, but plowed the waters of the Minnesota, still deep, and of a width but little diminished, changing our course now from the southwest to the northwest. Wood: On the south bank of the river, the shore now resounds with the blows of axes and all hands and the passengers are busy in cutting and carrying fuel for the boat. Here, in the woods, we found the red raspberry, and the choke-cherry, and precisely such a growth of woods and of grasses, as we used to see in the rich little intervals of New Hampshire. With a small supply of wood, we hurried on again, being now in the Great Woods; that immense body of timber, twenty or thirty miles wide, which commences at or near Crow Wing

[15] Pierre Charles Le Sueur in 1700 traveled up the Mississippi and Minnesota rivers, and built a fort on the Blue Earth River near its junction with the Minnesota. He took back with him to France a large quantity of what he supposed was copper ore, extracted from the banks of the Blue Earth. Folwell, *Minnesota*, 1:40–42.

on the Mississippi river, and runs 150 miles south, here crossing the Minnesota river like a vast belt.[16]

"Wonderful stream! We still thread its deep, crooked channel, measuring 8 or 9 feet deep, with no difficulty except the too great length of the boat. The face of the country everywhere denotes great fertility. Here we see fresh tracks of the buffalo, where they have crumbled down the steep bank of alluvion, in their haste to drink at the river. Now, far to the north of us, opens a vista of wide interval covered with grass reaching away between the forests on each side of the river, until the scene dissolves in the hazy blue of the far off horizon. — Hot! Oh, How hot! We stop for more wood; not a breath of air. Such heat, we never before experienced; and as for assisting to wood, it was wholly out of the question. The least exercise, produced a violent throbbing of the temples and darkness of vision. We tho't of Calvin Edson and 'sighed for such a frame as his.' That day, at Traverse de Sioux, the thermometer stood at 104 Fahrenheit, in the shade.

"*Cotton Wood River.* Sunset found us emerging from the Great Woods, and all exhausted with the intolerable heat. The Yankee staggered up against the north bank of the river, and there lay panting in the water like a weary Newfoundland dog; while the great sun with his furnaces blazing, sunk behind the distant Missouri. That night, there was no dancing upon the Yankee; but there were several musquitoes to combat, and there was no sleep 'till morn. The ice was nearly exhausted; much of the dry fuel was exhausted, of which it was indispensable to have a supply to make a full head of steam on our return down the river, in order to run the short bends and pass the snags with any sort of safety. At about 9 o'clock in the evening, some of the ladies being almost sick,

[16] The Great Woods, or "Big Woods," as they were usually called by early Minnesota settlers, were composed of hardwood trees. With the progress of settlement this great forest gradually gave way to farms and villages, and now only small remnants remain.

a spirit of mutiny which had been all day gathering, came to a head; and a party was organized to oppose the extension of our trip 200 miles further, to Lac qui Parle. — After discussing the subject, a vote was taken, however, and a very large majority were in favor of proceeding. We were then near the mouth of the Cotton Wood River — in a region becoming more beautiful every mile we should progress, and were approaching a point where the river widened into a sort of lake, affording very easy navigation for at least 80 miles higher, and we had reached within 15 miles of Joseph Laframboise's house, where we wished to leave him and his family, and especially as he promised to make us a present when there, of a fresh slaughtered steer.

"All were anxious to see the remainder of this glorious country, of which Nicollet says:

"'The whole country embraced by the Lower St. Peter's and the Undine Region exceeds any land of the Mississippi above Wisconsin river, as well in the quality and quantity of its timber as the fertility of its soil.'[17]

"But then the excessive heat, the want of dry fuel, the want of ice, the prevalence of musquitoes, the chance of sickness amongst women and children, the great distance from St. Paul, nearly 300 miles, and the possibility to say the least, of some accident to the boat by which we might all be left in a far off wilderness, were urged as reasons for returning. The third night brought no rest. Sun an hour high, the next morning, the Yankee was still moored and but just getting up her steam. — The crew of the boat were weary and disheartened, and there was a degree of reluctance manifested, which made it evident that our further progress would be very slow. The great expense of the trip, although not urged,

[17] Nicollet's "Undine Region" was the region of the Blue Earth Valley. See Joseph N. Nicollet, *Report Intended to Illustrate a Map of the Hydrographical Basin of the Upper Mississippi River* (26 Congress, 2 session, *Senate Documents*, no. 237 — serial 380). Goodhue misquoted Nicollet slightly, and the quotation is here changed to Nicollet's wording.

doubtless had also its influence; and at about 7 o'clock in the morning, it was determined to head the Yankee down stream. We accordingly nailed a board upon a tree, stating the date of the boat's arrival, her name, etc., and the name of the Captain and some of the passengers, and turned back.

"*Homeward Bound*. Now leaps the Yankee down the swift, crooked river. A refreshing breeze springs up — the band discourse enlivening music, the women are again in high feather, and the men also; for there seems to be something of the excitement of danger mingled with joy at our returning, as the boat sweeps the short curves and now steers through a grove of willows, across an obtruding point, or is swept from bow to stern by the obtruding branches of a tree, or plunges into the darkening shadows of a forest. Now the boat seems rushing with suicidal desperation upon a bristling snag in the shortest bend of a curve; a back stroke takes her stern back against the willows on the shore, where she lies until the current swings her bow into the right direction to run clear of the snags, when she again strikes down stream as if her life depended upon her speed. — All safe. Anxiety of passengers is relaxed; but not so of the Captain and the pilot. The Captain always at his post on the hurricane deck through the whole trip up and down, stood, watchful as a spider. In his memory and the pilot's, was a chart of every bend, every snag, every change of the river. It is not too much to say that in the exercise of all the memory, and all the judgment of the force and bearing of the currents and all the prompt coolness requisite in the management of the boat, constantly, but especially in repeated critical emergencies, no Captain but a Harris, seconded by the prompt action of such a pilot and such engineers as he had on his boat, would stand even a reasonable *chance* of conducting such a boat 300 miles down such a river for the first time without damage. Mr. Armstrong, the pilot, was assisted at the wheel by Mr. Brissette.[18] We

[18] Edmund Brissett settled in Minnesota in 1832. Williams, *Saint Paul*, 85.

would do full justice to Mr. Girdon, clerk, who, by his constant and careful attention to the wants and convenience of the passengers, so well compensated for the absence of the Captain from the cabin. Our pleasure was much enhanced by the stirring music of Messrs. Foster, Morgan, and Kirk, of the 6th Regiment band, aided by Mr. Eldridge with his violin, who also called the changes in cotillions.

"*Cannel Coal.* At noon on the 4th day, we reached the mouth of the Blue Earth river, up which the Yankee ran for a few rods, and nailed up a shingle. Much did we desire to wander 6 miles up that stream to the ruins of the trading post — a spot made historic by the adventures of La Coeur in 1698; but time forbade. We contented ourselves with wandering for an hour along the pebbly beach in search of curiosities. We saw a very perfect specimen of petrified wood, and some cornelians and agates, and a variety of odd shells; but what interested us more, was the discovery on the shore of several small specimens of what appeared to be mineral coal, precisely resembling the kind called cannel coal. Capt. Harris has one of the specimens; the Rev. Mr. Neill has a small specimen of it, which will be examined by a chemical test. A Frenchman living there, said there was a large, solid body of it in the bank of the river, a few miles up the Blue Earth.

"Again we are on our rapid way down stream. Fifteen miles below the Blue Earth, we came suddenly upon Turtle Bend, the high-water mark of the Wayne. Here the captain used the precaution to warp the boat down stern foremost below the snags, by the use of anchors and cables. We took down the board which the Wayne challenged us to bring back to Saint Paul, and put another in its place, and sped onward.

"At the place where we took rails for fuel on our way up, we landed and took on board all that remained; and speeding onward, soon rounded to for the night at Traverse de Sioux. Having been destitute of ice for several hours, we hastened to the Mission-house of the Rev. Mr. Hopkins, where we found plenty of cool well water. Mr. Neill and others had a pleasant interview with the families of the missionaries, remaining with them over night, while in the cabin of the Yankee, all who wished joined in the joyous cotillion.

"*The Fifth Day*. Bright and early on Friday morning, with a supply of cold water and new milk on board, having distributed presents amongst the Indians on shore, the Yankee was again on her way, plunging rapidly along. We passed an hour or so at the village of Little Six, where we found very sturdy beggars, and were annoyed with demands upon us for the satisfaction of various promises which had been made by passengers on the Anthony Wayne. Little Six and a hundred more came on board, when his majesty made a long speech to Mr. Wells, the only person present who could understand him.[19] He said 'he demanded presents for wharfage — that they must be paid for having their corn-fields trampled down by the whites, although it was true, their corn was not much, being damaged by the freshet — that it had been said about St. Paul, that his people believed that the freshet was a judgment sent upon them by the Great Spirit on account of steamboats coming up that river; but his people in fact believed no such thing, but were glad to see steamboats, especially if they brought suitable presents.'

"Having distributed two bolts of calico, and other presents amongst the Indians, we were off again, and at sunset reached Fort Snelling, where a shade of gloom was thrown over the company by news of the death of Mrs. Cooper, wife of Judge Cooper, of our company, and of the death also of Mrs. Ethridge, mother of another one of our company. Touching at Mendota we again proceeded homeward; but before rounding to amidst the enthusiastic shouts of welcome, such as St. Paul knows how to greet her friends with, at the Lower Land-

[19] James Wells established a trading post on Lake Pepin in 1831. He was a member of the first territorial legislature. *Minnesota History*, 20:307 (September, 1939); *House Journal*, 1849, p. 3.

ing, the following resolution was unanimously adopted and agreed to be signed as a card by the whole company:

" 'The undersigned, fellow passengers on board the steamboat Yankee, on the excursion just made by that boat for a distance of nearly 300 miles up the Minnesota river, and back again, without the slightest accident, while the boat encountered the constant hazard of navigating waters never before traversed by a steamboat, express their unqualified approbation of the skill, patience, and untiring attention of the Captain, officers, and men of the boat, to their comfort and safety.'

"Thus ended this eventful voyage of exploration, so replete with novelty and stirring incident, that it will be remembered while life lasts; and thus by a series of efforts, has been demonstrated the enviable commercial position of our young town.

"Not 20 years ago, near the south end of Lake Michigan, a few cabins clustered upon the low sandy shore of that lake. Well do we remember the time. Upon one side was stretched the restless lake, and elsewhere, in every direction a vast expanse of marshy prairie. The picturesque scenery of Fox river, the enchanting vallies of the O'Plain [*Des Plaines*] and the Dupage rivers, and the bewitching liveliness of the Rock river valley, had yet yielded no allegiance to the husbandman. Chicago actually suffered for want of the necessaries of life. Transient steamboats arrived there with cargoes of restless Yankees. Hundreds of those who arrived, glanced at the forlorn hopes of a town which had no trade, in a country which produced nothing as yet but swarms of mosquitoes; took in a bird's eye view of the marsh, or rode out perhaps as far as Berry's Point or Flagg Creek, and then taking the first boat, bade forever farewell to the 'Eelenoy in general and Chicago in particular.'

"Precisely such, is the history of the growth of St. Paul. With at least equal commercial advantages here, hundreds of those who arrived expected to find Minnesota a cultivated

Eden, without a barren spot — and St. Paul a Milwaukee or Chicago, in which however, corner lots could be had on time at a merely nominal price, and quarter sections adjoining the town, be entered at $1.25 per acre. Such people have been disappointed. They have been blown away like chaff before the wind. They are gone, carrying with them, doubtless, unfavorable reports of a country about which they know nothing; but they have left behind them in Minnesota, hundreds of substantial, energetic men, who have the foresight and judgment to comprehend the advantages of our town, and who will stand manfully up and aid in developing the resources of Minnesota. They are the men to build up a city and to profit, utimately, in its growth. Ten years hence, when St. Paul is numbered, as it will be, with the great cities of the Mississippi, their enterprise and their sacrifices will be gratefully remembered."

12. On to Suland

IN THE SUMMER OF 1851 TOOK PLACE THE GREAT EVENT FOR
which Minnesotans had been eagerly waiting since the establishment of the territory — the negotiation of treaties with the
Sioux. By these treaties the Indians sold to the United States
large tracts in Iowa and Minnesota, including most of southern Minnesota between the Mississippi River and the western
boundary of the state. The place selected for the treaty with
the upper bands, the Sisseton and Wahpeton, was Traverse
des Sioux, a trading post and mission station on the Minnesota
River near the present town of St. Peter. The treaty with the
lower bands, the Mdewakanton and Wahpekute, was held
at Mendota.[1]

On June 29, 1851, the two treaty commissioners named by
the president, Governor Ramsey and Luke Lea, the United
States commissioner of Indian affairs, with about thirty interested persons, Goodhue among them, left Fort Snelling on
the steamboat "Excelsior" for Traverse des Sioux, where they
arrived the next day. There, on "an inclined expanse of
prairie, nearly surrounded by a bend of the river," they de-
posited their baggage and provisions, pitched their tents, and
awaited the Indians.[2]

The Indians, however, straggled in in small groups from
day to day, and it was not until July 18 that they had assembled in numbers sufficient to warrant the beginning of
negotiations. Meantime, during the long days of waiting, the
treaty party, in their primitive tent village, endured violent
thunder storms and deluges of rain, combatted swarms of

---

[1] On the negotiation of the treaties and their provisions, see Folwell,
Minnesota, 1:266–304. The texts of the treaties may be found in United States,
Statutes at Large, 10:949–959.
[2] *Pioneer*, July 3, 1851.

gnats and mosquitoes, and lived on a fare of beef, biscuits, and pilot bread "harder than the horns of thunder." The Indians provided entertainment with ball games, dances, mock battles and buffalo hunts, and exhibitions of horsemanship.[3]

In a series of lively and entertaining letters which were published in the *Pioneer*, Goodhue reported in detail the events at Traverse des Sioux, the appearance, dress, customs, and mode of life of the Indians, the speeches of white men and Indians during the negotiations, and the dramatic scene of the signing of the treaty. Because of the length of the correspondence and also because it has been republished elsewhere, it is not reprinted here.[4] Instead, selections have been made from Goodhue's editorials on the treaties, which give an excellent idea of the attitude of prospective settlers in the "Suland," and of Minnesotans in general, on the subject. They reflect the exhilaration of the people over the successful negotiations, which gave place before long to impatience over the delay of Congress in ratifying the treaties; and they reveal how the restless settlers, refusing to await what to them was merely the unwinding of so much legal red tape, even before the ratification of the treaties in June, 1852, swarmed across the Mississippi River and staked their claims in "that broad

[3] *Pioneer*, July 24, 1851.
[4] The accounts of the treaty at Traverse des Sioux, in the form of "Editorial Correspondence," appeared in the issues of the *Pioneer* from July 3 to August 7, inclusive. Goodhue left the treaty ground for St. Paul on July 21, and on the same day William G. Le Duc, correspondent for the *New York Tribune* and other papers, arrived at the Traverse. An arrangement was made between the two that Le Duc should use Goodhue's notes for his account to that date, and that Goodhue should have access to Le Duc's notes covering the treaty from then on. The *Pioneer* accounts are substantially reprinted in Le Duc, *Minnesota Year Book for 1852*, 27–70, and in Thomas Hughes and W. C. Brown, *Old Traverse des Sioux*, 33–73 (St. Peter, 1929). With the treaty party was Frank B. Mayer, an artist who made sketches and kept a diary, which has been edited by Bertha L. Heilbron and published under the title *With Pen and Pencil on the Frontier in 1851: The Diary and Sketches of Frank Blackwell Mayer* (St. Paul, 1932). The portion covering the Traverse des Sioux treaty may be found on pages 145 to 189. Goodhue also attended the treaty with the lower Sioux at Mendota, his account of which appeared in the *Pioneer* for August 7 and 14.

Canaan of fertile lands," hoping, with good reason, as it
turned out, that any illegalities would be adjusted later.

The first of Goodhue's editorials on the treaties appeared in
the *Pioneer* of July 3, 1851:

"At length, Mr. Lea, the Commissioner of Indian Affairs,
has arrived, and in company with the other commissioners,
has gone up to Traverse des Sioux, about 100 miles up the
Minnesota river, to attend the treaty; the chiefs and braves
being already assembled there for that purpose. It is gratifying
to know, that this treaty is deemed, at Washington, of sufficient importance, to call the Commissioners here in person
to attend to it; and with the aid of Gov. Ramsey, who has
unbounded influence with the whole tribe, and with the hearty
co-operation and assistance of those traders who have, by a
long course of honorable and liberal dealing with them, have
their favor and confidence, there is every reason to believe
that a treaty can and will be effected. Of the value of the
treaty to Minnesota, and its importance to Saint Paul, there
can be but one sensible opinion. Thousands upon thousands,
in and out of Minnesota, are anxiously and impatiently waiting for this treaty and for the opening of the magnificent
country, which is spread out west of us, like a beautiful map
— a country full of game, and heavy timber, and delightful
prairies and rich bottom lands — its resources of natural wealth,
not only not exhausted, but, as yet, scarcely seen.

"We now inhabit but the margin of Minnesota — a portion
of it, which might be pared off, and would hardly seem to
diminish the size of the Territory. Our population is pressing
hard upon the Indian possessions. Saint Paul, increasing in
buildings, in business and population, with magic rapidity,
looks earnestly across the river for the unceded lands. The
wigwam is in sight of our office, from which, the growing
importance of our town and territory, already demands the
issue of a daily paper. The wild Sioux is daily in our streets,
beholding our progress with amazement. The civilization of

those bands, even nearest to us, by any present agencies and during the living generation, is utterly hopeless; and the welfare of the Indians requires their speedy removal, from a neighborhood which makes them daily more dependent, and in which they learn the vices but attain to none of the virtues of a civilized life."

The treaty with the upper Sioux was signed on July 23, and in a long editorial in the *Pioneer* of July 31, Goodhue exulted over the event and upbraided the editor of the *Democrat*, Daniel A. Robertson, who, in the issues of his paper for July 22 and 29, had insinuated that there was more behind the treaty than met the eye. He had commented that Governor Ramsey and "Messrs. Sibley & Co." were "the real parties to the Treaty," that the "Indians were like potters' clay in the hands of those who trade with them," and that Lea was "in the situation of a *green horn* with a pocket full of money among old gamblers." Robertson had reference to a provision of the treaty which stipulated that $275,000 of the $1,665,000 to be paid the Indians for their lands was to be used for their removal to the reservation provided for them, for their subsistence during the first year after their removal, and "to enable them to settle their affairs and comply with their present just engagements." Their "present just engagements" were, of course, their debts to the traders. Immediately after signing the treaty, the Indians had signed also a paper in which they acknowledged their obligations to the traders and pledged themselves to pay them.[5] Goodhue's editorial follows:

"The news of the treaty exhilarates our town; and it looks as fresh and lively and blooming! — It is the greatest event by far in the history of the Territory, since it was organized. It is the pillar of fire that lights us into a broad Canaan of fertile lands. We behold now, clearly, in no remote perspective,

---

[5] *Statutes at Large*, 10:950; Folwell, *Minnesota*, 1:282. The Indians' agreement with the traders may be found in 32 Congress, 2 session, *Senate Executive Documents*, no. 29, part 2, pp. 22–24 (serial 660).

like an exhibition of dissolving views, the red savages, with
their tepees, their horses, and their famished dogs, fading,
vanishing, dissolving away; and in their places, a thousand
farms, with their fences and white cottages, and waving wheat
fields, and vast jungles of rustling maize, and villages and
cities crowned with spires, and railroads with trains of cars
rumbling afar off — and now nearer and nearer, the train
comes thundering across the bridge into St. Paul, fifteen hours
from St. Louis, on the way to Lake Superior. Is this a dream?
What, but a dream, then, is the history of the Northwest for
the last 20 years?

"The treaty is made. It is a good treaty. It has been skill-
fully negotiated. The amount to be paid to the Indians is
not larger than they ought to receive, and certainly not as
large as it would be beneficial to our Territory to have dis-
bursed, for the increase of our business and the home consumption of such products as we shall have to sell to the
Indians. There are men in the world who have more than a
single idea, and that an addled one, in their heads. Such a
man is Commissioner Lea — a gentleman who has conducted
the treaty with a full and perfect knowledge of the various
interests involved in the treaty, the interests of this Territory,
the interests of the Indians, and his duty to the Government.
There are wretches base enough to malign any man, however
good, and any motive however pure. The press, as well as the
pulpit, has its bigots, its Mawworms. As the beetle with its
little black eyes cannot see beyond the apple or the leaf it
crawls upon, so a little partizan editor is incapable of taking
a liberal and extended view of any subject; and if he is a
Democrat or thinks he is a Democrat, although he may be as
haughty as Lucifer, and have as much upstart pride in his
composition as would starch all Secretary Smith's tall cravats,
he is as much of a monomaniac about Democracy, as Aunt
Betsey is, in 'David Copperfield,' about 'donkeys.' Is this
treaty to be opposed, is half the Territory to be hissed onto it

like a pack of senseless curs, because the treaty has been effected without the agency or advice of the Winnebago Fur
Company organ? All we ask, is his open, avowed opposition
to the treaty. Come out, like a white man, and make up an
issue before the people, and tell them, if you dare, that you
have come to Minnesota for a purpose so vile and selfish, as
to oppose the acquisition, or the possibility for many years,
of the acquisition of this fine Indian Territory of more than
90,000 square miles, which if acquired, will add immediate,
immense wealth to Minnesota, and make Saint Paul third only
in the rank of cities on the Mississippi.

"There was once a wretch vile enough, from selfish and
personal motives, to fire the Alexandrian Library; but compared with the pitiful scoundrel who would attempt to rob
Minnesota of the lands, the population, the wealth, which
this treaty, if ratified, will give us, that incendiary was a
saint, who deserved to be canonized. Must every thing, however vital to the interests of the whole Territory, be dragged
down and swashed and wallowed about, in the vile vortex
of politics? Why, there is not a solitary human being in Minnesota, who is not deeply interested in the treaty, although
some are certainly more interested than others; and if there
are any opposed to it, they are actuated only by that vile
spirit of envy, 'which drags angels down.'

"To the Indians themselves, the treaty is now indispensable
to their very existence. Especially the ensuing winter, without
the treaty, these poor wretches must die off by hundreds.
The high water has ruined their corn, and they will entirely
lose their summer buffalo hunt, by having spent the season
in coming to, remaining at, and returning from the treaty.
Whenever they came from their remote homes to the treaty, it
became almost a settled thing that they *must* sell their lands,
or perish by starvation next winter. They have nothing to
subsist on, and perish they must and will, unless they can subsist upon faith and credit of the treaty by the Senate. This

is a fact, to the Sioux Indians, a most serious and appalling fact, and to the Government a truth which ought to be stamped upon the memory of the Senate in burning letters, that many thousands of these poor wretches, have assembled at the treaty, by the invitation of the government, and in full faith that a treaty would be made and ratified and that they should subsist, notwithstanding they lose their whole summer hunt and corn crop.

"The Commissioners must, under these circumstances, have had everything, in time, in their own way; and we should be ashamed of human nature, and ashamed of our government, if the Commissioners were to drive the best bargain they could, and obtain their lands for the least possible amount. What could the Indians do? Without a solitary day's provisions on hand, feeding from the hand of government from hour to hour, without even the possibility of returning home, without obtaining some supplies from the Commissioners — these 2000 people, who represent the Upper Sioux attending the treaty at the Traverse, were as much at the mercy of the Government, as a poor woman with a family of starving children, is at the mercy of the pawn-broker, to whom she carries the last article of furniture from her home, to pawn or sell for something to eat. Nay, worse. There may be competition amongst pawn-brokers; but our Government alone can buy land of the Indian. If any thing better than a mean, huckstering spirit, worthy of a nation of peddlers and pawn-brokers, pervades our national government, there is no probability, and we may say from a knowledge of the provisions of the treaty, no *possibility*, that the treaty will be rejected, for the reason that it provides for the payment of *too much*, for the purchase of this vast country, larger than any State, and which, when sold, will pay into the treasury of the United States, not less than $50,000,000, after making a liberal deduction for waste lands and for donations of lands for public purposes.

"Looking at the subject then in every light, whether in reference to the absolute necessity of the treaty to the Indians themselves, or to the clamorous demands of 10,000 whites to occupy and settle the Sioux lands, a demand so loud, so pressing, so imperious, that it will be next to impossible to resist it; a pressure, which is hourly increasing, and must soon break over from the East and the South, treaty or no treaty, into those lands which Congress guaranties to the Indian the undisturbed possession of; or whether in reference to the interests of the Treasury, or of the duty of Congress to extinguish Indian titles in Minnesota, as they have been extinguished elsewhere; or whether, especially in reference to the fact, that if this treaty is now ratified, Minnesota will make but two states, divided by a line extending east and west, but that if the treaty is not made, the East, or ceded part of Minnesota, will make one state, and the West side, or unceded part, be eventually formed into two more states — in every view of the subject, we can see no reason why the treaty should not be received with universal favor, provided it is liberal enough to the Indians to comport with the dignity, justice and generosity of this great nation, towards its wards — the helpless, homeless, houseless Indians, who are vanishing like the dew before the rising sunshine of our national greatness."

In the *Pioneer* of December 25, 1851, it is evident that Goodhue had revised his prediction that, if the treaties should be ratified, Minnesota Territory would "make but two states, divided by a line running east and west," and had come to believe that the territory would "soon come into the Union . . . as *one* State." But his belief in the existence of "coal banks" on the Blue Earth River was evidently as strong as it was when he journeyed up the Minnesota River on the "Yankee" in 1850, for here he uses the mythical Blue Earth coal beds as an argument for the ratification of the treaties:

"This is the long session of Congress; and whether that august body will do any thing until the 4th of March next, but intrigue and plan and arrange for President-making, is uncertain. After the 4th of March, commences the summer session. As the Presidential Conventions will be over and the candidates for that office nominated in the spring, or early in the summer, we may expect that some time in the summer, if not sooner, the business of the ratification of treaties will come up and be acted upon by the Senate.

"The intervening period, will be one of suspense and extreme anxiety to Minnesota, to St. Paul, and we may well say, to the whole valley of the Mississippi river; every foot of which, from the Lakes to the Gulf of Mexico, is deeply interested in its ratification, and in the early development of all the resources and trade of this river to its sources. It is also a question of deep and intense interest, to the multitude of hardy settlers upon the frontiers of the Sioux lands, and we may say throughout the United States, who are, even now, restrained with the utmost difficulty, from entering these choice lands, for the purpose of cultivation, mining and trade. The opening of the coal banks alone, upon the Blue Earth river, to supply the demand for coal, and especially for the consumption of steamboats, renders the early, nay the immediate possession of the lands embraced in the treaties, indispensable to the steamboat business of the river. Galena, Dubuque, St. Louis, Burlington, New Orleans, every town on the river, as well as St. Paul, has a vital interest at stake in the ratification of the Sioux treaties.

"To the Indians themselves, it is indispensable. To the Government, it is vastly important, in an economical view. With the treaty ratified, with the possession and occupancy and settlement of these lands, Minnesota will soon be a State, say in two or three years. Without these lands, Minnesota will remain a dwarfed and blighted Territory for years, an annual tax upon the Treasury of the United States. With that territory, Minnesota will not only soon come into the Union as a State, but the whole of it, except the portion reserved for a permanent Indian possession will come in as *one* State. If the west side be settled up simultaneously with the east side of the Mississippi, our population will be homogeneous, united now and forever, in their relations with each other, as one State; but if the east side first harden into the gristle and frame and shape of a State, by itself, the west side, when it shall be settled, will never be united with the east side, as a portion of the same State; the Treasury will then be taxed for years with the support of another Territorial Government west of the river, embracing the lands for which these treaties are made. Again, there is not only a great deal of money expended, to effect these treaties, but the terms of the treaties are far more favorable to the Government, than the Indians will ever again consent to, and the amount they are to receive is actually less than the Government ought to be willing to pay to the poor wretches.

"But aside from all this, it will be impossible, we speak advisedly, it will be utterly impossible to dam out the white population another year. They must and will go in; and unless the treaties be ratified, Government will have to witness the humiliating spectacle of seeing these Indian lands over-run with farmers and mechanics who cannot be kept out, or *attempt* their forcible expulsion by military power."

Goodhue's conviction that ratification was "no longer a question of expediency, but one of necessity" was the basis of an editorial in the *Pioneer* of March 4, 1852:

"Nothing now before the public mind of Minnesota, is of half as much importance as the ratification of the treaties. Divorce bills, railroad bills, ferry charters, liquor laws — all other objects of public or private concern, sink into insignificance, compared with this. However our people may be divided on other questions, upon this, we are unanimous, that the treaties must be ratified. Heretofore, we have generally agreed that the treaties were expedient; but in the present conditions of things, it is no longer a question of expediency, but one of necessity — of necessity to the whites, of necessity to the Indians — and we might almost say, of necessity to the Government.

"With but a narrow portion of territory, entirely on the east side of the Mississippi river, of ceded lands, including a large share of swamps and land that is not arable, Congress rightly judged that it was needful to the growth and development of Minnesota, to extinguish the Indian title on the west side of the river. In anticipation of this, the Organic Act very properly provided for the exercise and enjoyment of political rights, on the west side of the river, as upon the east side. *It was hardly worth while for Congress to give a territorial government, to the narrow strip only of Minnesota, that was ceded.* — When Congress gave Minnesota a government, it also gave a pledge to extinguish the Indian title. Without the lands on the west side, Minnesota was a mere *rind*, a mere *paring*, a mere *husk* and *shell* of a territory. Government well understood this. Would $20,000 or $30,000 a year, be expended for the government of a mere county, a mere handful of our people? Or, did government contemplate the existence and growth here of a giant State, advancing with rapid strides to the dignity of a sovereign of the confederacy?

"The usual liberality of Congress, the experience of all other territories, the very creation of a territorial government for us, but above all, the appropriation of money last year for the express purpose of effecting treaties and extinguishing the Indian title, was proof, *was demonstration,* that the lands west of the river were to be ours. — Our own people and immigrants from abroad, over the face of the whole world, have acted upon the faith that the Indian title would be extinguished. Hundreds have sold out their possessions at home, and moved here, expressly to occupy these lands. The Indians have also acted upon the same expectation — they have permitted the settlers to come into their midst and live — they have fed upon the substance of the white man; for having, last season, done nothing but attend treaties, and being ever since ready, like the children of Israel before their Exodus from Egypt, for their departure, 'with their loins girt about,' they have had nothing to live on but what they could borrow, beg, or steal. The government ought to know and to understand, that the Sioux have been saved from starvation the past winter by the whites; and that but for their aid, a voice of lamentation and suffering from the Dakotas, such as was never before heard, would have filled the ears of their Great Father.

"If the Sioux Agent had possessed the power (and five hundred Sioux Agents could not have done it!) to keep the white settlers out, since the treaty, it would have been cruelty and starvation to the Indians, to have kept them out. Settlers have not only gone over, but have built houses and stables, and cleared lands, not dozens of settlers, or scores, or hundreds, but thousands of them — not near the river alone, but every where from the line of Iowa up, along the waters of Cannon river, the Vermillion, and the whole length of the fertile Minnesota, and upon the waters of the Blue Earth. Men are exploring for coal and minerals around the head waters of the Des Moines — the whole country west, for a vastly greater extent than the whole part of Minnesota, east of the river, is now swarming with settlers and alive with daring men of enterprise; some with families, living in brand new log houses, and others without; but none of them having the remotest idea of doing any thing short of staying where they are, and buying their lands of the Government, whenever they are offered for sale.

"Meantime the Indians, who just begin to understand that if the treaties are not ratified, they are in danger of losing their homes without getting any equivalent, payment or annuities for their lands, are becoming exceedingly jealous; and do not hesitate to theaten violence to the settlers who have come in, in case the treaties are not ratified and settlers do not leave. That the Sioux Indians, the most war-like of all the

tribes in North America, will form war parties and attack
the settlers — that we shall have an Indian war — (for the
settlers will never abandon their homes alive,) is just as inevitable as fate, unless the treaties be ratified.

"Let every person attend the mass meeting at the Capitol,
next Monday evening. Let Minnesota send up a voice to the
Senate that cannot be misunderstood. 'THE TREATIES MUST
BE RATIFIED.'"

The meeting which Goodhue thus urged Minnesotans to
attend was held on the afternoon of March 8. According to
the account in the *Pioneer* of March 11, thousands of people
from all over the territory assembled at the Capitol, "filling
every corner of the building, and blocking the doors and
windows, while on the outside, were hundreds anxiously and
breathlessly listening." Goodhue explained to the assembly
the object of the meeting, and moved that a committee of three
be appointed to draft a memorial to Congress urging ratification. The committee appointed pursuant to the motion, consisting of the editors of St. Paul's three newspapers, Goodhue,
Robertson, and Owens, speedily drafted a memorial couched
in urgent language, which was adopted and forthwith sent
to Washington.

Whether or not the memorial affected the final decision of
Congress, it failed to move that body to haste in its delibera-
tions on the subject. When the Senate committee on Indian
affairs, to which the treaties had been referred, took them
up for consideration in April, ratification was opposed by
Southern senators, who wanted no accessions of lands or
settlers to a Northern territory, which before long would be
seeking admission to the Union as a free state. When ratification was finally accomplished on June 23, it was by a small
margin of votes. It was to this opposition from the Southern
element in the Senate that Goodhue addressed an editorial
in the *Pioneer* of May 27, 1852, entitled "The Policy of the
South Toward the Northwest":

"There are some things yet, that excite our marvel. During the present century, not only has Florida been purchased, but Louisiana, and added to the national domain, at an expense of many millions. Texas has been annexed, at a vast expense. New Mexico and California have been added to our national empire, at the price of a bloody war. In all these measures for extending our eagle empire, the great, free west, has contributed her full share, of men and of treasure. We have never stopped to inquire, whether any of these acquisitions were more designed to promote the aggrandizement of the South than of the North. In whatever conflicts that have ensued, in Congress or out of Congress, in all the contests of extremists, for and against slavery, the States of the Northwest have uniformly acted with honorable impartiality, invariably sustaining by their votes, all the rights guaranteed to the States by the Constitution, to their fullest, amplest extent.

"The votes of the Northwest have built up a levee, to protect the South from the inundations of abolitionism. Through the Mississippi river, the Northwest has poured a perpetually increasing stream of produce and of commerce, into the lap of the South. A noble railroad is now extending from Lake Michigan to the Gulf of Mexico, to bind us with a band of iron to the South. The national laws of trade, the course of rivers, habitual, well-worn channels of intercourse, their interest and our interest, all bind us to the South. There is not a possibility, without maintaining and increasing the volume of trade flowing South through this valley, for the South long to make any pretension ever *to divide the empire of trade on the Atlantic, of which New York is the centre.* If the South would be true to herself, and to the Northwest, every acre of land drained by the Mississippi and its tributaries, would find a commercial mart at New Orleans, or Mobile, or Charleston, or Savannah, and at such other towns South of this valley, as might be made most accessible to us by railroad, or by steamboats; for by the laws of trade, exchanges of products seek the nearest routes *across* isothermal lines — products of the equator moving North, and products of the temperate and polar regions, moving South.

"Yet what do we behold? When the Northwest asks the South to aid in opening and extending her settlements — asks, that at a trifling expense, 30,000,000 of acres more of fine lands shall be opened for settlement, by the extinguishment of the title of the Sioux Indians — when we ask for these measures, calculated to benefit and enlarge the trade of the South, by giving her more customers, more produce, more steamboats, what does the Northwest behold? Opposition from the South? We pause to see if it be so. The great Northwest, anxiously waits to know, if the South really intends to spurn us, with haughty contumely. We await in silence the action of the Senate upon the treaties of Minnesota; and well will the Northwest note and remember *who are her friends.*"

On June 26 the steamboat "Excelsior" steamed up to the St. Paul levee with the news that the treaties had been ratified. How much it meant to Minnesotans is revealed in Goodhue's account of the reception of the news in the *Pioneer* of July 1, under the title "A Glance at St. Paul Last Saturday Evening":

"On Saturday night last, looking down 100 feet from Bench street, we saw up stream, the Excelsior, moving up toward Mendota, and down stream, near the bend, the Old Franklin going down and the West Newton coming; and this scene, near the sunset of the glorious day that brought us news of the ratification, seemed to fill the heart of our town with joy.

"It was one of those glorious, eventful hours, which those who live here will long remember and describe to their children, when Saint Paul shall become a thronged city. The unfinished excavations and grades on Third and Fourth and Jackson and Sibley streets, rendering them impassable — the hope of ratification almost quenched, the loss of the costly hotel and of Mr. Baker's house, on the Wednesday before[6] — in fact the darkness of despair almost shrouded us, when the Excelsior came with the news, confirmed soon after by the West Newton — and if ever the light of joy blazed suddenly in the face of a sorrowing town, like lightning in a black cloud, it was here; the news flashed over town —no need of telegraphs; for various extras were out with the news, in half an hour, scattering across the whole Territory.

"At sunset, the three steamboats disappeared and our people piled up fire barrels and kindled up blazing illuminations, along the bluff, notwithstanding the moon took the shine all out of the bonfires; and speeches were made by Mr. Baker and Mr. [William D.] Phillips and we know not by whom beside. In fact, it was one of the nights we might read of, but such as few if any three year old towns have experienced. Nothing was wanting but the ringing of one half dozen church bells; which was omitted simply for want of some concert and arrangement to have it done."

[6] The hotel was built by J. Daniels at a cost of $12,000, and had been opened for business only a few days before the fire, which occurred on June 23. According to the *Democrat* of June 30, 1852, "The new building adjoining, belonging to Baker & Nickerson, worthy mechanics, was also consumed."

13. These Are the Things

GOODHUE'S LOVE FOR MINNESOTA, HIS FAITH IN ITS DESTINY, colored every issue of his newspaper. With the optimism and impatience characteristic of the pioneer, he wanted his dreams for the territory to become immediate realities. If he had had forewarning that the time allotted him would be so short — that he would live to see but the bare beginnings of Minnesota's development — he could hardly have been more impatient to hasten its progress. Weekly in the *Pioneer* he called attention to the needs of the territory, urging that something be done about them with the utmost dispatch.

One need which he considered "of vital importance" was a bridge across the Mississippi at St. Paul. "It is the most southern point probably on the river," he wrote in the *Pioneer* of December 12, 1849, "where a railroad can be carried over on a bridge, so as to make a continuous line of iron rails between the Atlantic and Pacific oceans. It would converge to this point, all the main East and West roads — all the avenues of trade, travel and business, extending East and West, from the source of the Mississippi to as far south as the natural radius of the business of St. Louis, at least; making St. Paul the busy focus of converging roads and railways, and a free bridge here, the gateway between the two oceans." He urged that all Minnesotans "unite in asking Congress for a donation of the Sioux lands, as soon as a treaty is made and ratified, sufficient to build at Saint Paul, a substantial bridge — a National bridge, to be free in all coming time, for all but the enemies of our beloved country." [1]

Minnesota's wretched mail service tried the editor's patience

[1] The first bridge across the Mississippi was built, not at St. Paul, but at St. Anthony. It was a suspension bridge, and it was first opened to traffic in 1855. Atwater, *Minneapolis*, part 1, p. 349.

to exasperation. The mail came up from Prairie du Chien by team, over a road on the east side of the Mississippi which Goodhue described as "rough, hilly, impassable much of the time," with many streams to be crossed. There were times when several weeks went by without mail from outside the territory. In his paper for April 22, 1852, Goodhue urged as a matter "of the *first* and *highest* importance, that a mail route be opened *this* season, on the west side of the Mississippi river, from St. Paul to Dubuque; and that next winter, we have a daily mail route through, if we have to pay for it by private contribution. . . . if the road were opened, there would soon be towns, villages, daily stages, and Minnesota would never again be caught on the 16th of April, isolated." This route, he explained, would be shorter by one-third than that on the east side of the river, and the road could be kept in better condition. But it was not alone bad roads that he blamed for the delay in the mails. In the *Pioneer* of February 26, 1852, the Prairie du Chien postmaster came in for a sound drubbing:

"We received a mail last Friday. It is provoking, that our whole Territory has been put on an allowance of only one mail a week; when the Government has paid for carrying two mails; that we have been thus starved for news, because the old ass who is P. M. at Prairie du Chien, has been either too obstinate or too selfish and indolent, to make up and forward two mails a week. It takes this administration to keep such men in office. Why, this P. M. is so notoriously negligent of his duty, that he not only robs a whole Territory of half its mail accommodations, but he does not pretend to sort and distribute his mails, when he sends them; but here comes through to St. Paul, week after week, a part or the whole of the mail of St. Croix and Lake Superior, to be sent back again from there. Yet knowing the utter unfitness of that man for the office — for any office — and knowing it for years, he is still retained, to favor some spooney of his, who has the President's ear."

Production Goodhue considered Minnesota's greatest need — manufactures, "every sort of manufactures that can be named," and, above all, agricultural production. Time and again he urged the people of Minnesota to raise enough crops to supply their own needs. "There is waste industry and unemployed muscle enough, at this moment," he wrote, "in St. Paul and St. Anthony, if wisely and energetically exerted in agriculture here, to produce a surplus of provisions for the Territory and leave the balance of trade abroad, in our favor. There is land enough, as good land as the Almighty ever finished up, lying uncultivated, between St. Paul and St. Anthony, to profitably employ every man and boy, capable of manual labor, in this Territory. . . . There is something wrong — some screw loose in society, when young men cannot be tempted away from the towns, to labor upon these rich lands that every where surround us — there by a few months of patient toil and self-denial to make themselves comfortable homes, independent free-holders." [2] In order to "convince *some* of the thirty lawyers in our town, as well as other professional gentlemen, including the whole of that genteel class of loafers, who are waiting for something to *turn up* that the best thing they can do is to turn up the sod," he tried to show, in the *Pioneer* of October 10, 1850, how "any industrious man can soon make a fortune in Minnesota, by farming." He used as an example a ten-acre crop of potatoes, and, taking into consideration all costs, including the original cost of the land, he estimated the clear gain from a single crop "a fine ten acres and $778.50." In the issue of the next week he asked in a heading "What Is Requisite for Minnesota?"; and he answered his question in the article under it:

"Not a better climate, not a better soil, not purer water, not more of Government patronage; not better facilities for commerce — not anything, in short, but *more production*. Before we can really thrive we must produce amongst ourselves,

[2] *Pioneer*, May 13, June 3, 1852.

all of the oats, corn, wheat, potatoes and other vegetable productions that are needed. High prices, extravagant rents and
large incomes, will not avail much, until we can prevent the
enormous annual drain of specie, which flows down the river,
to pay for produce, and the freights on produce. To produce
something at home, to pay off the annual balances due us in
the river trade, is what we want and is the only method by
which our wealth and our river business can be much increased. With the exception of lumber and cranberries, we
pay for everything we wear, and all that we eat, or nearly
all, out of Indian payments, Government contracts, and the
expenditures of the annual Territorial appropriation for the
government of the Territory. All this out drain of specie, for
provisions, ought to be stopped at once. It is bleeding us to
death. It makes Minnesota worth every thing to the country
below and nothing to herself.

"Stop this weakening depletion, and our territory would
increase faster in wealth, than any other part of the world.
This is a matter, not only of interest to us all, in the aggregate, but to every individual of us. — No man is more truly
a benefactor to our Territory, than he who helps to stop one
of these bleeding veins, and to stay the specie carried in
through the Government arteries, so that it may circulate
amongst us. It is not only a work of profit, but a work of
patriotism, to cultivate our soil. —

"We are pleased to see one example of this kind, the present season, by one of our citizens, whose example is almost a
law,[3] and we hear of extensive farms being opened up along
the Mississippi, by men who see and feel the importance of
such improvements. Every man, in every one of our villages,
ought at least to cultivate a garden next season. The great
idea is to save money — we can *make* money fast enough in
Minnesota, if we could only stop the leaks, we should be

[3] The reference is probably to Governor Ramsey, who had a farm a short
distance northwest of St. Paul. *Democrat*, August 26, 1851.

getting rich, and a trade of exchange and barter would soon grow up between the country and villages, which would make us thriving and independent. To commence this thing, let every man manage to put a ten acre lot in cultivation next year, all who do so, the whole territory will be benefited by it — in autumn, the balance of trade below, will be in our favor — we shall be out of debt — and shall be able to lay up much of the large expenditures amongst us of public money, for those expenditures will still remain as large as if we produce nothing, but a few furs and cranberries. An argument to convince the people of Minnesota that any soil or climate is better adapted to agriculture than ours, is useless. We have nothing to do, to secure unrivaled prosperity, but for every man to lay hold of the plough-handles."

One great hindrance to production in Minnesota, Goodhue felt, was the holding of lands for speculation by nonresidents. "These gentry" he wanted "to see . . . used up in every possible way," for they "ride upon the back of Industry." "Much of the choicest lands between here and the St. Croix," he wrote, "is taken up by non residents, who do not improve, and never intend to improve it. Lands so hung up for speculation, might as well be an impassable swamp; and every entry so made, may be considered as good as submerged. The true policy is, for every man to have a small piece of ground and to cultivate it — to produce something out of it — and let his neighbors settle down close to him, and do the same thing; and thus schools and all institutions of civilization will be fostered." [4]

The improvement of the rapids in the Mississippi River at Rock Island and Des Moines, known as the "upper" and "lower" rapids, was the subject of frequent comment in the *Pioneer*. These rapids were serious hazards to navigation. Except during high water, freight had to be lightered through them, consuming much time and greatly increasing costs. Be-

[4] *Pioneer*, February 20, November 6, 1851.

THE MINNESOTA PIONEER.

BY JAMES M. GOODHUE & ISAAC N. GOODHUE.

Democratic Principle, Democratic Men and Democratic Measures.

TWO DOLLARS A YEAR.

VOLUME II.

ST. PAUL, MINNESOTA TERRITORY, THURSDAY, MAY 9, 1850.

NO. III.

MINNESOTA PIONEER.

PUBLISHED EVERY THURSDAY MORNING
By JAS. M. & ISAAC N. GOODHUE.

OFFICE ON THIRD STREET, NEAR THE UPPER LANDING, ST. PAUL.

TERMS:

THE PIONEER will be furnished to subscribers at Two Dollars per annum, invariably in advance.

No subscriptions received for less than six months.

All letters to this office must be free of postage, to insure attention.

RATES OF ADVERTISING.

Advertisements, per square, (12 lines or less) first insertion $1 00
For every additional insertion 50
Business cards, ... yearly.

All advertisements sent without direction, will be made to conform to the column.

St. Paul Business Directory.

H. L. Moss,
Attorney and Counsellor at Law, and General Land Agent, St. Paul.
Particular attention paid to Collecting Debts, Buying and Selling Real Estate, Paying Taxes, Entering Lands, Securing Pre-Emption Claims, and entries made by Military Land Warrants.

Henry A. Lambert,
Attorney and Counsellor at Law, and Solicitor in Chancery, St. Paul.

Rice, Whitall & Becker,
Attorneys at Law.
Will give their entire attention to the business of their profession.

Babcock, Amos & Wilkinson,
Attorneys and Counsellors at Law, St. Paul, Minnesota Territory.

Amos & Wilkinson,
Attorneys, Counsellors at Law and Solicitors in Chancery.

PROF. WEBSTER.

Eugene Aram and the Crime of Murder.

During the reign of George II., all the literary world was astounded by the arrest, for the high crime of murder, of a man who had until that time been the envy of the scholars of his age. This man was named Eugene Aram, and known of the natural sciences, and as a metaphysician and philologist, had become so famous, that his opinion was considered on every point. His life was a noble one, for not wealthy, for scholarship was no more productive that it is now; yet he was not in want. His fireside was adorned with a wife who had been the companion of his youth, and a large and promising family, which would probably have reaped the benefit of his self-denying existence, but for the events of his after life. The name of this man, was Eugene Aram.

Katharine of Russia.

Dark and dreadful was the night of the 26th of November, 1869, and heavily fell the snow flakes; no darker were the prospects, and heavier was the heart of Katharine, a wanderer in the wilds of the dense forest, surrounding the town of Marosburg. Misfortune had compelled the indignant peasant to abandon his favorite haunts of second memory, and seek anew strangers that which was placed him in the midst of his friends.

Accompanied by his first born, a sprightly youth of fourteen, and bearing the weary arms a tender infant, the expressive image of her whom he had late—

"Good God! what do I hear?" ejaculated the pious minister, Skorowski, as on subdued cries of distress, falling upon his ears during a temporary cessation of the storm, attracted his attention to the frozen embankment upon which rested the deserted infant. She longed to join her pious and devotion, but woman's curiosity, and respect for the General in Chief, who ordered her to the strength of his attachment by procuring her release from confinement...

age, the General granted her request on condition of her returning to him where she had completed her march.

The night was dismal, and the undertaking a fearful one, but the difficulties of the road it would be hard to relate...

I shall now give the statement of a man selected at random from amongst a number, such as himself, congregated in this place as a returned convict, and one who had gone through the several bodily and mental agony. He said—"I was two years and a half at picking pockets; one week after I was transported...

"I am now twenty-eight, and have known all connected with the begging trade since I was 14. I took to screening writing on the stones, I got my bread and board, and a cloth tied round my jaws, and wrote on the flags—

"Illness and Want,"

through I was never better in my life...

A CONVICT'S TALE.

Dull at the Start, (Old Bailey,)

ginning in the 1820's, surveys and plans were made from time to time for the removal of the rapids, but none of them materialized. It was not until the 1880's, after the heyday of steamboat navigation on the Mississippi had passed, that the rapids were made navigable. In the fall of 1851 a convention was held at Burlington, Iowa, to memorialize Congress for the removal of obstructions to navigation in the Mississippi, and Minnesota was represented at the convention by Goodhue.[5] In the *Pioneer* the editor was persistent in his demands that Congress, "in justice to the South and the North-West," make "ample, immediate appropriations, to render navigation practicable, safe and easy, at all stages of water, across both rapids." "If we were a member of Congress," he declared in the issue of August 28, 1851, "we would thunder for this in the ears of Congress, loud enough to shake down the walls of the Capitol." On April 29, 1852, he took the national legislature to task under the heading "Why Is Congress Reluctant?":

"It seems impossible that Congress can overlook the immense national importance of making the navigation of the Mississippi unobstructed, from St. Paul down to the Gulf of Mexico. Why is it? Can it be because the States down the river, are so ravenous for grants of public land, that the Government is unwilling to give us an appropriation of money for the Rapids, in addition to grants of land to the States, for fear of doing too much for the West? The West wants cheap communication more than lands: and the main artery more than little rivers. If we had a railroad from St. Paul to New Orleans, we should not rest quiet, if it were obstructed at Rock Island and Keokuk; but having a river which is better, with only two obstructions in it, which might be removed for less

[5] Mildred L. Hartsough, *From Canoe to Steel Barge on the Upper Mississippi*, 266–268 (Minneapolis, 1934); George B. Merrick, *Old Times on the Upper Mississippi: The Recollections of a Steamboat Pilot from 1854 to 1863*, 226 (Cleveland, 1909); *Pioneer*, October 30, 1851; *Minnesotian*, October 29, 1851; *Democrat*, November 11, 1851.

money than the cost of a week's idle debate in Congress, we sleep over it and let Congress sleep over it, for a quarter of a century, and continue to let our little steamboats crawl and scratch and scrabble over the rocky bottom of the river every year, carrying only a shirt-tail full of goods at a time, and that in lighters. Make the navigation of this river what it ought to be, and our boats would double in size and capacity, insurances and freights and the cost of pilotage, would soon fall one half. In every foot of lumber we raft, in every bushel of grain we ship, in every cup of coffee we drink, we are taxed, in consequence of the want of cheap navigation on this river. The whole West, from Pembina to the Gulf of Mexico, ought to light down upon Congress and sting that stupid body, besiege it, harass it, beleaguer it, into immediate compliance with the demand of half a continent."

On the subject of railroads, Goodhue, at first enthusiastic for their early construction, later revised his ideas to some extent. A railroad between St. Paul and St. Anthony he always regarded as an urgent necessity, because of "the daily increase of business" between the two towns, and because "whatever can be done to promote the growth of Saint Anthony will directly benefit Saint Paul." The road would be easy to grade, cheap to construct, and would connect "a great and increasing steamboat business on the Mississippi." In the *Pioneer* of April 3, 1850, he suggested that the people of the two villages take upon themselves the building of such a railroad, which would be a section of a future "Mississippi, Lake Superior and Hudson Bay railroad," connecting the Mississippi River with Lake Superior.

On March 27, 1850, he advocated the construction of a railroad to Dubuque, "at no distant day." "How greatly would the distance as well as time of communication, be shortened by a railroad!" he wrote. "What a saving in risk and insurance! What unlimited agricultural resources, would at once be developed, along the line of such a railroad!" Two months

later, on May 16, he urged "the immediate and vigorous
prosecution of the work, upon the Chicago and Galena railroad." "Hating distances, risks and delays," he wrote, "commerce is now forcing a passage overland by railway, from
Chicago straight to lake Erie; and nothing will do, but the
connection of Chicago by railroad, with the Atlantic cities.
The same laws of trade which give existence to the road east
of Chicago, require, nay, *demand*, its extension west to the
Mississippi. That railroad completed, will speedily concentrate
upon it, all the travel and freight to and from the eastern
cities, for the whole length of the Mississippi above its western
terminus, and for hundreds of miles below its western terminus, and all the business of the north temperate zone, west
of the Mississippi river."

On June 5, 1851, he recommended that St. Louis "put a
railroad along up the Mississippi as fast as possible." "When
the railroad from lake Michigan to the Mississippi shall be
completed," he wrote, "and a daily line of steamboat packets
from its western terminus to Saint Paul, will be requisite to
do the business of Minnesota, some of our neighbor towns
down the river, will find that the trade of the upper interior
of North America, *might have been* worth cultivating. Even
Saint Louis, is not too large, to learn, that in these days of
competition, cities as well as men, must struggle to maintain
their position. They must keep open the outlets of the remote
springs of trade that supply them with business."

By the fall of 1851 the *Pioneer's* editorials on railroads had
become surprisingly conservative, considering that they were
written at a time when the West, indeed the whole country,
was clamoring for railroads. While Goodhue was often in-
consistent in his attitude, in general he had come to believe
that railroads should not be built paralleling rivers but at
right angles to them; and that, in any event, railroads should
not be built until the region had population enough and capital enough to build them without going into debt. In an edi-

torial in the issue of October 23, 1851, the editor expressed his doubt that a railroad could ever compete with the navigation of the Mississippi; and he drew a sorry picture of what railroads would do to Chicago:

". . . Is not the world getting railroad mad? Are not railroads, all pointing eastward and intersecting New York roads, draining away the business of the Mississippi Valley, destroying the trade of Western towns and centralizing all commerce in New York City? The jobbing business, where is it going? To New York. What will the ganglion of railroads, that pass through Chicago, do for that city? Chicago will be like the middle of the hour glass, through which commerce will pass, in a swift, narrow stream, between the East and the West. To the extent that railroads supersede lake navigation, Chicago will lose the aliment of commerce, that has given it a growth so extraordinary. She will sit upon her sandy beach, with drooping plumage, as poor as the bird without a gizzard and with but one short, straight, intestine through her emaciated body. She will do a lumber business it is true, and a fair retail business; but she will be mortified to hear the hourly whistle of the locomotive hurrying up to thrust its fiery nostrils into the waters of Lake Michigan, and away again in a twinkling, drawing away to New York, the Western merchant with his produce.

"But if such will be the result to Chicago, of the competition of railroads with lake navigation, what will be the result to St. Paul, of a railroad in competition with the river? Very different; a railroad will not pay; for the distance along the river, could not be materially shortened by a railroad, as it is along the lakes — then there is far less peril in river than in lake navigation; and again, the course of the Upper Mississippi, from St. Paul to Galena, from N. W. to S. E., is in the natural and direct course of our trade that seeks the Atlantic around the foot of Lake Michigan, and of our trade down the river, with St. Louis and New Orleans. Except New York and New

Orleans, towns are few, very few, that are not in danger, under the railroad system, of becoming mere thoroughfares for railroads, and mere tributaries to one or the other of these cities.

". . . As for St. Paul, it being at the head of navigation, its river trade entirely secure from the competition of a railroad either South or East, and with an interior of undeveloped natural wealth and resources, unsurpassed in value and extent, the commercial position of the town is absolutely impregnable, whether the rapids be improved or not. It has nothing to fear from the railroad system, which is revolutionizing elsewhere, the whole system of trade, and which even threatens the commercial supremacy of St. Louis as well as of Chicago."

Under the heading "Industry vs. Banks and Railroads," in the *Pioneer* of November 27, 1851, Goodhue urged, as an antidote to the railroad mania, "regular, steady, laborious production, that fills the corn crib with plenty and covers the back with warmth":

". . . Travelling South lately, upon the Mississippi river, which passes our very door, the highway of North America, almost from the Arctic regions, to the ocean, we found along its shores, on both sides, farmers, mechanics and all sorts of men, who had bought stock in railroads to the East, who were neglecting their farms and workshops, spending their time in idle talk and speculation, instead of production, waiting impatiently for the construction of railroads, the panacea of poverty, the patent highways to wealth, by which they all expect to get rich. In Grant county, Wisconsin, we found the railroad mania raging. Farmers, mechanics, every body had it. There was but little surplus produce – prices were high; but the whole country was perishing for want of a railroad to Milwaukee.

"The roads to the Mississippi, where boats were daily passing to take their crops to a cash market, either up or down, were execrable; full of rocks, and gullies, and mud holes and tree tops and stumps and ungraded hills and unbridged streams and whatever else makes locomotion dangerous and expensive, not to say impracticable. But instead of mending their ways, every man is bawling out for a railroad. It costs them more to get their freights to and from the river, upon the execrable roads, than the freight to and from St. Louis; roads that could be mended by their own industry, without paying out a dollar of money; yet they neglect to mend these roads, and only clamor for a railroad. They have tried the Mississippi market; that does not save them from hard times; and they will find the result just the same, after they have tried a railroad.

"One remedy they have not tried; *i.e.*, hard work. Thrift and economy and a rigid avoidance of debt, these things are what we want in the Valley of the Mississippi. . . . As for railroads East, let those who want the trade of our valley, build them. Produce enough to make railroads pay to this valley, and the cities of the East will build them. Railroad building is not the business of farmers and mechanics. Their business is to produce; and if they neglect to do that, railroads will not pay. Capital will make your railroads for you, as soon as they are worth making. Give the river, and the towns upon it, whose shores you inhabit, their legitimate trade. In the natural course of things, if the trade of this valley is not drained to the East, New York and the capital of New York and other Atlantic cities, will come to St. Louis and Burlington and St. Paul and to New Orleans, and every where along its shores, to share in and profit by that trade. We have the Mississippi river, which God has given us. If New York has any railroads to give us, equal to the river, let her bring them along.

"The Valley of the Mississippi has enough to do to produce freights, without producing better means of transporting those freights, than nature and Robert Fulton have given us. If we plunge into railroad operations, we go into debt, then comes banking, idleness, speculation, bankruptcy. Learn a lesson in time. The West is not too old to learn. New England has made a net of railroads all over their territory — has made herself as poor as a church mouse, by building railroads. What is the result? Why New York taps the whole of her vast system of railroads, designed to aggrandize and enrich its emporium, Boston, and makes them all tributary to her own gigantic trade. Just so the West may impoverish itself in building railroads every where, to drain Eastward the trade that naturally flows South, to impoverish ourselves and depopulate our towns, and leave us at last without any West — all polarized towards New York, without a Western interest, without Western influence and deeply indebted in Wall street, tied up with railroad bonds, which we have foolishly and voluntarily fastened upon ourselves as with a chain, to be forever led at the triumphant chariot wheels of old Gotham."

In the *Pioneer* of January 29, 1852, Goodhue expressed the opinion that the construction of a railroad paralleling the Mississippi, as well as a road from St. Paul to Lake Superior — both of which he had previously urged — were "chimerical" projects:

". . . We regard the construction of a railroad parallel to the Mississippi river, to connect with any of the lines of railroad extending eastward, to be a very chimerical scheme, for yet these many years. When the business of the Upper Mississippi, shall correspond in amount with the business and travel upon the Hudson, there will be more sense and reason in holding railroad conventions: St. Paul will then be ready, co-operating with St. Louis, Galena, Chicago, Milwaukee and other business places South and East, to take the subject in hand and have the work accomplished.

"In the meantime, we have not the slightest objection that the gassing politicians of Dubuque or of any other town *back amongst the sloughs,* that affects to be interested in the trade of this river, should vary their usual winter employment of making lines of *paper steamboat* packets, and *resolving* their *own* to be the great emporium of the Northwest, by building paper railroads from their own place, straight through, by the great bend of the Minnesota, to the Red river of the North, and supplying the road with paper depots and station houses and paper trains and locomotives, propelled by gas.

. . . .

"Not less chimerical is the idea of constructing a railroad from St. Paul to Lake Superior, unless it were a road expressly for the purpose of intersecting a railroad built by British capital, from the Gulf of St. Lawrence to the British shore of the Pacific – a work not likely to be accomplished, for some time yet. With a short canal around the S[aul]t Ste. Marie, freights could be taken from Buffalo to the Western extremity of Lake Superior, at about as low rates as from Buffalo to Chicago. A town, therefore, at the west end of Lake Superior, could obtain freights lower than St. Paul can and would undersell us. Thus, if a railroad were built from St. Paul to Fond du Lac on Lake Superior, the trade of the Upper Mississippi would flow up stream, and move off to the eastern cities, through the Lakes. The steamboat business of this river would be dried up; for not a pound of goods could be brought to St. Paul, in our flat, small, river boats, if they were brought in direct competition with the capacious holds of the Lake propellers, sailing to Fond du Lac; and so far from benefiting the trade of this river and especially of St. Paul, which now supplies the whole trade north of us, by building a railroad from St. Paul to Fond du Lac, it would be found that our mill was at the *wrong end of the race*, and that the stream of commerce was flowing away from the town.

"But why talk and write all the chimerical nonsense, why utter all the windy vaporings that are uttered, about building railroads that will cost *millions*, through a country not yet inhabited, and much of which never will be? When will men become reasonable and practical?

"Have we not the Mississippi river, made on purpose for trade? Have we not natural advantages and resources of trade that need all our capital and resources, properly to develop them? . . .

"More and more are we daily convinced, that the true commercial interests of the valley of the Mississippi, are identified with the navigation of the river. When the east and west lines of commerce cut off the north and south, steamboats will peter out, (as a miner would say,) and the west, instead of doing her own carrying trade, will surrender it to soulless railroad corporations."

In "A Revolution in Steamboating on the Mississippi River," in the *Pioneer* of June 3, 1852, Goodhue proposed a plan, "not to discourage the railroad, but to make it an ally, an aid and assistant to the steamboat," thus setting "forever at defiance, the competition of the railroad as the great carrier." To do this, the steamboat "must nearly equal, if not excel the locomotive . . . in speed and cheapness of conveyance." His plan was this:

"First then, we want the rapids improved, speedily and thoroughly.

"Then we want the Government of the United States to establish a line of daily mail steamboat packets, to run seven months in each year between New Orleans and Saint Paul, and all the year as far up the river as St. Louis; fifty thousand dollars to be paid annually, for this mail service. . . .

"These mail boats ought to be built with entire reference to the comfort and safety of passengers, and speed of conveyance. They ought to carry no freight but the mails, unless it might be such rarities and luxuries, as the stewards of boats are usually allowed to traffic in. The price of cabin passage (and there should be none other) ought to be about double the price now made. There ought to be no delay at all, but to change mails, and that right speedily. Every boat ought to take her wood from a flat boat, while running. The time from

New Orleans to St. Paul and back, ought not to exceed thirteen days. The boats now upon the river ought to be converted into freight boats, except such as might be wanted in the trade of other waters. These freight boats ought to be conducted with strict reference to economy, so as to carry for low freights — no passengers at all, unless it be those of the cheapest description."

This arrangement, according to Goodhue, would result in a complete separation of passenger and freight business; less traveling time and better accommodations for passengers; cheaper freight rates and less risk to freights "upon slow, strong, cheap boats"; and financial gain to steamboat companies, for passengers would have fewer meals on fast boats, and the boats, making twice as many trips as formerly, would make more money.

As far as Minnesota was concerned, Goodhue astutely summed up the railroad situation in the question, quoted above, "Why utter all the windy vaporings that are uttered, about building railroads that will cost *millions*, through a country not yet inhabited?" It was to be another decade before any rails were laid in Minnesota, and then only over the ten miles between St. Paul and St. Anthony; and it was more than another decade after that before railroad building really got under way in the state.

In the *Pioneer* of January 22, 1852, Goodhue bundled up all "The Wants of Minnesota" in one editorial:

"We want the treaties ratified. There can be no division of opinion on that subject. With the treaties ratified, our Territory will be rapidly progressive; without the treaties ratified, Minnesota will be stationary, if not retrograde.

"We want the Chippewa treaty ratified.[6] The interests of our brethren at Pembina require it. We want treaties made,

⁶ Soon after the negotiation of the Sioux treaties of 1851 a treaty was made with the Chippewa at Pembina, whereby those Indians ceded to the United States about five million acres in the Red River Valley. This treaty was not ratified. Folwell, *Minnesota*, 1:288, 291.

for every foot of Indian territory within our limits, east of the Mississippi river. We want the pine lands purchased, surveyed and sold, on the head waters of the Mississippi river. Not only do the interests of the Territory require this, but the whole valley of the Mississippi river, cries aloud for it. The river itself, is not more indispensable to the great valley which it irrigates, and to the business of the multitude of steamboats which it carries upon its waters.

"We want ample provisions made, by a grant of public lands, to place St. Paul, the emporium of the Northwest, in uninterrupted railroad connection with the railroads of the Atlantic cities.

"We want the military reserve taken off of the beautiful tract of land, which lies now like an useless and uncultivated blotch, upon the finest portion of our Territory — a sort of military carbuncle which is unbecoming to the face of the country, on the west side of the river. Out with it! Let us have on it some beautiful gardens and smiling cottages and productive farms.

"We want ten thousand farmers, with strong hands and courageous hearts, with their plows and their oxen and cattle and sheep, and their wives and children, who are not particular on which side of the river they settle, to raise large crops, and obtain large prices and enjoy vigorous health, and build up valuable institutions of religion and learning, for present and future generations.

"We want manufacturing capital enough, invested in sawmills, planing mills, lath mills, shingle mills, lathes, and the manufacture of wooden ware and the building of boats, to manufacture into all possible uses, every pine log that can be cut on the Mississippi river and its tributaries, to supply the home demand and to furnish the demand of the whole vast region of hard wood lands and prairies, to the mouth of the Mississippi river. We want thousands of lumbermen, to supply the pine logs; and we want the permission of the Government, to buy the pine lands north of us, and to continue in and to extend, this our legitimate business, for our own profit and the evident profit and advantage of the Great West.

"We want a plank-road or a railroad, between St. Paul and St. Anthony, *now*. The business and welfare of both towns and the prosperity of the fertile valley of this river, filling up, every where with settlers, from here to Pokegama, and our increasing intercourse with Pembina and Selkirk, demand at least the commencement, of a system of easy, cheap and rapid communication from St. Paul northward.

"We want good school houses and good schools in them.

"The voice of five hundred neglected children in St. Paul, cries out in united reproach against us, that of the half dozen expensive edifices in this town, whose spires glisten in the light of the rising sun, *not one of them*, is devoted to the mental and intellectual culture of the rising generation. How long shall we remain destitute of liberal and ample accommodations and provision, for the education of every child, rich or poor, in St. Paul.

"We want to see every child, boy and girl in this Territory, either at school, or bound out to some honest trade, or inured to habits of steady industry; so that industry and honesty, may come to be regarded as synonyms, in Minnesota; and that no pursuit that is not useful or productive, shall be considered honest.

"We want to see all our people distinguished for thrift without meanness, for strict temperance in all things, for religion without bigotry, for intelligence without pedantry; for charity, for strict punctuality in the payment of all debts, for abhorring and reprobating all tricks and chicaneries and unfair advantages, by which men deceive and defraud each other, and call it *smartness*.

"We want that there should be such intelligence and such a standard of enlightened public opinion, as will awe down roguery and rowdyism, and enforce correct conduct with a power far mightier than the penalties of statutes.

"These are the things that Minnesota wants, far more than the arrant bigotry and the proscriptive policy of party politics — far more than an array of Whigs and Democrats, to quarrel about issues that do not exist, and to promote certain men and carry them, by compact party discipline, upon the shoulders of a faction, to places of honor which they could never attain to, by the force of their individual, personal efforts to rise to distinction.

"The men who aid in and cherish, the purposes and aims which we have above set forth, are your true Democrats, your liberal, practical, working Democrats; and they are the men, and the only men, in our Territory, who are really, heartily and sincerely, laboring to promote the greatest good of the greatest number. These are sober, honest truths. People of Minnesota! We ask you to ponder them."

14. Local and Transitory

ON THE EDITORIAL PAGE OF THE PIONEER, FOLLOWING THE REGU-
lar editorials, was a column or more of brief items, headed,
during much of the period of Goodhue's editorship, "Local
and Transitory." It contained comments on matters vital to
the interests of the territory, as well as information on early
Minnesota that has not been recorded elsewhere. Many of the
items are humorous, most of them are interesting, and some
of them are obviously space-fillers. Many of them have been
quoted elsewhere in this book along with Goodhue's editorials
on the same subjects. A number of others, on a variety of
miscellaneous matters, also deserve another fate than the limbo
of the "transitory," if only because they exemplify the personal journalism of that time.

Patent medicines were the subject of many a paragraph on
Goodhue's editorial page. He deplored the prostitution of the
press "to the use and profit of quack medicine venders," and
announced that he would "advertise no remedy which we
ourselves refrain from taking." "Our terms," he wrote, "for
advertising patent medicines are $50 per column, if the medi-
cines are such as will really benefit mankind; if they are *not
such*, they cannot find a place in the Pioneer." [1] Typical of his
comments on patent medicines was a paragraph in the *Pioneer*
of June 10, 1852:

"One of the best evidences of the intelligence of the people
of Minnesota, is the fact that there appear in our journals, so
few advertisements of humbug quack medicines. When newspapers are filled with whole columns of certificates about the
miraculous cures effected by some specific — it proves that
readers will tolerate all sorts of flap-doodle — that they are
ignorant, stupid fools, who can be stuffed with words. Now

[1] *Pioneer*, July 25, 1850.

an editor is no more bound to take a quack advertisement into his columns, than the captain of a steamboat is compelled to take a maniac, or a leper into his boat as a passenger. And be it remembered, that for every such passenger who comes on, half a dozen cleanly passengers will get off, in disgust. We do not mean to condemn all patent medicines; for some of them are of acknowledged merit; (and we will advertise none other.) But we mean to condemn *the most of specifics* — the most of such medicines, popular medicines of the day, as are certified to by the 'hon Mr. Funkhollows, and the Miss Susan Nippers,' of our time. Here is a specimen which we cut from an exchange, of Miss Susan's certificates, who was suffering from general debility, sick headache, heartburn, indigestion, tapeworms, consumption, rheumatism in the shoulders and hips, and besides these, she didn't feel very well herself. At length she says:

" 'I was brought so low that my most impudent friends didn't expect me to live from one end to the other. About this time a friend recommending as the last resort, that I should try a few bottles of the Pectorial Oxinated Compound Saxafarilla Extract of Wild Cherry Wine Bitters, satisfaction given or money refunded, to be taken, destroy the label as soon as possible — no pay no cure, beware of counterfeits — none genuine without the proprietor is on the wrapper. I took three bottles of this truly invaluable medicine, and it gave me immediate relief in three months."

"Psychologists," or "mesmerizers," who visited Minnesota now and then and gave exhibitions of their "science," were a special abomination to Goodhue, who usually referred to them as "suckologists." His attitude toward phrenology, too, remained unchanged from the days of his lectures on the subject in Galena and Mineral Point. On September 4, 1851, the *Pioneer* published an advertisement of Fowlers and Wells, who announced "A New Volume of the American Phreno-

logical Journal." [2] It is questionable whether Fowlers and
Wells reaped a large profit in Minnesota from their advertisement, for in the same issue of the *Pioneer* appeared this paragraph:

"We publish to-day the advertisement of Fowlers & Wells,
because it is sent to us to publish. But we assure our readers,
that in our opinion, a more arrant humbug was never hatched
than this same Phrenology. It has neither fact nor philosophy
to sustain it — nothing but the prurient vanity of mankind.
We never yet saw a disciple of Fowler, who was not an
empty, conceited fool. The 'Water-Cure' may be well enough;
but if it has any real merit, it is unfortunate in having for its
champions, Fowlers & Wells, the high-priests of humbug and
quackery."

Woe to the man who decamped from Minnesota without
paying his debts, "especially to the printer"; for the *Pioneer*
editor saw to it that his character was "properly appreciated."
Such an unfortunate was one Dr. Rich, whom Goodhue dealt
with in the issue of September 4, 1851:

"Dr. C. Rich and family (he professed to be of the Eclectic
school of medicine) left by the Nominee, last week, between
two days — being in debt to many people in St. Paul, and especially to the printer. Thus reminded of the old maxim that
'Riches take to themselves wings and fly away,' we cannot
help heartily and meekly responding to the language of Agur's
petition, 'Give us, Lord, neither Poverty nor Riches.' Cheerfully would we forgive any poor fellow his debt, who was
man enough to say, 'Sir, I owe you, but I am poor and cannot pay you.' As for that man, dressed in black broadcloth,
for whom we have labored and received nothing, who is too
proud to work and too poor to pay — if such a fellow sneaks

[2] Orson S. Fowler and his brother Lorenzo became editors and publishers
of the *American Phrenological Journal and Miscellany* in New York in 1842.
In 1844 S. R. Wells joined the firm, which became Fowlers and Wells. In
1863 the Fowlers withdrew from the partnership. Orson Fowler was in the
class below Goodhue's at Amherst. *Dictionary of American Biography.*

out of Minnesota, in debt to this office, we will try to have the man's character properly appreciated, wherever he may go.

"Dr. C. Rich is about 33 years old, 5 feet 10 or 11 inches high, slender, bilious, black-haired, black eyes, smells like an apothecary shop, and looks like the ghost of a bilious fever. Wherever he finds employment as a physician, there will be bread for an undertaker; and if he does not *lose* his patients, it will be because he can *find* none. As a surgeon, he would only do to call in case of a broken neck or a musket shot through the heart; or as a physician, in the last stages of cholera or consumption, when 'it is too late.' — But, to do him justice, he was a very good collector of his own fees, and would take the last shirt from any poor patient who by accident or miracle survived his treatment."

Early St. Paul was a poor place for a man in his cups to stage an escapade, for on his recovery he might find himself the subject of a paragraph in the *Pioneer*, such as the following, from the issue of November 28, 1850:

" 'Humble Come Tumble Down Seven Pairs of Stairs.' — We have read of old Putnam's ride down the precipice at Stony Point, on horseback, and have seen some rough riding in the circus, and have heard of English fox hunting over ditches and stone walls, and of their steeple chases, where they ride through swamps and over five barred gates, or every one by the nearest course he can, in a *steeple chase*, of perhaps thirty miles; but we do not know of any riding to compare with that of Sergeant Findley, of the U.S. Dragoons, at Fort Snelling. Our readers know of those successive flights of wooden stairs, leading down from the end of Bench street, by Mr. Randall's store, to the Lower Steamboat Landing.[3] Sergeant Findley, who was down from the fort, rode his horse, pell mell down all those flights of stairs, to Mr. Randall's store door, and then took the horse back up the stairs, by the

---

[3] The stairs from the levee to the top of the bluff at Jackson Street were built in 1849. *Pioneer*, August 16, 1849.

same way he came down, without injury to horse or rider. The horse must have been perfectly sober."

Tall stories and hoaxes were a part of the literary equipment of most frontier journalists, and they were a special delight to Goodhue, who enhanced their effect by sandwiching them between comments on serious and important matters. Typical of such tales was one in the *Pioneer* of October 3, 1850:

"Sergeant J. of Fort Snelling, come down from the fort the other day, to St. Paul, and amongst his purchases, bought a ham and put it on his wagon. Just as he reached [Samuel J.] Findley's Ferry, opposite the fort, the ham proved to be so lively with skippers, that it leaped out of the wagon and escaped upon the prairie; and it was not until a couple of dragoons had pursued it half an hour, that they succeeded in capturing it with a *lasso*."

And this, from the issue of December 26, 1850:

"Since our last publication, the weather has been mostly very moderate. They have a way of moderating the cold, on the Saint Croix, which is rather novel. Instead of the common mercurial thermometer, they carry out with them, in their pockets, common *razor strops*, which by sliding in their cases, they can regulate for themselves, so as to keep the weather very comfortable. Others having no faith in mercury, which is liable to congeal, use spirit thermometers; these are prepared by simply pouring whiskey into the throat."

Goodhue's most successful hoax appeared in the *Pioneer* of February 20, 1850, under the heading "Singular Petrifications":

"At the mouth of Crow River, a navigable stream entering the Mississippi on the west side, thirty-five miles above St. Paul, there are said to be visible in the bottom of the river, several petrifications in the shape of men and horses. The Historial Society should make arrangements to obtain some of these specimens of petrified zoology."

The story was taken seriously and was copied by news-papers outside the territory. A few weeks later Goodhue re-ceived the following letter from a St. Louis man:

Sir: — You will I hope excuse the liberty I take of addressing this letter to you, being an entire stranger to you. My object in writing it is, to enquire of you some particulars with respect to a notice I observed in the St. Louis *Union* of the 29th inst., copied from your paper, of a number of petrifactions in the shape of men and horses which are said to be at the bottom of Crow River, near its mouth. If not too much trouble, will you be good enough to let me know, at your earliest convenience, more about the mat-ter, and if there is any possibility of getting at them?

I am about establishing a Museum in this city, and am desirous of collecting all the natural curiosities I can get for the same. If there are any specimens of fossils, minerals, &c., &c., or in fact anything in the way of curiosities in your neighborhood, that could be sent to this city, I would pay liberally for them. . . .

In the *Pioneer* of May 16, 1850, Goodhue acknowledged the letter, and went on to say:

"In answer to it, we can only say, that it is generally under-stood here in Saint Paul, that the Secretary of the Territory had all the petrifactions in question (four horses and riders, beside a few fragments) raised at the expense of the Treasury and put in a small new stable erected for the purpose in the rear of the Central House, Saint Paul, at the expense of four hundred and thirty-one dollars to the Government, which has been duly audited and allowed in his accounts. Secretary C. K. Smith, who is also Secretary of the Minnesota Historical So-ciety, is now absent. On his return, a few weeks hence, a let-ter addressed to him on the subject, will no doubt receive prompt attention. Crow Wing river is 128 miles above Saint Paul. To prompt further search for similar petrifactions at the mouth of the Crow Wing, we will now make an offer of fifty dollars for each sound, petrified horse, mare, or gelding, the same for each petrified man or woman, and half that price for ponies and children, delivered in boxes on the bank of the

river, ready to be shipped down to St. Anthony on the steamboat Gov. Ramsey, in good condition."

But even this barefaced fraud went unsuspected in some
quarters, for in the *Pioneer* of June 20, 1850, appeared the
following:

The petrified men and horses recently discovered at the bottom
of Crow River, Minnesota, near its mouth, have been housed in a
building near St. Paul, erected for the purpose, and are under the
care of the territorial officers. — *Philadelphia North American.*

"Yes: but as oats in Saint Paul are scarce at one dollar per
bushel, the Secretary enlisted them in the new company of
dragoons and they were shipped down on the Dr. Franklin,
No. 2, last week, under command of Capt. Garland, U. S. A.,
to hunt the Sacs and Foxes out of Iowa."

Goodhue's petrified cavalry is remindful of Mark Twain's
hoax about the petrified man, which, as a newspaper reporter
in Nevada, he perpetrated several years later. At the time that
Goodhue wrote, Samuel Clemens was a young boy of fifteen,
working as an apprentice on a newspaper down the river at
Hannibal, Missouri. The newspapers of the river towns
exchanged with one another, and it is conceivable that the
youngster may have been familiar with the *Pioneer.* Another
reminder of Mark Twain, and his famous remark that the
report of his death was "greatly exaggerated," is found in
Goodhue's account of Robert Hughes, who, although well
known in St. Paul, was not, it may be surmised, a pillar of
the town's society. In the *Pioneer* of September 25, 1851, appeared the following paragraph:

"Robert Hughes. — Robert was well known about Saint
Paul; but for several days past, nothing has been seen or heard
of him. Robert mostly frequented that old fortress of temperance, known as the Fremont House.[4] Fears begin to be enter-
tained, that Robert has 'taken water;' which if he has done,

---

[4] The Fremont House was a small hotel just east of the *Pioneer* office on
Bench Street. *Pioneer*, May 6, 1852.

would be likely to prove fatal to him. He was seen the day before his disappearance carrying a pail of that fluid — a suspicious circumstance, as he was known to have an aversion to aqueous fluids, amounting almost to hydrophobia. Robert may turn up again — in fact, he cannot well be spared until after election — but it would be well to have his obituary notice in readiness."

The issue for the next week carried another item about Robert:

"Turned up again. — Bob Hughes, who, it was feared was drowned, requests us to say that the report of his death is undoubtedly premature and greatly exaggerated. He was wanted to be absent for a few days, so as *not to be a witness.* We did not inquire who issued the negative subpoena, requiring Bob's absence from Court."

One June 24, 1852, the *Pioneer* reported Hughes's death, and this time the report was not an exaggeration:

" 'Now, lies he there and none, so poor, to do him reverence.' Whatever remained of poor old Bob Hughes, after the spirit had left him (Bob was knocked into the river last week, while playing with a bear, and drowned,) was carried up through 3d street, in a rough box, drawn upon a dray, at the expense of the town. Rows of decanters, in the groceries, stood arrayed on both sides of the streets, as the corpse passed, with tin labels, like aprons, suspended in front of them; but none of the secret societies turned out."

While the two paragraphs below, the first from the *Pioneer* of August 21, 1851, and the other from the following December 25, are too mild to be considered typical of Goodhue's references to the rival *Democrat,* they do indicate how slight was the excuse he needed to produce a gibe:

"The 'Sheboygan Lake Journal,' writing for an exchange with the Pioneer, says: 'We want a Minnesota paper *bad.'* We will send the Pioneer; and if the Journal wants a Minnesota paper *worse,* we must refer it for an exchange, to our neighbor, the Democrat."

"The Democrat of yesterday says, 'week after week, the editor of the Pioneer displays his wit,' &c. That praise is only in the *positive* degree. Not to be outdone in compliment, we may, with equal truth compliment our neighbor in the *comparative* degree; and say that the editor of the Democrat, weaker and weaker displays *his* wit."

Reverence was not a trait that was overdeveloped in the editor of the *Pioneer.* Even when the occasion was a funeral, Goodhue found it hard to resist bantering the Sons of Temperance. Thus he wrote on June 27, 1850:

"At the funeral of Mr. [John] Lumley, whose death occurred last week, from exposure to disease on board the Lamartine, the Sons of Temperance, of whom Mr. Lumley was a member, marched in procession, wearing white scarfs. Upon the whole the display they made of clean linen, certainly gave them an unusual appearance."

Nor was veneration of those in high places one of Goodhue's outstanding characteristics. It was probably just as well that the *Pioneer* had no subscribers in England, for they doubtless would have been scandalized to read this item in the issue of July 11, 1850:

"Barnum, it is said, having been encouraged by his success in procuring Jenny Lind's appearance in this country, is now making great efforts to bring Queen Victoria out next year. He has already obtained the consent of Prince Albert; and the only opposition now to overcome is the Ministers."

Not all the music produced in Minnesota met the standard set by Goodhue's beloved Sixth Regiment Band at Fort Snelling, according to an item in the *Pioneer* of May 27, 1852:

"A stranger in Saint Paul returning last Sunday from a walk by one of the churches, said he was much disappointed in the morals of Saint Paul; that he had not supposed that any people could be found here, bad enough to run a gang of saws on

Sunday. Upon further inquiry, we found he had mistaken the performance of the choir, in one of our churches, for the noise of a gang of saws in a steam saw-mill."

An interesting example of Goodhue's reporting is found in the *Pioneer* of June 21, 1849:

"The current of St. Paul's affairs was gliding along smoothly enough, when of a sudden a voice was heard in the lower square at about dusk one evening last week, speaking like a trumpet on the subject of temperance. The sensation among the hearers we found, after having come too late to listen, was considerable. The meeting having been announced for the second night, we were there. The speaker was a Mr. Ross, of Canada — rather under the middle age, of a somewhat dignified demeanor, and considerable power. Many of his sentiments were just, and many of them appropriately expressed. His anecdotes were good; for we recognized some of them as of the old staple stock, which have stood the test of time excellently well; and if they had not been good, would have worn out long ago. Most of his illustrations were undoubtedly original — one in particular was so strikingly different from those used by men of ordinary taste, that we shall probably incur no risk in fully according the merits of its invention to Mr. Ross. It was something like this: 'If this earth were one v-a-s-t ipecac; and this ipecac were made into one pill; and this pill were rolled down into the bowels of the deepest hell; hell could not vomit up a being so destitute of benevolence as the whiskey seller!' — Mr. Ross informed the audience that he received his literary education in Kingston. He spoke under the advantage of some personal experience in intemperance, and undoubtedly has an honest conviction that whisky is a very bad thing. He spoke with his back against a liquor shop, and evidently didn't fear the devil.

"He closed with taking up a collection."

15. A Daguerreotype of the Past

FOR THE LAST ISSUE OF VOLUME THREE OF THE PIONEER, PUB-
lished on April 15, 1852, Goodhue paused to "glance back at the
past of Minnesota, before entering upon the future." He described St. Paul as it was on the day of his arrival in 1849,
locating the few buildings in the town as he remembered
them; and he gave a résumé of the events of the territory's
first three years, highly colored by his own interpretations.
While the article, headed "The Pioneer – End of Volume 3,"
did not quite close his career, it might well have appeared as
his valedictory:

"When the traveler in his progress over an unexplored region, reaches the summit of a dividing ridge, beyond which,
in misty expanse, lies the untracked future, he sits down upon
a rock and takes a retrospect of his journey; a daguerreotype
of the past. So now do we, having as a journalist passed
through three full years, the entire period of the Territorial
existence of Minnesota Territory, to the second grand epoch
in its history, when the Sioux treaties are about to be ratified,
and our progress as a Territory is to be onward – when, as
Napoleon said to the Army of Italy, 'Soldiers we are precipitated beyond the Alps!' So we may say, that we are precipitated beyond the Mississippi and our career is now westward across the plains and the forests, to the banks of the
White Earth and the Missouri; so we, here pausing, before we
enter our fourth volume, glance back at the past of Minnesota,
before entering upon the future.

"The 18th day of April, 1849, was a raw, cloudy day. The
steamboat Senator, Capt. [Orrin] Smith, landed at Randall's
warehouse, Lower Landing, the only building then there, ex-

cept Roberts' old store.[1] Of the people on shore, we recognized but one person as an acquaintance, Henry Jackson. Took our press, types, printing apparatus all ashore. Went with our men, to the house of Mr. Bass, corner of Third and Jackson streets. He kept the only public house in St. Paul;

JACOB W. BASS'S HOTEL
It was called the "St. Paul House" in 1849.

and it was crowded full, from cellar to garret. Mr. Bass was very obliging and did everything possible for our encouragement.

"The next thing, was a printing office; and that it seemed impossible to obtain. Made the acquaintance of C. P. V. Lull and his partner, Gilbert. They furnished us gratuitously, the lower story of their building, for an office – the only vacant room in town; being the building on Third street, since fin-

[1] William H. Randall's warehouse was owned by Freeman, Larpenteur, and Company at the time of Goodhue's arrival. Robert's store was built in 1844. His advertisement in the St. Paul newspapers of 1849 read: "Louis Robert, forwarding and commission and dry goods and groceries.—Corner of Jackson and River sts., on the north side." Information for this and the following notes, as well as for the map on page 252, has been obtained from advertisements in St. Paul newspapers of 1849; records in the Ramsey County register of deeds office; Williams, *Saint Paul*; Upham and Dunlap, *Minnesota Biographies*; and various other sources.

ished off and now occupied as a saloon, by Mr. [Thomas W.] Calder. The weather was cold and stormy; and our office was as open as a corn-rick; however, we picked our types up and made ready for the issue of the first paper ever printed in Minnesota or within many hundreds of miles of it; but upon search, we found our news chase was left behind. Wm. Nobles, blacksmith, made us a very good one, after a delay of two or three days.[2] The paper was to be named 'The Epistle of Saint Paul,' as announced in our prospectus, published in the Feb. preceding; but we found so many little Saints in the Territory, jealous of Saint Paul, that we determined to call our paper, 'The Minnesota Pioneer.' One hindrance after another, delayed our first issue to the 28th of April, ten days.

"Meantime, Rev. Mr. Neill, arrived. It was encouraging to find a young man of education, courage and capital, ready to enlist all that he had or hoped on earth, in the fortunes of our town. Stillwater and St. Paul, were then running neck and neck, as rival towns. Not a foot of pine lumber could be had nearer than Stillwater; but about this time, one of the mills at St. Anthony was put in operation; but there were only then a few buildings at the Falls of St. Anthony. We looked about St. Paul, to buy a lot. Mr. Larpenteur's house was built, also French's house and shop, (now a tin shop,) and the little shop, then the Drug Store of [Dr. John J.] Dewey & [Charles T.] Cavileer, now Major Noah's office, next door west of Calder's (then our printing office) also the office of Judge Pierse (then the fur store of Olmstead & Rhoades [David Olmsted and Henry C. Rhodes].) Mr. Lambert's house was partly finished.[3]

"As you go up Third street, and Bench, the next buildings

[2] Cornelius P. V. Lull and S. Gilbert were carpenters. William H. Nobles was a wagon maker as well as a blacksmith. In 1857 he led a government expedition to survey a wagon road from Fort Ridgely to the Pacific, and discovered the Nobles Pass through the Rocky Mountains.

[3] Auguste L. Larpenteur's house later became the Wild Hunter Hotel. A. R. French made saddles, harnesses, trunks, and carpet bags; Jacob J. Noah and Allen Pierse were lawyers; and Henry L. Lambert dealt in real estate.

were two old tamarac log houses, a little east of where Mr.
Neill's church is; then passing the school house, there were
two more of the same sort, in the street, in front of the houses
now occupied by Mr. Benson and Mr. Hollinshead, near the
junction of St. Anthony, Bench and Hill sts. Beyond, was
the house John R. Irvine lives in, and nothing else but the
symptoms of two or three balloon frames. The Fullers were
at work putting up a small store, with their own hands.[4]

MAJOR NOAH'S OFFICE

"Returning, on the right, was the old underground dead
fall, in the ground opposite John R. Irvine's house, then at
the junction of Third and Bench streets, was Vetal Guerin's
log house, (now Le Duc's,) then the building in which Mr.
Curran lives, at that time unfinished, then the old bakery next
door east, then Mr. Hopkins' at the corner; turning the corner to the head of Randall's stairs (not then built) was the
old building still there, (now belonging to F. Steele,) which
Henry Jackson used to own, where he kept grocery, postoffice, and a tavern, free for all the World and the World's
wife — up along the bank of the river, stood and yet stands,

[4]Lyman L. Benson was a member of Goodhue's favorite livery firm,
Pattison and Benson, mentioned frequently in the foregoing pages. William
Hollinshead was a lawyer. Irvine was the owner of a large section of St. Paul,
which became Rice and Irvine's Addition. David L. and Alpheus G. Fuller
sold general merchandise.

the building occupied as a store by Wm. H. Forbes, the St. Paul Outfit, next was a little log building, the nucleus of 'the Central House,' next the old log Catholic church, where the Rev. Mr. Ravoux faithfully labored, and sometimes saw miraculous visions during the time of Lent, then the log house belonging to Mr. Laroux [*Timothy Lareau*], which is now being metamorphosed into a neat building.[5]

IRVINE'S LOG HOUSE

"This brings us back to Vetal's, the junction of Third and Bench streets. Half a dozen other buildings along Roberts street, and Mr. Hoyt's neighborhood, in addition to the above, constituted St. Paul. But let it be remembered, that the fashionable drinking place then, was that little log house next east of Goodrich's brick store. Mr. Bass was busy in hurrying

[5] Vital Guerin came to St. Paul in 1838 as one of its earliest settlers. William G. Le Duc established the first book store in Minnesota. He later settled at Hastings, where he manufactured the first flour from Minnesota spring wheat. M. Curran established the World's Fair store at the corner of Robert and Third streets in 1851. Daniel Hopkins opened his general store in 1847. Forbes came to Minnesota in 1837, and later took charge of the St. Paul Outfit of Pierre Chouteau Jr. and Company. Father Augustin Ravoux was pastor of the Catholic chapel from which St. Paul received its name.

up a new saloon; the building, now occupied as the Clerk' office by Mr. Wilkinson, on the spot where the Minnesota Outfit stands. The ground west of Roberts and north of Third streets, was covered with any quantity of hewed timber stripped from the forest opposite town.[6]

"We looked about for a lot; and saw that the two ends of the town must soon unite in the middle. Along the lower end of Third street, owners of lots had the coolness to ask from one hundred to two hundred dollars a lot. Between Lambert's and where the Sligo Iron Store is, on Third street, the price was $75.00 and soon after, $90.00. We bought a fractional lot with Dr. Dewey; and on our half of it built the middle section of the building where the Pioneer office is, for a dwelling house, and lived in it through the next year, without having it lathed or plastered.[7]

"But to return a little. We were at length prepared to issue our first number. We had no subscribers; for then there were but a handful of people in the whole Territory; and the majority of those, were Canadians and Half-breeds. Not a Territorial officer had yet arrived. We remember present, at the

[6] Benjamin F. Hoyt settled in St. Paul in 1848, where he sold real estate on week days and served as a Methodist preacher on Sundays. The present editor has been unable to locate Goodrich's brick store and the "fashionable drinking place" next to it. Morton S. Wilkinson was register of deeds of Ramsey County. From 1859 to 1865 he was a United States senator from Minnesota. The Minnesota Outfit of Pierre Chouteau Jr. and Company was in charge of Dr. Charles W. W. Borup. Wilkinson's office, according to newspaper advertisements, was on Third Street one door below the Minnesota Outfit.

[7] In the Pioneer for May 5, 1852, Goodhue stated that his description of St. Paul in April, 1849, contained some inaccuracies. "We ought to have stated," he wrote, "that Louis Robert's house was built on Bench street"; and he added that "a Frenchman kept a grocery in that old log building on the bank of the river, below Robert's ware house." Three more buildings should be added to the list — buildings which Goodhue mentioned in the Pioneer of October 23, 1851, as standing in April, 1849. These were the house later remodeled for and occupied by Governor Ramsey, which later became a hotel known as the New England House; an old log building on the corner of Bench and Robert streets just east of Louis Robert's dwelling; and Benjamin Brunson's house on Robert Street. The locations of these dwellings are indicated on the map on the next page.

BUILDINGS IN ST. PAUL IN APRIL, 1849

KEY TO THE MAP

This map is based on the original plat of St. Paul made in January, 1849, by Benjamin W. Brunson. The locations of the buildings are at best approximate. The orderly arrangement of the plat existed on paper only. Actually, the streets in April, 1849, were merely ungraded dirt trails, and it is impossible from the descriptions of Goodhue and his contemporaries to show buildings in their exact locations. Numbers circled on the map indicate buildings mentioned by Goodhue, but built after April, 1849.

1. Randall's warehouse
2. Robert's store
3. Bass's hotel
4. First *Pioneer* office (later Calder's saloon)
5. Nobles' blacksmith shop
6. Larpenteur's house
7. French's house and shop
8. Dewey and Cavileer's drug store (later Noah's office)
9. Olmsted and Rhodes's fur store (later Pierse's office)
10. Lambert's house
11-12. Log houses (later Goodhue's second house)
13. First Presbyterian Church
14. Schoolhouse
15-16. Log houses
17. Benson's house
18. Hollinshead's house
19. Irvine's house
20. Fuller's store
21. Guerin's house (later Le Duc's)
22. Curran's house

23. Bakery
24. Hopkins' store and house
25. Jackson's store
26. Forbes's trading post (St. Paul Outfit)
27. Central House
28. Catholic Chapel
29. Lareau's house
30. Hoyt's house
31. Bass's saloon (later Wilkinson's office)
32. Minnesota Outfit
33. Brown's building (later Marshall's Sligo Iron Store)
34. Goodhue's first house (later the *Pioneer* office)
35. Robert's house
36. Log grocery
37. Ramsey's house (later the New England House)
38. Log building
39. Brunson's house
40. *Chronicle* office (later the *Minnesotian*)
41. *Register* office (later Simon and Masterson's)

date of our first issue, Mr. Lull, Mr. Cavileer, Mr. Neill, and perhaps Maj. [Edward] Murphy. The people wanted no politics and we gave them none; they wanted information of all sorts about Minnesota; and that is what we furnished them with. We advocated Minnesota, morality and religion, from the beginning. Wm. B. Brown, built a shell of a building, (being the south end of the Sligo Iron Store now,) which Mr. Neill occupied for a meeting house. It was half filled with hearers on Sundays; for Sunday was like any other day; or perhaps rather more so.

"The first officer who arrived, was Chief Justice Goodrich; who, through chivalry and kindness, in defending a woman, involved himself in difficulties and troubles, greater and more undeserved, than have ever been suffered by any other man in Minnesota. The Governor came — a good man, who has been a true friend to Minnesota — Secretary Smith came, a man whom we first detected and exposed as an infamous old villain, and the whole Territory has since agreed to the verdict. Judge Meeker and Judge Cooper came, who have been tolerated. Mitchell, the marshal, came; a weak, vain, unprincipled man, who was wicked chiefly through weakness and by being made a tool of. Moss, the U. S. District Attorney, was then a resident of Minnesota; but as we never have noticed him, so it is probable we never shall, unless he should do something.[8]

"The town grew rapidly. The boats came loaded with immigrants; but then, as now, a great many feeble, weak-hearted folks, were frozen out and went back down the river, not being made of the right sort of stuff. Mr. Owens came up, with the 'Register' press, from Cincinnati, one No. of that

[8] Although it was Henry L. Moss's fate to remain unnoticed by the editor of the *Pioneer*, he did "do something" for Minnesota. He took a prominent part in the movement for the organization of the territory; he served as United States district attorney of Minnesota from 1849 to 1853, and again from 1862 to 1867; and he helped to secure from the government land grants for Minnesota railroads.

journal, having been printed in that city. Col. James Hughes also came, from Ohio, with the Chronicle, which was issued soon after, from the building where the 'Minnesotian' is now published. Soon after, the 'Register' by M'Lean & Owens, was issued from the building that is now the law office of [Orlando] Simons & [Henry F.] Masterson, St. Anthony street. After a few months, the Chronicle & Register, were united, in the old Chronicle office, under the firm, name and

SIMON AND MASTERSON'S OFFICE
The building on the right was a fur store.

style of Owens & M'Lean & Hughes & Quay. Mr. Quay soon left the office; and soon after Col. Hughes sold out and Mr. M'Lean become sole proprietor of both offices, and Owens editor, Maj. M'Lean being appointed Sioux agent at Fort Snelling.

"Being cursed with a bad batch of Federal officers, and hard pushed to make a living in competition with two other presses, we though favorably of a proposition to get up a Democratic organization; for with the exception of $1500.00, which we had already expended in defraying the expenses of the Pioneer, and what patronage Galena had liberally extended to this journal, we had nothing or next to nothing to keep it alive. At the solicitation of the Democracy, more fully organized than it has ever been since, we stood on and defended a

Democratic platform. Neither wing of the party is free from the charge of abandoning us and our cause. We fought through one campaign and were defeated. Through the jealousy of a part of Mr. Sibley's Democratic friends, we were defeated.

"We were determined to rally and make another fight. On the eve of the very first party election, Mr. Rice, with all the friends he could carry with him, went over to A. M. Mitchell, the Whig [candidate for] Delegate, and pledged themselves to his election for Delegate, in 1850, (at the next election.) Mr. Rice was one of our Central Democratic Committee, to call Conventions. Mr. Rice after a long absence, returned from Washington. The rupture in the Fur Company, in the meantime had taken place, and riven the two factions, splitting the party wider apart than ever. We remonstrated, expostulated, urged harmony and concession; but all in vain. As well might a man attempt to hold together, by straddling, two masses of ice, suddenly cracked asunder, in passing through a gorge.

"The election approached. In spite of all our exertions, the old factions, Rice and Sibley, embracing Whigs and Democrats, began to solidify into parties, for the election of Delegate. We would gladly then have united with any ten Democrats, who would stand up independent of both factions, and nominate and support, as a party Democrat, any good man. Olmsted offered himself; but not as a party man. He was brought forward by the Chronicle & Register, which he had bought and which was then edited by L. A. Babcock, his niece,[9] as the 'People's Candidate.' We would not support *him*; both because we thought him unfit, and his election impossible; and also because we would not, if we could avoid it, be dragged into the support of a ticket nominated as a people's ticket. We could not do it, consistently with our party obligations. We preferred and finally determined, to nominate and support Mr. Sibley, a known, tried Democrat, a

---

[9] This is an obsolete use of the word "niece" for "nephew."

faithful friend to Minnesota; and who, we are now satisfied, was justified in trusting himself very cautiously upon a platform which was designed to be a deadfall.

"To defeat Mitchell, we were thus compelled to abandon high party ground and fight one mixed faction against the other. We took the only possible plan, to defeat Mitchell. We did right; and that we know full well; and for the Whigs, by whose alliance we accomplished it, we will say, that they have generally acted in good faith with us, deserving the confidence we have had to repose in them; while, we, as Democrats, have also treated them with candor and fairness. And further, we say, that the most obnoxious and unscrupulous of the Whigs, from that time having joined the Rice faction, we have since had but little necessity to organize as Democrats; since Whigs have been ready to aid us in the reforms needed; and especially in the removal of some very obnoxious Whig officers.

"Viewing the matter in every way, it appears to us that our union against the Rice faction, was never firmer than it is now. At the same time, our Whig friends know perfectly well, that the time must come, when we as Democrats, shall oppose them, upon high party grounds; and we hope successfully. Being thus arrayed against Rice & Mitchell, we became, of course, obnoxious to Mr. Rice; and that is the reason why the Democrat was brought up here. Mr. Olmsted having covertly sold out the Chronicle & Register to Mitchell & Rice, with whatever Whig influence it carried along with it, the journal was taken along side of the Democrat and used as a tender. These two crafts, under one command, were then ordered to make all sail and bear down upon and capture the Pioneer.

"Their flag ship, the Democrat, ran up a Democratic pennant. The Pioneer met them both, starboard and larboard, sunk the old Chronicle, cut away the rigging of the 'Democrat' with chain shot, raked her fore and aft, until she can no longer respond to her helm or manage her guns; and at the

Liquor election, last week Monday, her political owner jumped aboard of her, pushed the Captain aside, seized the helm, and in a fit of desperation, ordered the crew to break into the spirit room.

"The bold, wicked attempt made, in the Liquor election, last week, to enlist the 'Organization' against the Liquor Law, to lay that down as the main plank in their party platform, on which to array the party, we regard not only as a gross insult to the good men who had been ensnared into their party, by false pretences of Democracy, which they have perpetually falsified; but it is absolutely fatal to the remotest possible hope or fear of their political supremacy, now or hereafter. And here, as Democrats now and forever, we solemnly protest, in the name of true Democracy, against the declaration thus made to the world, that Democrats in Minnesota, consent that the whiskey interest, shall be a part of any Democratic platform here.[10]

"The great feature of the year 1850, was the exploration by steamboats, of the Minnesota (St. Peters) river. These various excursions, ending with the trip of the steamboat Yankee, Capt. Keeler Harris, cost us much time and a great deal of money. We went into this work, not as some did, for the pleasure of it, but as a necessary, almost, an indispensable preliminary to obtaining an appropriation from Congress, for the negotiation of the Sioux treaties. Our accounts of the exploration of these fairy regions, were very extensively, almost universally, read; and the public mind was fired with a general wish for acquisition of the Sioux territory.

[10] On March 6, 1852, the Minnesota legislature passed an act prohibiting the manufacture or sale of intoxicating liquors in the territory, and providing that the act should be submitted to the voters at a special election. At the election on April 5 the act was approved. The territorial Supreme Court in 1853 declared the act illegal, since the Organic Act had vested the legislative powers of the territory in the legislature, which could not delegate them to the people. Goodhue was at first skeptical that the law could be enforced, but later he supported it vigorously in the columns of his paper. The Democrat was outspoken against it. Folwell, Minnesota, 1:264; Pioneer, April 8, 1852.

"The great event of 1851, was the negotiation of these treaties and the treaties of Pembina. Especial pains was taken, during the negotiation, and ever since, by the press of Minnesota, not to suffer the interest and excitement about the Sioux country, to subside. Our worst obstacle in keeping alive the public interest abroad, in Minnesota, has been the want of frequent, regular mails; a want that must be promptly supplied before the next winter, by having a mail route opened direct from St. Paul to Dubuque, cost what it may.

"The great event of this year, 1852, will be the ratification of the treaties, and an accession of sober, industrious immigration, far greater than we have now in the Territory. In one year from now, we confidently expect to be lost sight of, in the multitude of men and of enterprises that will surround us. Abundance of capital, and fresh, vigorous young men will come in with talent and activity to push on the column of civilization. We bid them welcome. If we have aided in quarrying out the material here, for a noble political structure, that was the task we found for our hand to do, and we have done it 'with all our might.' If, in the absence of established public sentiment and vigorous law, to punish offenders against public justice, and public decency, we have sometimes attacked the profligate and the shameless in high places, with vigor or even violence, let it be remembered that the time then was in Minnesota, when the press was the only engine, that could overawe and restrain the wicked — when mobs and violence and drunkenness, dreaded nothing but the fearless publication of the truth."

"In one year from now, we confidently expect to be lost sight of." Prophetic words! Less than four months after he wrote them, Goodhue had made his last "fearless publication of the truth." The *Pioneer* of August 5, in an item dated three days earlier, announced that its editor lay "dangerously ill," and rather indirectly indicated the nature of his illness: "Many persons in this meridian are lying prostrate under a complaint peculiar to the season, the dysentery. . . . This affection is caused perhaps by exposure to the intense heat of the sun for the few days past, and is much aggravated by care and labor." A contributing cause is suggested in the *Pioneer* of July 22, 1852, when Goodhue urged "every man in St. Paul" to "turn out next Friday morning at 7 o'clock, with an axe or spade, or with both, to assist in opening the road into Suland, on the west side of the river. . . . we can all turn out and do the work in one day if we will. Come prepared to stay all day, or send a hand or two. Ferriage free." It may easily be surmised that his part in the project was an active one. Also, at about this time, he fell from his ferry boat into the river, "and was obliged to use great exertion to keep from drowning." [11]

Goodhue died on the evening of August 27. It is evident from the newspapers and correspondence of the times that all Minnesota was profoundly moved by his death. From the many obituary columns, the words of the editor of the *Minnesotian*, in the issue of the next day, may be selected as best expressing the sentiments of the territory: "We have never seen a greater degree of dismay settle upon the countenances of any community than was visible in St. Paul on Wednesday, when it was announced that he was dying. All that he has done for Minnesota — and it is a vast deal — passed in general review before his fellow-citizens; and it was the general remark, that we could not spare him, except to be visited by an irreparable loss." And from a political enemy came perhaps the greatest tribute: "We never agreed — *politically* — yet he *had* a soul." [12]

[11] *Pioneer*, September 2, 1852.
[12] A. Jackson Morgan to Stevens, September 20, 1852, Stevens Papers.

INDEX

Index

Printed in the USA
CPSIA information can be obtained
at www.ICGtesting.com
JSHW082153140824
68134JS00014B/213